P9-AFD-704

The Happy Runner

Love the Process, Get Faster, Run Longer

David Roche
Megan Roche, MD

HUMAN KINETICS

Library of Congress Cataloging-in-Publication Data

Names: Roche, David, 1988- author. | Roche, Megan, 1990- author.
Title: The happy runner : love the process, get faster, run longer / David Roche,
    Megan Roche.
Description: Champaign, IL : Human Kinetics, [2019]
Identifiers: LCCN 2018035095 (print) | LCCN 2018047006 (ebook) |
    ISBN 9781492572589 (epub) | ISBN 9781492567653 (PDF) |
    ISBN 9781492567646 (print)
Subjects: LCSH: Running--Training.
Classification: LCC GV1061.5 (ebook) | LCC GV1061.5 .R63 2019 (print) |
    DDC 796.42--dc23
LC record available at https://lccn.loc.gov/2018035095

ISBN: 978-1-4925-6764-6 (print)

Copyright © 2019 by David Roche and Megan Roche

All rights reserved. Except for use in a review, the reproduction or utilization of this work in any form or by any electronic, mechanical, or other means, now known or hereafter invented, including xerography, photocopying, and recording, and in any information storage and retrieval system, is forbidden without the written permission of the publisher.

The web addresses cited in this text were current as of October 2018, unless otherwise noted.

Senior Acquisitions Editor: Michelle Maloney
Managing Editor: Julie Marx Goodreau
Cover Designer: Keri Evans
Cover Design Associate: Susan Rothermel Allen
Photographs (interior): Courtesy of David and Megan Roche
Photo Production Manager: Jason Allen
Production: Westchester Publishing Services
Printer: Sheridan Books

Human Kinetics books are available at special discounts for bulk purchase. Special editions or book excerpts can also be created to specification. For details, contact the Special Sales Manager at Human Kinetics.

Printed in the United States of America

10   9   8   7   6   5   4

The paper in this book is certified under a sustainable forestry program.

Human Kinetics
P.O. Box 5076
Champaign, IL 61825-5076
Website: www.HumanKinetics.com

In the United States, email info@hkusa.com or call 800-747-4457.
In Canada, email info@hkcanada.com.
In the United Kingdom/Europe, email hk@hkeurope.com.

For information about Human Kinetics' coverage in other areas of the world, please visit our website: **www.HumanKinetics.com**

E7323

CONTENTS

ACKNOWLEDGMENTS

We'd like to start by thanking our parents, for everything, but mostly for never telling us any of our ideas were bad, even when they were. That is probably the most relevant contribution to this book.

Writing a book is a big undertaking, even when the book is full of questionable ideas. Our big undertaking would not have been possible without the SWAP team. When we started SWAP, we promised athletes unconditional support on their life journeys. We never expected we'd also get that in return. Most of what you read about in the book was just wisdom from SWAP team members passed on to us in phone calls, e-mails, training log updates, and plenty of dog dates. SWAP, we could never have done this (or honestly much else) without you.

To our families, thank you for giving us the courage to say, "You know what? I am perfect *no matter what*." But even better, thanks for teaching us to say that while not taking ourselves seriously at all.

Thanks to Scott for reviewing early drafts, building us up and reminding us to take our own advice not to take things too seriously. Thank you Solmaz, Sydney, and Michael for providing feedback on an early draft, particularly your last question, "But where is Addie dog?" And thanks to the rest of our big running family all over the world for being freaking great.

Thanks to Michelle Maloney at Human Kinetics, who believed in us as authors when we weren't sure we believed in ourselves. Do you think this book has some groan-inducing lines in it now? Imagine what it was like before Michelle worked her magic.

FINALLY, THANKS TO ALL OF YOU FOR BEING AWESOMELY PERFECT IN EVERY SINGLE WAY, EVERY SINGLE DAY.

Addie dog wrote that last one, but we co-sign.

INTRODUCTION: THE HAPPY RUNNER

Every runner has the same finish line: death. That is a melodramatic way to start a running book. Heck, that's a melodramatic way to start a philosophy class or a eulogy. But it's true. And it's essential to ponder now, because later on, if you think deeply enough, running will constantly remind you of your own mortality.

To paraphrase comedian Pete Holmes, by talking about death at the beginning, we aren't trying to ruin your morning, we're just trying to help your breakfast cereal taste better (or your morning run be more fun). Zooming out can bring some clarity about what really matters to you, and what brings you joy.

Because if you don't zoom out now, a running life will do it for you when you least expect it. Whether it's slowing down with age, getting injured, or simply hitting the wall in a race or training run, being a lifelong runner means making friends with your own fragility. As a 25-year-old, you can get drunk on the trails or roads without a care in the world. But eventually, running makes you sober up rapidly through aging, injury, or weak performances. The morbid truth becomes suddenly apparent—as the high wears off, you realize you're a sack of bones and gristle, stardust with delusions of grandeur. Your finish line is the same as everyone else's. Ashes to ashes, dust to dust.

What does the ultimate finish line have to do with being a happy runner? That's the core question we sought to answer when we formed the Some Work, All Play (SWAP) running team. Our experiences showed us that the key to a sustainable love of the running process was to practice a perspective that supports unconditional self-acceptance in the face of an uncertain running (and life) future. So we started SWAP to provide runners with unconditional support on their journey toward self-acceptance. SWAP has excelled because we talk about injuries when healthy, about sadness when happy, about aging when young. As Holmes said, maybe if we do that, then we can help their Cinnamon Toast Crunch taste even better.

Why talk about the bad stuff with running? Because running does not follow a linear progression. Instead, it follows something more like the flight path of a drunken duck that swerves and then crashes into a lake. You'll progress, you'll get a bit worse, you'll progress some more, and then you'll gradually decline with age, before eventually dying. At some point in that trajectory, you'll peak without realizing it, only to have an epiphany one day that your best is behind you. In the face of a chaotic running journey, it's key to embrace the present no matter where it is. Entropy will win eventually, like it always does, so resolve to enjoy the game while it lasts.

The Happy Runner is the story of what happened when we decided that unconditional love and support in the face of an uncertain running future were just as important as expertise on training methodology. But long before the SWAP team started winning dozens of big races around the world, it began simply: as a love story.

If you groaned at that sentence, you are reading this book with the right tone. We promise lots of humor mixed with stories that might help you learn something about yourself. You are free to internalize what you find helpful and throw out what you don't.

We promise not to be self-serious (much). We understand that a lot of our wisdom can be characterized as "Snapple cap gains sentience and writes a running book." This book isn't even about us—we are decades away from the wisdom and life experiences and writing skills for a memoir. But through our stories and the stories of some of our athletes, we can talk a little bit more openly about the stuff that you don't see on social media feeds.

Because for us, at one point, we were unhappy runners.

Before getting to our unhappy runner story, a note on pronouns. (A sexier sentence has never been written!)

The awkwardness of a coauthored book is telling stories about one writer when both writers are behind each word. For the sake of clarity, references to one of us will use our name in the third-person ("David" or "Megan"). For references to both of us, we'll use first-person plural ("we" or "us").

Also, a quick "About Us" primer! We are big fans of comedy, sports, medicine, law, dogs, cereal, philosophy, and cereal philosophy. ("I cinnamon, therefore I toast crunch.") The book has some asides thrown in where we nerd out on these things. It usually gets back to running, we promise.

Before we talk about the importance of zooming out, we should zoom back to our origin stories. Like Peter Parker being bitten by a spider on a school field trip, we each had a specific moment when the superpowers of a running life became apparent. For us, it wasn't super-strength and the power to swing from buildings. It was the power to accept ourselves just a bit more. And also the power to wear brightly colored spandex, which we guess brings us even closer to Spider-Man.

Megan was born with an insatiable thirst for life. Her parents loved her deeply as she was, but they foresaw an obstacle in the distance— playing with others at school. They spent her first few years trying to wrangle their precocious-but-crazy daughter before she unleashed her boundless energy on her kindergarten class.

But the insatiable thirst for life could not be quenched, at least not yet. On her parents' nightstand was the Megan manual, a book called *Your Difficult Child*. As Megan started school, the book was heavily earmarked and underlined, yet it yielded no secret code. So when Megan's mom got a call from school, she was not surprised. Well, she wasn't surprised until she heard this particular complaint.

"Megan ran away. She ran away fast."

What was she running from? Where was she running? All those questions must have sprinted through her mom's head as little 40-pound Megan sprinted down the street, her bowl cut and back-pack bouncing.

They found Megan. Eventually. But the scene would repeat itself, like horror-movie sequels that get released like clockwork every

Halloween. Megan was a pint-sized Freddy Krueger, allowing her loving-but-tired parents no sleep between tantrums.

Then, one spring day when she was six years old, everything changed. Megan's father was frustrated. "Run around the house," he said. "I'll time you." At the very least, it'd be a minute of peace and quiet. Forty seconds later, she came back huffing and puffing. Only something had changed—this time, she no longer seemed on the verge of blowing the house down. "Can I do it again?" she said. "Time me!"

So she ran, and ran, and ran—a hamster on a wheel with the radius of a small house in suburban Pennsylvania. Her dad's stopwatch trigger finger got tired before her legs did. The rest of the day, she accepted herself a bit more, and she was a bit happier. The thirst was not so insatiable after all.

David was born with a nagging hunger. But that hunger was mostly just for lots of food, so it wasn't insatiable at all if there were French fries in the general vicinity.

If anything, his parents thought he should cry more. From day one, first the nurses, and later on family members, were confused by his deep stares and big eyes, which seemed to know some secret. He was a toddler living in his own head, thinking a bit too much at too young of an age.

That hunger for food was not just a joke. The one time David would cry was when dinner was a bit late. "How long, Dad?" he'd lament.

"Soon," his dad would say, toiling over a pot of spaghetti. David's go-to response became a family catch phrase.

"Soon is too long!" he'd say, storming off to his room.

At this point, the recipe is not hard to mix—an empathetic kid, living in his own head, with a love of food that was more Labrador retriever than human. Yes, you may have guessed it. He was very overweight.

David was the big kid in elementary school. Every summer, he'd go in the pool with a shirt on, the only contestant in a sad wet T-shirt contest. There's no shame in that (in retrospect), but it's not easy for a sensitive kid who heard every comment behind his back.

Then, one summer day when he was turning 11 years old, everything changed. His mom and dad made him an offer: "We'd love to run with you, then celebrate with ice cream."

"Yes!" David responded, joyful like always, with an added joie de vivre since ice cream was involved.

So they ran a mile. The next day, they ran another. Then another. By the end of the summer, a lot of the baby fat was left on the road, alongside some of the rubber from the bottom of his running shoes. David became more accepting of himself and happy in his own skin. Food became fuel. The hunger could be an asset after all.

―――――――――――――

Through running, we began our journey to self-acceptance. Despite a daily dose of sweat, though, something was missing for both of us. Sweating helped quell our hunger for life (and food), but it didn't make us fully happy or self-accepting, and it didn't answer the question of why. Why did we rely on sweat as a tool to get through the day?

Perhaps there was a clue the night of Senior Prom. Megan had outgrown the bowl cut she rocked with pride as a precocious kid, but she still didn't love social events. She spent prom night reading Steinbeck's *East of Eden* at her job as a barista in a Saxby's coffee shop in Pennsylvania.

By Senior Prom night, David had outgrown his muffin top, but he still didn't feel fully comfortable with himself. He spent prom night reading Vonnegut's *Cat's Cradle* in his room on a farm in Maryland. Well, Vonnegut sounds cooler than *Sports Illustrated* and comic books, so we'll stick with that story.

We didn't have dates to prom. And honestly, we were both convinced we might never have a date that was a better option than staying in and reading. It was the sad, alternate ending of a 1980s movie starring Molly Ringwald. *The [eating] Breakfast [alone] Club* would probably not have been a box office hit.

Something was missing. And that empty space was filled with insecurity.

So we still had no answers, even as we channeled our running epiphany into other sports. Megan went to Duke University to play field hockey, bringing her competitive nature and love of running into wind sprints. She got excited for the conditioning days that her teammates loathed, viewing each sprint as a race.

David went to Columbia University to play football, before moving on to bike racing his freshman year. He went from timing himself in football sprints, to racing himself on the indoor bike trainer. Those training days enabled him to escape the crowded streets of New York, a place where he felt out of place and trapped inside his own head all over again.

Our lives continued like that through college, a bit unsure and insecure for no good reason, all the way until David went to Duke for graduate school. On his last weekend in New York City, he met a woman from Megan's high school. "You should meet my friend," the woman said. "She's weird."

Now, out of context, that sounds brutal, like it was lifted from Megan's kindergarten report card. "She's weird," the report card probably said, "Plays well with dogs, awkward around humans." But if you knew the woman, Hannah Kligman, you'd understand that it was the best compliment she could give. Hannah would go on to become a smoke-jumping firefighter in New Mexico, with a penchant for archaeology—a modern-day Indiana Jones with a ponytail. Her worldview seemed a bit "different," but in the way that all the best ideas are a bit different. So for her, "weird" was a synonym for "delightful." Or, at the very least, "worth meeting ASAP (and bring your adventure shoes)."

David didn't know that at the time, though. So when he finally met Megan at a frozen yogurt shop in Durham, North Carolina, in 2010, he arrived out of curiosity more than anything. Megan was in the same apprehensive boat. The small talk began.

"What do you like to do for fun?" David asked.

"I like to go up."

"Like . . . up hills?"

"I like to get to the top of places."

When David ordered potato chips on top of chocolate frozen yogurt, Megan gave him a quizzical look and paused before saying anything.

"You're weird," she said with a big smile.

David paused too, before smiling even bigger. "So are you."

With some more conversation and a few bites of potato chips and frozen yogurt, our lifelong hunger was suddenly on the way to being satisfied. It had been unconditional self-acceptance that had been missing, and for some reason, we couldn't get there alone.

So our love story had its first chapter. And over the course of the next few months, we found our *why* for both life and running—unconditional love and the daily purpose that comes with complete, long-term commitment. Through running and love, we had found self-acceptance (a lot more of the time).

Self-acceptance is what it's all about. Everything else you read from here until the last page is designed to support your knowledge that you are enough NO MATTER WHAT. All-caps seems excessive, like we are shouting at you about happiness (thereby decreasing your happiness), but it's necessary to underscore the central thesis of the whole book. Your running and your perspective on your running can support unconditional self-acceptance. In that way, it's just like love itself.

It helped that we discovered love and more serious long-distance running together, both at the same time, which made these lessons intertwine into our eventual coaching philosophy. It wasn't a straight line to spiritual epiphanies, though. We are still swerving along our paths, as if we entered "Enlightenment" into Apple Maps.

When we met, David had long since quit bike racing, but Megan was still playing field hockey. On our first run together, we started at Eno River State Park in North Carolina and traversed leaf-laden, rocky trails like ladder drills and agility sprints, tiptoeing over the single-track like the world's most awkward turtles.

Slowly, Megan's ponytail went from turbo-bounce to the lowest setting (slow-motion shake), until she stopped. It was six miles from the start, and she had bonked. David was thrilled because he was having trouble keeping up on every uphill. Two naïve running babies!

Bonktastically, we walked back to the car, scrounged around for potato chips, and drove home with that euphoric giddiness that characterizes both the start of a relationship and the end of a run. As country music blared in the background (forgive us, we were in North Carolina), we talked excitedly about all the hill climbs and mountains ahead. The biggest blessing was not knowing just how big the mountains would be.

That night, we started studying training methodology to understand what we never learned on a college track team. We probed our limits (and sometimes past our limits), applying training methodology to ourselves in a trial-and-error (mostly error) fashion.

Little by little, over the next couple years, it worked. Megan walked on to the Duke track and field team and was top 10 at the conference championships 10K in 2012. That same year, David went to the trails and won the U.S. 10K Trail Championship. By 2013, we were engaged. On our honeymoon in 2014, we both won the U.S. 10K Trail Championship. In the years since, we went on to qualify for a combined nine Team USA appearances and moved up to longer ultramarathons. All the while, we learned about running (i.e., how not to bonk on six-mile runs) and life (i.e., how not to judge ourselves all the time) and love (i.e., how to support someone no matter what) together.

Disclaimer: Those results mean nothing. It just took achieving them to realize it (as you'll read in the first chapter).

Of course, there were ups and downs along the way, like any good trail run. Through it all, though, we were still the little girl that ran away from school and the big boy that thought too much, but with unconditional love and daily purpose, we could accomplish things that seemed impossible. Together, we were happy (a lot more of the time). Together, we became runners.

And together, we started the SWAP team to provide unconditional love and support to others, so we could help them become happy runners too.

———————————

Back to the mortality melodrama: what does unconditional love, self-acceptance, and happy running have to do with death? On a date a few weeks after that first trail run, we started to understand the principle that would lead to the creation of SWAP a few years later.

That year, North Carolina had an anomalous snowstorm on November 5. We MacGyvered some cardboard boxes into makeshift sleds and brought them to the Duke golf course under the cover of darkness.

"You go first," Megan said, squinting down the steep hill ahead. "I'll be right behind."

"Okay, woohoo!" David sped down into the darkness. Only we were young and dumb and hadn't planned ahead. We hadn't seen this section of the golf course before. And we didn't know that the rough backed up into a sand trap.

David screamed, as he picked up the pace and launched over the lip of the sand trap. In the movie version, Tom Petty's "Free Falling" would be the musical accompaniment for the next second. He hit the sand hard with a thud as the music came to a screeching stop. The wind was knocked out of him in a way that felt strangely reminiscent of his football years.

But Megan was following fast. As David was contemplating breathing, she too launched over the lip of the sand trap like Shaun White, as "Learning to Fly" played in her sledding montage. She landed right on top of David with another thud.

We laid there, under the stars in the sand trap, and we laughed for a minute. David's heart rate shot up to +O$_2$max as he worked up courage, lying prone in the sand trap with his heart beating out of his skull. For the first time, he tried a new trick, like launching off the lip of a halfpipe, spinning four times, and hoping for the best: "I love you, Megan."

Megan didn't pause. "I love you, too."

Stuck the landing!

We both barely had romantic relationships to that point, and the insecurity monster told us it was due to defects of our character. During lots of nights reading while our friends partied, we spent time in our own heads. And the conclusion was the same as countless lonely people with powers of extrapolation on any Friday or Saturday night—"I am weird. I will probably die alone. Can a dog count as a family member listed as a life insurance beneficiary? What about three dogs? Twenty?"

In that sand bunker and the preceding few weeks, we realized we might not fulfill the irrational prophecy in our heads where we die alone and out-of-place. We found love, and later overcame the tough times that face all relationships, because contemplating loneliness and mortality before we met let us understand the beauty of unconditional companionship after we met. We were open to love because we contemplated the alternative.

Similarly, what if the starting point of building a lifelong happy runner is contemplation of the fragility of the human body and the finish line that awaits everyone, long before you're forced to by injury or decline? What if affirmation of life comes most honestly from contemplation of death? That's not a unique thought—Socrates and Nietzsche and just about every philosopher (and prophet and college stoner) start from a similar place when thinking about the meaning of life.

Runners should do the same thing. The inexorable trail from where you are now to death is far clearer for runners than for most people who don't have daily feedback about their physical nature, just as it was for us on those lonely nights when we thought we might be alone forever with our 20 dog children.

Think about it. What are body failures or severe injuries other than reminders of the limits of what our body can do? What is slowing with age other than a reminder about where that regression line ends? The brain can expand to encompass the universe, with no limit to the ideas it can process or dreams it can hold. But the body plays by different rules. As said by the Faceless Men, a group of assassins in *Game of Thrones*, "valar morghulis." *All men must die.* Runners just get more reminders.

For many runners, the realization of their fragility comes in the form of a severe injury. Do you think a monk is contemplative? Do you think a coroner is morbid?

When it comes to contemplative and morbid thoughts, no one is quite like an injured runner.

It was a cold fall day in Washington, D.C., when David lined up for the 2013 Veterans Day 10K. He was fit, coming off a successful season on trails, and he had big expectations. In retrospect, he was a naïve "sweet summer child," a term *Game of Thrones* used to describe those children who had not had to face the harsh, decades-long winters that can happen in that book's world (between key plot points involving dragons and nudity). But, as all runners figure out eventually, winter was coming.

He felt "off" warming up. When the starting gun sounded, his legs felt like six pounds of mashed potatoes in a two-pound sack. He pushed through, figuring that he could at least churn out an acceptable performance. But something still didn't feel right.

The day after the race, he ran, like always. A slight pressure was bearing down on his right hip, but he didn't think much of it. That night, it began to throb like the drumbeat in a White Stripes song. He had a dream that someone came and popped his hip out, and everything was magically better. But he woke up and it was still throbbing.

The hip continued to worsen. When the orthopedic surgeon finally opened up the MRI a couple weeks later, the doctor audibly gasped, which is never a reassuring moment. "That is the worst torn labrum I have seen."

The surgery was scheduled for January. On the final prep visit, the surgeon provided the brutal honesty of a doctor who was short on sleep and time: "With this type of damage, the surgical outcomes are uncertain." David wasn't supposed to think in terms of days or weeks, but months and years. Winter had come, indeed.

The day before the scheduled surgery, a light turned on, brightening the dark thoughts in David's mind. The doctor had said that any subsequent damage to the hip didn't matter because it would require a full repair regardless. Light bulb moment! The doctor basically gave David carte blanche to do stupid, painful things to his hip. That was a crazy conclusion to distill from the doctor's advice, but the mind of an injured runner can be a crazy place.

That afternoon, David did an hour of aggressive physical therapy. He booked a flight to California, where Megan was starting medical school at Stanford. And he called the doctor's office and postponed the surgery.

Miraculously, the injury receded after three months off. Or maybe it was just the miracle of PT. Whatever it was, David had to face his own fragility after seeing his running mortality laid out on a gasp-worthy MRI.

When it came down to it, a few things were illuminated in his mind. The process of being a lifelong runner mattered, not the results along the way. Being a lifelong runner meant accepting the process of injury and decline, and having a "why" that withstood this test of time. Finally, since a running life is finite, every moment is to be enjoyed as enthusiastically as possible with your big running family.

Afterward, we talked a lot about life, death, and happy running. Could we help others have the same realizations—and sustain that perspective over time—without having to get severely injured? Two weeks later, sitting in a 400-square-foot studio apartment in California, SWAP was born with a simple mission statement: Develop a good process, motivated by a good why, fueled by kindness, enthusiasm, and belief.

When SWAP started out, we thought a lot about what it actually meant to be a happy runner, and we kept coming back to what "happiness" actually means. We read the writings of philosophers and scholars and authors. We watched TED Talks. We listened to Kelly Clarkson *and* Taylor Swift. And we found the universal truth—that there are no universal truths.

In *The Geography of Bliss: One Grump's Search for the Happiest Places in the World*, author Eric Weiner travels the globe in search of what makes different people and cultures "happy." The conclusion is that happiness is not what you have or what you do, but something simultaneously complex and simple. It's community, it's a sense of place, it's purpose and contentedness. It's not money or power or stress (at least for most people). Happiness plays by some general rules, but it is different to everyone. Humans and emotions are complicated.

Gretchen Rubin's *The Happiness Project* chronicled a one-year journey to find out if living a thoughtful, mindful life could improve happiness. Her conclusion? Heck yes, it could. But it wasn't easy. She quoted a saying, "Dying is easy, comedy is hard." In other words, finding the light in life is harder than finding the darkness. It's usually something that takes a lot of work, especially when adversity strikes.

Socrates, Epictetus, Buddha, and Nietzsche wrestled with the same questions long before any of us were born, and they couldn't figure out the universal $E = mc^2$ of happiness. So we shouldn't be discouraged in our Happy Runner aims; lots of people with higher IQs and better study habits than us didn't ace the happiness midterm either. If we purported to have universal answers, then you could throw this book in the trash as a dirty, rotten lie.

While there are no universal answers, there are some principles to mull over. The happiness research and philosophy could be stacked up to reach the moon. We won't try to summarize it all, and we won't try to reinvent it. As Rubin said in her book when discussing happiness studies, it's a lot like dieting: "We all know the secret of dieting—eat better, eat less, exercise more—it's the application that is challenging." But that doesn't stop there from being a thousand "miracle" diets that purport to know the secret. We promise you we don't have any secrets.

An additional challenge for a happy runner is determining how a running life applies these principles for happiness. The answer? We don't know. Different things work for everyone. We aren't even happy runners (or people) all the time! But after years of coaching, we have found that viewing those happiness principles in the context of running can provide some insights that help some people accept themselves unconditionally.

So this book presents some of the principles that might help you most on your happy runner quest. Just remember—we don't have the answers either. The one place we are the world's foremost experts is in our own ignorance. We have just been lucky to live enough running lives vicariously through athletes we coach to get better at asking the right questions.

For example, here's one of our favorite pieces of happiness research: the U-shaped curve of age and self-assessed happiness. Appropriately, it looks like a smile, with high points for kids and the elderly being joyful dimples. The lower lip is for people in their 30s, 40s, and 50s. Why are people happiest when they are young and old, but less happy when they are ostensibly running strong when it comes to life? And why are 85-year-olds so freaking joyful?

Weiner explained that much of the variation comes from the weight of expectations and stress. Rubin herself was living in the midst of that happiness lull, and it's what got her to start her happiness project in the first place. One proposed explanation for the offset: Children don't have to think existential, stressful thoughts (as often). They live in the present. The elderly think existential, stressful thoughts, but generally are not thinking too much about what they can achieve and whom they will meet next. In between, people strive endlessly—for finish lines, for mortgage payments, for a tomorrow that never comes.

In the book *Being Mortal*, Dr. Atul Gawande looks at how society and medicine conceive of death. His discussion of aging and happiness brings us one step closer to how to develop a happy runner. "When horizons are measured in decades, which might as well be infinity to human beings, you most desire . . . achievement, creativity, and other attributes of 'self-actualization.' But as your horizons contract—when you see the future ahead of you as finite and uncertain—your focus shifts to the here and now, to everyday pleasures and the people closest to you." That shifted focus makes happier people.

Finite and uncertain? Sounds like a runner's development. Everyday pleasures? Sounds like the daily running grind. Can we somehow bottle up this secret to happiness that old people have and sprinkle it on our running lives?

Gawande next recounts some experiments to test these ideas. In one study, a group of men were given a deck of cards with descriptions of people they might know, varying from close family members to celebrities, and they were asked about how they would feel about spending time with each. The twist? Some of the study participants were healthy, some had HIV/AIDS.

Generally, the younger participants wanted to spend less time with those closest to them, and more time with the celebrities. However, when the participant had HIV/AIDS, the age difference disappeared. Contemplation of an end point made study participants more focused on the people closest to them.

The study findings were duplicated when the younger participants were told that they were about to move away from loved ones. In that instance, close relationships and everyday pleasures were prioritized regardless of participants' ages. And it's not like age brings some type of infallible nobility and wisdom. When the older participants were told a medical breakthrough would add 20 years to their lives, they made the same decisions as the younger participants. Understanding the relative imminence of our demise and the uncertainty of the present makes us appreciate what we have.

As a runner, you don't have decades of improvement, unless perhaps you are reading this book in your elementary school classroom. You're always on the precipice of decline. Acknowledge that, and perhaps we can think a bit more like the happy elderly people. Love where you are, love who you are with, and be happy in the present. The finish line is coming for all runners, and no one wants to be the first to break the tape.

SWAP formed on the basis of these ideas, a lot like the first fish moving onto land back in the Cambrian period. It's easy to imagine the fish thinking, "Oh wow, this seems like a solid idea. Now what the heck do I do?"

Like ambitious fish out of water, we wrote down the first principles of SWAP. One side of the paper listed three life principles of happy running (the next section of this book). The other side of the paper listed a five-point training philosophy to make these happy runners healthy, strong, and fast (the next section after that). On another piece of paper, we sketched out all the answers about the meaning of life (cut for space).

The training philosophy centered on running like a kid at recess, constantly reinforcing how to run fast and free. The life principles centered on finding self-acceptance and joy in the daily process. Or in the SWAP formulation, it was all about living like a puppy.

If you don't have a dog, that may sound simplistic and naïve. We were in that skeptical boat once, too. When we met, neither of us had lived with a dog before. When we saw dogs on our runs, our adrenaline surged as fight-or-flight took hold. "You better check yourself before you wreck yourself!" our body language would scream, usually at a fluffy goldendoodle that wanted to say hi.

Then, in 2012, our worldview changed with one wag of the tail. We were driving through rural North Carolina, on our way to Hanging Rock Park to hike. Our relationship had hit a rocky section (as will be described in chapter 1), and we were escaping the stresses of our busy lives for a day. As we drove through a small town called Walnut Cove, Megan uttered her most common catchphrase, "Pull over, I have to pee." That same second, we saw a sign in front of the hardware store: "Free Pups."

We stopped, because even people who don't love dogs can't help but stop for puppies (and full bladders). We walked to the hardware store and came to an unattended pickup truck. On the tailgate was a see-through crate. And in the crate were six puppies.

No one was in sight. We looked around quizzically, wondering if someone was playing a practical joke on us. Is Ashton Kutcher in the hardware store? Are we getting Punk'd?

The puppies were just a few pounds—we'd later learn they were five or six weeks old, the product of some unsanctioned Romeo and Juliet action between a spaniel and a retriever on neighboring farms. Five of the puppies were boys, all pitch black. One of the puppies—the smallest—was a girl, spotted like she thought *101 Dalmatians* was a fashion show. And that girl would not stop wagging her tail.

Gust of wind? HELLO, WIND. A leaf in the crate? I WANT TO BE YOUR FRIEND, MR. LEAF. Two strange hoomans walk up to say hi? I WILL LOVE YOU FOREVER, DAVID AND MEGAN.

We fell in love, right then and there. Eventually, after our five-minute love story had climaxed with a snuggle through the crate, the owner of the pickup truck emerged from the store. "Take one if you want," he said while holding his overalls. "Like the sign says, they're free."

Later, we'd learn that six-week old puppies from a farm in rural North Carolina that had grown up in a barn without supervision are . . . surprisingly . . . not completely free. But before Addie ruined our carpets dozens of times over, we learned her origin story. The farmer's nine-year-old daughter picked her out of the litter a bit too soon. The little girl saw something. Even at a few weeks old, that puppy had a special ability to love everyone unconditionally.

We never made it to Hanging Rock Park that day. That little, unnamed black-and-white puppy became Addie the Adventure Dog. Addie talked and lived in all caps.

I LOVE YOU AND YOU AND YOU.

I LOVE FOOD AND FETCH AND TOYS AND SLEEP.

I LOVE DOING EVERYTHING AND I LOVE DOING NOTHING.

We knew nothing about dogs, and honestly we taught Addie very little in the years since. If you have met her, that'd be apparent from her inability to do any tricks other than snuggle. But that unconditional love resonated with people. In the years since, Addie has been the gateway dog (the dog that spurs someone to adopt their first pet) for 14 different families. She has been in 29 states, ran thousands of miles, and even learned not to ruin every carpet she sees (just some of the really fuzzy ones).

But way more than she learned, she taught. She taught us that unconditional love—of others, yourself, and the moment you are in—does not have to be the product of simple ignorance. It can be a worldview that makes you and everyone around you a bit happier.

Dogs like Addie have that age curve mastered, right? They live in the present and value what they have. They aren't thinking about their stock portfolio depreciating, and they aren't wondering if there are other owners out there who might give them more kibble. They love, they run, they eat, they do it all over again with their tails wagging the whole time.

Addie was listed as one of the SWAP coaches because she embodied what we saw as the point of coaching. SWAP was about providing puppy love to runners and providing an opportunity for puppy epiphanies, all without taking the whole process too seriously.

Humans aren't puppies though. It's an unfortunate reality.

Given that runners have a more complex worldview than dogs, SWAP needed to figure out how to drive home these points without simply providing tail-wagging from incessant enthusiasm and head-patting from positive reinforcement.

We kept coming back to death, something that Addie dog might not think about, but we did all the time. Contemplation of our own lonely mortality enabled us to love deeply. Experiencing our own running "deaths" through injury enabled us to cherish all of the experiences along the way. Maybe a training philosophy built on the inevitability of adversity could help others be puppies without the treacherous middle steps of loneliness or injuries.

It was worth a try. The ambitious fish stepped onto the beach, decided, "I guess this is what the heck I'm doing," and started walking. What happened next, in retrospect, was shocking.

Rapidly, SWAP athletes started having breakthroughs. In the years since, they have won some of the most prestigious races in the world, all while tolerating some cringe-worthy jokes and lots of exclamation points from their coaches. AND SOME ALL-CAPS LOVE FROM A DOG LIFE-COACH THAT DOESN'T EVEN HAVE THUMBS TO TYPE WITH. But it goes beyond race performances. SWAP athletes have started to think a bit more about finding fulfillment in the process of training and finding simple joys in the process of life.

If you mix a unique training philosophy with unconditional love, relentless enthusiasm, and a dose of perspective, it turns out that you can help runners become more like puppies. And a human puppy has the tools to become a happy runner.

This book features the principles we have found important in supporting the development of a happy runner. These principles don't unlock the answers to life and they won't lead to puppy joy overnight. After all, everyone has different life situations and brain chemistries. There's a whole chapter on complications to everything. Even dogs deal with depression and anxiety. For some people, this approach could be completely wrong, and that's okay too.

But others might find the tools to start their own happy runner mission. For some of you out there reading, by starting the process of thinking about life, love (of self and others), and mortality, before you know it, you may become a little happier and a little speedier. And the coolest part? You might find yourself not caring about your results much at all, starting a friendship with the insecurity monster between your ears.

You live, you love, you run, and you die. The whole time, no matter what, you are enough, unconditionally. This book is about connecting those ideas.

PART I

THE HAPPY RUNNER RULES

Have you ever been struck with a sense of wonder and joy when standing on top of a mountain? The answer is probably yes. Why do you think that is? Your answer can vary from the simple ("wow, that's a big freaking mountain") to the complex ("billions of stars had to live and die to create the raw materials for the mountain under my feet, and that thought activates dopamine release in the prefrontal cortex"). No matter what the reason, a mountain summit can feel magical.

Now think of what happens when you run up the little hill outside your house. Do you get the same feeling? Probably not, unless you took a mountain-sized hit of something that releases a lot of dopamine before leaving the front door. It's just an everyday, boring hill. It's mundane.

The goal of a happy runner is developing a perspective that allows you to find the magic in the mundane. If you run enough to get anywhere close to your potential, the daily act of running becomes mundane by definition. There are some mountains along the way, but if you view the journey as just connecting summits, then you'll miss out on the everyday beauty. In the moment, cherishing that everyday beauty brings purpose and contentedness. And later on, when faced with the fragility of your running life, you'll look back with sadness and regret if you have to wonder how much magic you missed by failing to appreciate the journey.

In that way, running is just like life. Life is mundane as crap when you think about it. People talk about time being short, but it really isn't in the moment. If you want proof, go get your car registered at the DMV. That is just a few hours of awareness of time passing—now multiply that by the hours in a day and the days in a lifetime. Life is long—it only flies by in retrospect.

And it's usually full of regrets if you don't learn to bottle up that daily, mundane magic. The ultimate scholar of the 1980s, Ferris Bueller, said it best: "Life moves pretty fast. If you don't stop and look around once in a while, you could miss it." For running, looking around means embracing the process, including the ups and downs on the way. It means the same thing for life. If the goal is just to connect summits, you'll probably grow to be indifferent about all the time you aren't on top of a mountain.

But Professor Bueller, someone might ask, how can you look around when you're just trying to find out where you are going? This section of the book gets into a bit of that, all revolving around a theme from one of Kurt Vonnegut's more famous quotes. "I urge you to please notice when you are happy, and exclaim or murmur or think at some point,

'If this isn't nice, I don't know what is.'" It's about pausing along the way to appreciate the mundane.

So we know running and life are largely mundane. What about something that connects the two—love? In this case, love just means a deep emotional connection with someone or something. A number of philosophers throughout history posited that love is one of the purposes of life and one of the strongest emotions we can feel, and most people that have experienced it probably agree. But even the most affectionate, passionate love reaches an equilibrium point. That is where the universal rule of entropy comes in.

A closed system, like a long-term relationship or a running life, loses energy over time. Entropy is often summarized in the phrase "all things fall apart." And that's true, all things do fall apart . . . unless energy enters the system.

For love, it's all about bringing energy into the bond that strengthens it even as everything else changes and falls apart around it. That's why long-term relationships require a renewed daily commitment. It's why a running life requires an evolving appreciation of the joy of each day. Heck, it might work for dogs, too.

When Addie dog was a puppy, David noticed a strange experiment going on that would test this theory. Megan constantly told the kibble-saurus how she felt about her. So one random Sunday, David got out his lab coat and tested his hypothesis. He had a love-counter in his brain, ringing up every time Megan said "I love you" or "You are the best" or "Thanks for being perfect" to that little fluff-ball. By noon, it had reached 50, and he gave up.

Now, that may be excessive, especially for creatures that have slightly longer memories. ("WHEN ARE YOU GOING TO FEED ME DINNER?!" "You got dinner 5 minutes ago." "NOPE, DO NOT REMEMBER THAT.") But we are constantly asked why Addie dog is so joyful and loving, and David's answer is always to tell that story. When you are told anything 50 times in a few hours, maybe you start to believe it a bit. You definitely don't risk taking it for granted.

The message here is not to repeat yourself over and over. It is simply that the warmest love becomes room temperature unless constantly reinforced. For relationships, that means that it may help to express your love and affection and admiration, enthusiastically and consistently, whenever and however you can.

In any relationship (whether it's romantic, friendship, or doggo), love can be something that becomes boringly mundane. It's easy for other things to take center stage, like who is taking out the trash or when you'll find time to run. Petty grievances can feel huge in these settings, kind of like a guitar solo of annoyance getting all of the attention while the drumbeat of unconditional love and bass line of friendship get ignored.

On top of that, society often encourages us to "play it cool," to hold in these thoughts and feelings. That's some crazy stuff when you think about it. What makes you feel better in life, when your friend/partner tells you how great you are or when they express an ironic, detached witticism? It's probably the simple expression of love. You can be the person that extends that joy to others and to yourself. Always be honest, but don't be "cool." Screw being cool.

So try your own experiment. Change your e-mail signature line from "Regards" to "You are great!" for people you care about. Tell your dogs they are the best dogs in the whole world. Let your loved ones know they are loved, deeply and personally, bringing a brilliant light to the world with their presence.

Or, at the very least, just count how many times you tell people how amazing they are (because they are). Try to tick that number up just a few notches. Watch what happens.

It might be nothing. But wait just a bit, and you could change everything in their world and how they perceive themselves in it, strengthening your bond in the meantime.

And perhaps even more importantly, do that in your own head too. Who is awesome? You are awesome! What do you love? The daily act of running! What do you want to be? A lifelong happy runner, bringing joy to the world with your presence, totally uncool and totally okay with it!

It's more complicated than that, though. Sometimes, running sucks (just like there are moments where any relationship sucks). Sometimes, your mental health doesn't let anything rise above room temperature. It's really, really hard. But we're all fighting entropy, one of the most powerful forces in the universe, so it's okay for it to be hard. The next few chapters try to explain how you can push back against entropy and learn to love the mundaneness of a running life.

—1—

Embrace the Process

No one gives a crap about your marathon PR. No one cares how many races you have run or how well you placed. Even if you win the biggest race of the world, you'll find out that the few people who do care about that have the collective memory of a family of fruit flies. "What have you done for me lately?" they'll imply with their comments on social media. "What a failure," some of those same people will say behind your back.

Your own brain may start telling you the same thing. The ego monster can never be satisfied, like a virus that has to kill the host. The finish line drug requires bigger and bigger doses to get you high, and eventually it might kill your love of running (and your love of self) entirely.

When we are talking to our athletes, especially ones who are heavily invested in races and self-evaluation, we'll underline and bold a line in the intro e-mail. **<u>We don't give a [fudge] about your results.</u>** This chapter is about why we send that counterintuitive message.

The basic takeaway? If you run for results, your happy runner journey is at the mercy of forces you don't control. It's okay to care about results, but not to let them define your self-worth as a runner or person. A process-driven running life is the first step to being a happy runner long term. Because you are enough, every day, no matter what.

It's not just that you don't control results, it's that they don't really matter for happiness much anyway. One of Gretchen Rubin's secrets of adulthood summarizes it best: "What you do *every day* matters more than what you do *once in a while*." On top of that, research shows that people emotionally adapt to whatever level they reach in work, hobbies, or anything else. It's a perpetual merry-go-round of striving, ending up where you started no matter what you do.

We get that this line of thinking can seem ridiculous. You can almost imagine us wearing tie-dyed running tights and saying, "It's all about the journey. Enjoy the ride. You are a precious, blooming daisy. Have you ever just looked at your hands? Like *really* looked at them?"

We get it. It isn't so easy to say, "I don't care about results, man" unless maybe you grew up on a commune that produced hemp oil and prayer flags. For most people, it's really, really hard to turn off our win-everything, crush-everyone primal brain screams. "Do it all! Do it better! Conquer the village and subjugate the villagers! Then conquer the next village and subjugate those villagers too!" That's culture and evolution, all mixing together in a potent brew that makes it difficult to achieve unconditional self-acceptance.

But it is our undeniable nature, at least for most of us. So this chapter isn't about turning off the brain to our results-focused nature entirely. Instead, it's about turning that scream into an inside voice that can be mindfully reasoned with.

"Be mindful" and "be present" are two statements said so often that they lose almost all their meaning, kind of like "have a nice day" and "for the last time put down the freaking toilet seat after you are done." But here at the outset, it's important to think about what mindfulness and presence really mean, because those traits are among the strongest predictors of happiness.

Buddha is attributed with the following quote: "Do not dwell in the past, do not dream of the future, concentrate the mind on the present moment." That is a wonderful aspiration. Life is lived in the present moment, so letting your mind overemphasize the past or future implicitly devalues what you have right here, right now. Mindfulness is the method to achieve presence.

"Mindfulness is simply being aware of what is happening right now without wishing it were different; enjoying the pleasant without holding on when it changes (which it will); being with the unpleasant without fearing it will always be this way (which it won't)." That quote is from mindfulness expert James Baraz, outlining his interpretation. The overarching message? Accept the good and the bad of the journey as they come, rather than elevating fleeting outcomes. Think of your life as if you're a puppy, not as if you're undergoing a performance review in purgatory. Your best will never be enough unless it's always enough.

Of course, that perspective is darn near impossible sometimes. But in your running life, you can practice mindfulness to achieve enlightenment . . . or at least escape a mental prison where your self-worth depends on beating that never-ending merry-go-round of striving. Over the next few pages, we'll outline some stories from running and life that show the pitfalls of chasing results and the benefits of focusing on process. The end goal? Accept that results aren't the goal at all, but a pleasant by-product of the process along the way.

Process Is Life

This quick section of the chapter is cowritten by Captain Obvious, the superhero with the catchphrase, "Yeah . . . duh." By "process," we mean the day-to-day movement through life and running. By "results," we mean focusing on races or even workouts or any benchmark of self-judgment. Process is where almost all of what matters about a running life happens.

Let's start with the physical processes. A lot of our emotions are influenced by neurobiology and psychology. In some people, consistent running can help modulate serotonin, a key neurotransmitter that plays a role in everything from mood to social behavior. Dopamine is another key neurotransmitter, and endorphins are hormones that impact mood, and both are impacted positively by running (and pizza, or intimacy). Studies show that running positively influences brain chemistry and happiness in some people (runner's high!). A neuroscience saying is that "neurons that fire together, wire together." So practice all this good-mojo brain chemistry in the daily run, and you may be able to raise your happiness setpoint over time. (Depression, anxiety, and other mental health issues talked about in chapter 4 complicate things, so as always—remember it's okay not to be happy, too.)

Results can produce all those brain chemicals too, but just periodically. Plus, there is the added risk of failure and conditional self-acceptance. Think back to pizza (yes, please!). Results are like possibly having pizza once in a while. Process is like having all different types of pizza all the time.

And it truly is all about the full range of pizza options that you can experience along the way. Each run is an opportunity to experience all the emotions related to the human condition in a low-pressure environment. Ken Chlouber, the founder of the Leadville Trail 100 Run, said it best: "Make friends with pain, and you'll never be alone." The daily run lets you make friends with pain, joy, fear, success, and every other emotion (including a true love of pizza). Periodic races don't offer the same opportunity, they don't influence your life as much, and some don't even have finish-line pizza (blasphemy!).

You can still really, really care about results. They can drive your daily process. Just remember that when it all comes down to it, they are one of many days in an ongoing process. Results can be a means to an end, but they are almost never an end in and of themselves.

Over time, you can even learn to put results in their proper place by relishing failure. Fear is one of the biggest enemies of happiness, and fear of failure is common among runners. So make friends with failure! Gosh, if you count failure *and* pain amongst your friends, no one will want to mess with you and your super-squad of emotions.

Plus, emphasizing each day in your worldview guards against what Tal Ben-Shahar calls the "arrival fallacy" in the book *Happier*. When something far-off gets to you (like a race or promotion), it's rarely accompanied by sticky happiness growth. Instead, it's the "atmosphere of growth" that was most important all along. Sounds like process and results, doesn't it?

Last important point: running can suck. It can suck bad. Not every day is a beautiful Instagram photo, or even a janky Myspace page. Lots of days are more like YouTube comments sections—gross and terrible, telling you that you're fat and ugly and smell like musty socks.

But that is all a part of the process. By emphasizing the day-to-day experiences and long-term atmosphere of growth over results, the bad stuff can be good too, just another story to tell on your adventure. The Yellow Brick Road would be way less interesting without the Wicked Witch.

Thanks, Captain Obvious, that whole section was a no-brainer. But coaching has showed us that lots of people end up defining themselves by results, even knowing all these facts. And as a consequence, they end up living much less life, failing to relish the emotions, experiences, and memories along the way. They effectively turn down the knobs on their self-love because of running. And here's the really fascinating part—sometimes they cling to the very thing that makes them feel worse about themselves. So for those people that are still skeptical, we offer another, potentially less obvious reason: you may not control results as much as you think.

What We Control and What We Don't

To paraphrase Disney's Queen Elsa, when it comes to running, you gotta "let it go, let it go." When you hold on too tightly to control and results, you're holding onto a mirage. It's okay to think the mirage is actually a pond when you're not thirsty. Results are fun to chase during the good times of health and peak fitness. But at some point, things will be going a bit worse with your running and you'll be desperately parched, only to realize that there's nothing to drink.

It all gets back to our general lack of control. Success and failure, health and injury, life and death—all can be fickle and uncertain. That's not to say we can't control anything. We can! But a lot of what we perceive as self-determination is more like a game of roulette that matters a ton to us, and not so much to the house.

In the universe's casino, we have some control over the games we play and the way we play them, but not the outcomes. If you think you have full control over your odds, you will eventually make wrong decisions for your long-term running happiness.

In many ways, our desire to control our own destiny is a lot like how we predict the weather. In theory, it's all clean and straightforward. In reality, we live in a universe characterized by chaos and entropy.

Let's look at how models are used to predict the daily forecast and how that can serve as an analogy for how we forecast our own running results. The weather models usually involve a few variables: a set of initial conditions (a map of temperature, pressure, etc.), an understanding of physical relationships (i.e., how air cools as it rises), and historical data that clarifies how similar initial conditions interacted with physical laws in the past. The best weather model is essentially an informed best guess.

Watch weather forecasts over time, though, and you'll notice that best guesses can sometimes be wildly inaccurate. Even with reams of data, controlling for almost every variable, chaos can come in and blow it all to smithereens. Hurricane models, for example, create a "cone of probability," which plots the range of potential paths for a storm. You've probably seen the cones on TV, usually around the same time that a meteorologist stands in a flooded Walgreens parking lot as debris flies by. "It's windy," the meteorologist says. "A bit rainy too. I have a master's degree. Somebody call my agent."

However, until the weatherperson is getting blown sideways in a parking lot monsoon, questioning their life decisions, these cones of probability are just best guesses. That's why the long-range forecast can be so wrong so often. Weather is subject to chaotic unpredictability that means outcomes are difficult to ascertain with certainty no matter how well you understand and control the initial conditions. So too is running, or anything else outside of computer simulations. Life is often just blackjack night at the universe's casino.

Sometimes, that means that doing everything right can still end with everything wrong. You can control every variable, work as hard as you can, and generally be an exemplary running student, only to fail the final exam. But here's the thing—by going to a process-oriented mindset, you can opt out of tests altogether, making your running about celebration rather than evaluation. And the happiness research supports that approach, generally indicating that happiness levels do not change (sometimes even going down) with increased accomplishment and recognition. That's the main takeaway of this chapter—your luck will run out eventually, so don't bet your self-worth on results in the first place.

Chaotic Unpredictability and the Futility of Results Chasing

When we last left our story, it was 2013 and SWAP had just formed. We had a dog named Addie that taught us to lighten-the-heck up and love deeply. Addie helped engrain a happier outlook with her exclamations. YOU ARE PERFECT. I AM PERFECT. THAT SQUIRREL OVER THERE IS PERFECTLY DELICIOUS. It was all a fairy tale.

Oh wait, it was not like that at all. Even though we had a magical talking dog, it wasn't all puppies and unicorns. Sometimes, it was more like Mad Max, feeling like we were being chased by hordes of mercenaries looking to ruin our day. YOU ARE PERFECT, we'd say, parroting Addie's wisdom. "I will eat your entrails for breakfast," the hordes would respond. Unfortunately, positivity can't always win.

The big thing to remember is that setbacks and failures are inevitable no matter what you do. And it's not just you, everyone goes through tough times no matter how positive they are and how hard they work. We sure do! Megan once dropped out of the 2015 U.S. 50K Trail Championships due to extreme fatigue just a few miles into the race, as if she was a rhino felled by a tranquilizer gun. Around that same time, David nearly dropped out of the U.S. Mountain Running Championships, thinking on a steep climb, "It would be delightful to go lie down on that rock and sleep, waiting for the vultures to come for my useless body." After some twists and turns and doctor visits, based on her symptoms of fatigue and nausea, Megan was tested for both mononucleosis and pregnancy (they should give 25% off for the combo pack). The mono test came back positive. Over the next few months, we'd both be exhausted. It turns out that there was another downside to not getting many kisses when we were young.

And that was just one of many failures, obstacles, and demons. That's the nature of life, though, isn't it? From the outside, it may have seemed a bit like a fairy tale, but that was only true if you counted the talking dog sidekick. GUESS WHAT? THE SALTY WATER THAT COMES OUT OF MOM AND DAD'S EYES IS DELICIOUS AND NUTRITIOUS. AND AFTER I GET MY FILL, IT OFTEN GOES AWAY WITH CUDDLES.

Here's the thing—everyone shares that same story. Results come and go for every lifelong athlete, often influenced by things that seem random and are mostly outside of our control. It may be mono. It may be genetics. It may be injury or depression or really anything else you can imagine. The happy runner epiphany is taking the pressure off of results, cutting yourself (and others) some slack, and understanding that it's about the process all along. Results are judged by finish lines. Process isn't judged at all. Process is just life.

Amelia Boone shows what happens when you reorient your thinking about running, and life, altogether. In 2016, she was on top of the world. She had moved into a new sport, trail running, and already qualified for the Western States 100. She had been a world champion in Obstacle Course Racing, and now she was on the path to chasing similar results on trails.

But the stone-cold reality of human fragility gave zero craps about race results.

Her hip started hurting in February, around the time she won the Golden Ticket to Western States by finishing second at the prestigious Sean O'Brien 100K. She thought little of it, just another obstacle to overcome through force of will.

She pushed and pushed, ready to shock the world in June at the big Western States dance. One of her final long training runs was on tap in April, and she hammered her legs off. The times? Amazing. The climbs? Practically molehills. Nothing could stop her.

Well, nothing but the right femur that had nearly broken all the way across.

That little pain had morphed into one of the worst injuries imaginable for a runner. She'd be lucky to walk for weeks, let alone run. So she had a lot of time to think. In mid-2017, she described her conclusion:

> "Maybe, just MAYBE—I could change my relationship with racing. Maybe that's what I needed—maybe I could learn how to handle the pressure constructively, and maybe I could finally nut up and do what was right for ME, not what I thought everyone else expected. And maybe being sidelined was the catalyst I needed to change that relationship by taking control of that relationship.
>
> "Someone asked me the other day if I wanted to win another world championship. 'Sure,' I responded, 'that'd be fantastic.' He responded that I didn't sound that enthused.
>
> "And I wasn't. Because I'll let you in on my racing goals this year. There's just one.
> ***"To race happy."***

Amelia cared about results still—it's almost impossible not to. In fact, it's healthy to care. But her brush with possibly never being able to run again made it clear that results were just checkpoints in the broader journey as a runner and person. She zoomed out and saw what mattered to her.

As she summarized: "I love this sport, I love this community, and I'm saying yes to happiness.

"Podium of life, here I come."

Amelia reframed results, and it led her to being a happy runner for the first time in her life. The final diagnosis? A fractured femur, but the perspective necessary to make her soul whole.

The takeaways from Amelia and many other lifelong, happy runners: finish lines, no matter how prestigious, don't bring long-term happiness. Embrace the process, and you may find contentedness (and every other emotion that adds richness to life) along the way, reaching your long-term potential too. Focus on results, and there's a good chance you'll never win in the end.

Talent as an Uncontrollable Initial Condition

Of all the initial conditions that matter, talent may be the most important. It's like the commercial slogan, "Maybe she's born with it. Maybe it's *Maybelline.*" Come on, Maybelline, we all want to scream, that is not true at all. We all know that she was almost certainly born with it. What else are you lying about?!

Here, what the Maybelline principle means is that genetics and talent are important, whether it's a beauty pageant or a running race. However, talent is complicated. An example from a different sport can show just how complicated it can all be.

The NFL Combine is held each April, a glorified talent competition for a few hundred promising prospects. Each of the invitees goes through a series of tests, focusing on speed, strength, and agility. They work out in spandex without pads, for just a few days, with their NFL futures on the line. Behind closed doors, NFL executives often call it "The Underwear Olympics," like it's the Victoria's Secret Fashion Show for jocks.

NFL teams invest millions of dollars in talent evaluation, culminating in the Combine. There are some notorious examples of the talent show going horribly wrong. In 2008, Vernon Gholston jumped nearly out of the stadium, with a standing vertical leap of three feet.

Combined with his 6'6", 260-pound frame and 4.6-second time in the 40-yard dash, he appeared to be a freak among freaks, a guaranteed star. The gold medal at the Underwear Olympics moved him all the way up to the sixth overall pick in the draft by the New York Jets. But he never recorded a sack in the NFL and was out of the league after a few years on the bench. Though, to be fair, that could be the natural result of having to play for the Jets.

On the other side, NFL stars sometimes fail to impress in underwear. Perhaps the most disconcerting moment of the Combine each year is when the prospects stand in front of a dull, gray background, hands at their sides and shirtless, as flashbulbs take their official photos. The resulting photos look like the outtakes from a post-apocalyptic Hanes advertisement.

In 2000, a quarterback from the University of Michigan looked particularly drab and shlubby. He was pasty. He was flabby. He was gangly. His name was Tom Brady, and he fell all the way to the 199th pick in the draft. He went on to become one of the greatest quarterbacks of all time, still playing into his 40s.

While there are some infamous misses, NFL Combine performances do generally correlate with NFL success, particularly for "skill position" players who rely on speed and agility. The Underwear Olympics feels like it should be unfair, like the stories of Tom Brady and Vernon Gholston are universal. After all, what does shirtless photography and padless jumping have to do with football success? We are constantly told it's how hard we work that counts, right?

But multiple studies have shown that Brady and Gholston are the exceptions that prove the rule. As runners know too, talent matters. Tom Brady shows there are some things that can't be measured initially. Most of the time, though, the initial condition of raw talent plays an outsized role in the results that come later on, for football players and runners alike. So putting results up on a pedestal is giving too much credit to largely genetic metrics that are out of your control entirely.

If running had something similar to the NFL Combine, it might be the mile run at middle school field day. There have been no studies on performance at field day versus running results as adults, likely because that idea seems simultaneously creepy and boring, as if Pennywise, the clown from *It*, was in the sewer whispering, "Come down here, I can do your taxes." To fill the gap, we did an informal survey of athletes on the SWAP team to see if there was a general pattern.

More than 50 percent of the pro athletes won or finished in the top few at the mile run at field day or in gym class. Non-pros on the team fell in a more normal distribution, with most in the top half of their class, but not the very fastest. There were some Tom Bradys in the group—people who underperformed in middle school relative to their adult race results. But for the most part, fast kids make fast adults.

Now, what exactly the elementary or middle school mile results show is uncertain. It could be as simple as showing the intangibles—the drive to care enough about a blue ribbon to push hard enough to perform to your potential, foreshadowing a dedication to training later. Or it could be something less psychological, like muscle fiber composition or $+O_2$max. It could even be related to epigenetics—changes of genetic expression based on external factors. No matter what we mean by running "talent," it's one of the most important elements in predicting results.

$+O_2$max is the prototypical metric of talent for runners. To measure $+O_2$max, runners are usually strapped to a ventilation machine as a treadmill is cranked up from walking pace to puking pace, measuring aerobic capacity (around the effort an athlete can sustain for 7 to 11 minutes). The fastest runners generally have higher $+O_2$maxes. However, $+O_2$max is only partially trainable—it'll improve 10–30 percent as a runner starts out, then it'll level off, with performance increases after that explained by other variables. So where an athlete starts plays a big role in determining where they end up no matter what they do in between.

Every physiological element of running success plays by similar rules—a starting point that can change different amounts based on age, background, and training. But even if a variable is highly trainable, like lactate threshold (a measure of the effort an athlete can sustain for around one hour), the starting point matters. When it comes to being an elite athlete, talent alone isn't going to teach you to dance, but it's essential to get you into the club.

That's not to say you can't improve beyond your wildest dreams. Recent studies indicate that some physiological variables like muscle fiber expression are trainable far more than previously thought. Where you are now might be nothing compared to what you can become. Heck, a lump of coal can become a diamond! But a baked potato probably won't be a diamond anytime soon. And either way, wanting to be something you are not is one of the quickest tickets to existential despair. You can practice enjoying the day-to-day process no matter where it leads.

The Power of Circumstances

Results also depend on circumstances largely outside of your control that impact you during your journey. For some people, results chasing is unfair to yourself because it doesn't consider circumstances like stress, family, and everything else that makes you who you are.

For example, professional runners often live a Spartan lifestyle in order to absorb massive training loads. In some training camps, there are competitions to see who can walk the fewest steps in between runs (not the recommended use of your Fitbit). They might run 20 miles a day over the course of two runs, but walk less than 2,000 steps the rest of the time, like puppies that alternate between practicing their zoomies and perfecting their snoozles. I NEED TO ABSORB THIS FETCH STIMULUS. New GPS watches with wrist-based optical heart rate may provide a clue why.

Many new watches constantly keep track of heart rate, like the watch designers read Edgar Allan Poe's "The Tell-Tale Heart" in design school. The constant stream of data provides some fascinating insight into stress, with the metric heart rate variability (HRV) taking center stage. HRV measures the variation in time between heartbeats. Counterintuitively, a healthy heart in an unstressed person has high HRV. In fact, at rest the heart can vary around 10 to 15 beats per minute in a single inhalation–exhalation cycle. But add distress and that all changes.

Stress triggers the nervous system to grab the wheel, a variation of fight-or-flight response. As a result, when stress is high, HRV is low. The heart goes on autopilot.

Of course, there's chaos within HRV system predictions. Taper periods can paradoxically drop HRV from decreased training load, mimicking a state of stress. Illnesses can paradoxically increase HRV, mimicking a state of recovery.

While it's subject to debate, HRV has been held out as a proxy to predict everything from performance to recovery to illness in athletes. Your watch may even be secretly judging your stress right now.

Megan's watch is a judgmental jerk. She got her Garmin because, in her words, "It's sexy." It was her first foray into wrist-based heart rate, which does not seem fully reliable for running yet, so she did not pay much attention to it. At least, she didn't pay much attention to it until she paired her watch with her phone a few days later.

The watch app had reams of data summaries for her to peruse. Like a kid on Christmas, she unwrapped her data presents. And the "Stress" page, prominently using HRV, told the unfortunate truth of being a working runner. "What's your takeaway?" David asked.

Megan responded simply, "Life is stressful as heck."

Her HRV and stress levels varied wildly based on seemingly routine life events. That big stress spike two weeks ago? That was from standing on her feet all day in the hospital. The little stress spike two hours ago? That was getting really excited when the hospital cafeteria had chocolate milk. The lesson?

Megan thought for a second. "Run hard, rest often, and live easy."

That's why those professional runners sometimes try to live the sleepy-sloth life. And it makes sense intuitively for anyone who has tried to train for running while living a busy life. For two years while on rotations in medical school from 2015 to 2017, Megan tried to do it all. In practice, that meant a lot of alarm clocks set for 3 a.m., which would give her enough time to run on the treadmill at 24 Hour Fitness before arriving at the hospital at 5 a.m. to round for her surgery rotation. At first, it worked. But like a tell-tale heart, stress kept beating in the background.

It culminated in early 2017, when David asked how she was feeling. Megan quoted one of her idols, Leslie Knope from the TV show *Parks and Recreation*.

"Everything hurts, and I'm dying," she said.

David laughed. "But what exactly hurts?"

"Well, let's see," she said. "My hip feels like it's in need of some grease. My back feels like a package of stale rice cakes. And I'm so sleepy that I'm not sure if this is a good dream, a strange nightmare, or real life. There's a one in a million chance I have a good season."

David quoted one of his favorite characters, Lloyd Christmas from the movie *Dumb and Dumber*. "So you're telling me there's a chance?"

Megan was not amused.

Sure enough, Megan had a difficult few months, characterized by constant little injuries that derailed training and led to subpar results. She was still loving the process, but did the process have to involve so much fatigue that the bags under her eyes sometimes made her look like an under-caffeinated raccoon?

As runners, we cannot choose our parents. Talent is out of our control entirely. And when it comes to circumstances, we have some control, but countless considerations beyond running factor in. Money matters (some), family matters (a lot), chocolate milk in the cafeteria matters (more than money but less than family). Those initial conditions are further subject to chaos theory—unpredictable, nonlinear deviations from expectations.

Talent and circumstances set in motion a range of possible results, like one of those hurricane cones of probability for our running potential. A talented person with a chill life may have a cone that points up a little higher. But a person with less physical talent who trains better and embraces the process can win a race between the two, and they can be a whole heck of a lot happier either way.

That difference between initial conditions and results is a product of embracing the process. And the process is where happy runners are born.

The Benefits of Loving the Process

Decisions made in pursuit of results have a scary way of ending in a crisis. What happens when you reach some of the finish lines you worked so hard to chase and realize that nothing changes? Many people realize too late that the process was the point of it all in the first place.

David was fortunate to have his midlife crisis early on. As SWAP grew in 2014 and 2015, he mostly found himself channeling Addie dog's wisdom. I LOVE LIFE AND EVERYONE AND FOOD MOST OF ALL. But stress was mounting in the background as he tried to balance coaching and working as a lawyer. Instead of living in the moment, he found himself living to finish a to-do list.

It all came to a crisis point in December 2016 at a major biannual gathering of environmental lawyers, policy-makers, and scientists. Around the room were most of the top people in the environmental field. As the musical *Hamilton* would say, it was "the room where it happens," the place you have to work your butt off to get to, and work your butt off to stay in. And sitting there, getting ready to give his third presentation in as many days, all David wanted to do was go home and cuddle with Addie and Megan.

That's crazy talk, right? David spent five years making pennies doing public interest work, working his way up lists of lawyers to watch for the future of environmental law. All the while, his goal was the abstract call to arms of stoners and tech start-ups everywhere: to "change the world." It just took him all that time to realize that he was chasing an abstract result, rather than enjoying the process of the work.

He re-booked his return flight home, spending an extra $400 just to get back to Megan three hours earlier. The next day, he took the leap to leave the prestigious career path, with a couple hundred thousand dollars of student loans behind it, to chase the daily process he loved: running coaching.

In retrospect, the choice probably should not have taken so long. He never considered an hour spent coaching as "work." That's the dream, right? Well, the inertia of expectations and sunk costs held him back. $200,000 on education to be a running coach? Giving up on a prestigious career path that might end as being a CEO or senator? It took that trip, his third in the last few months, to snap him out of that results-oriented mindset. Through coaching, he could help people every day. Maybe not as many, maybe not in a way that would impress at family reunions, but in a way that was meaningful to him. Most importantly, he loved every second of the process of coaching. So, he leapt.

The importance of finding meaning, purpose, and love in the process—and the downsides of failing to think about that before it's too late—is perhaps most evident for lawyers. How a lawyer determines their calling has lessons for how we think about structuring our running decisions.

Every year, at law schools across the country, a cattle auction commences. At the start of their second year, aspiring lawyers are wined and dined by big firms during "on campus interviews." The law students are usually a tad bit naïve—at this point, most have a faint idea how law works, but know little about the life of a lawyer. They are talented and a confluence of circumstances put them in this position, and they're asked to make a decision that could shape the rest of their lives.

On one side are the big firms, with $160,000 starting salaries in big cities, touting prestige and holding back a snicker whenever the phrase "work–life balance" comes up. On the other side are law students, many motivated by the results of getting the job rather than the process of living the big-firm life. If they say yes to the big firms, they are rewarded with prestige, a pat on the back from professors and their school, and high fives from classmates. If they say no, they're unlikely to graduate with a job at all, left to fend for themselves in the hinterlands of public service, government, or small practice work.

One year of intro law classes plus a mountain of inertia pushing them to say yes, then they are asked to make one of the most important decisions of their lives. And many have no clue. It's results versus process with lifelong implications.

It shouldn't be surprising, then, that many lawyers are unhappy. Just 44 percent of big-law lawyers report satisfaction with their careers. One study of 6,200 lawyers found that making more money and having a more prestigious job made lawyers even more unhappy. Some love it, but way too many don't.

It's quite the conundrum for a first-year law student, and it can be boiled down to the same decisions runners face too. Focusing on results can often get you far at first. Focusing on process might not provide as many short-term rewards, but it usually supports long-term happiness.

Process Focus Makes You a Better Runner, Too

The difference between running and lawyering is that process focus often creates the best runners over time. It all gets back to how running progression happens through a series of aerobic, neuromuscular, and musculoskeletal adaptations that build on each other for years and decades.

Aerobically, the body improves oxygen processing capacity by increasing the number of capillaries to carry blood to working muscles, decreasing the amount of oxygen those muscles need in the first place, and turning fuel into energy more efficiently. Essentially, the gas mileage goes up while the engine gets bigger, turning a Kia into a Tesla.

On the neuromuscular front, the brain gets better at transmitting signals to the body to perform complex movement patterns, decreasing ground contact time, making faster cadences feel easier, and improving how the nervous system operates. Just like you learn to play the piano or dance, you learn to run efficiently.

While aerobic adaptations act as the engine turning fuel into power and neuromuscular adaptations act as the computer making the gas pedal more responsive, musculoskeletal changes improve the chassis to handle the load. Consistent, minor stress on bones, joints, and muscles provides the stimulus for them to grow back stronger. Consistent stress, plus enough rest to avoid breakdown, and the result is growth into a nearly indestructible, far-faster runner.

All of these adaptations are cumulative, involving positive feedback cycles over time. As will be discussed in the training section, easy running is the base to ensure you don't break down, letting your musculoskeletal system adapt to handle more stress and improving your aerobic system too. Then, if you do a small amount of faster running consistently, improvement in neuromuscular efficiency starts making all of your paces faster (including easy ones), improving your running economy, or how much energy it takes to go a given pace. Better running economy means more aerobic development, and more aerobic development means even faster strides and intervals. Like a snowball rolling downhill, running fitness gains momentum over time. As coaches, we know an athlete gets it when they first describe a run with the magic phrase: "it feels like I am riding a bike with a tailwind."

The transition from beginner runner struggling to run up a hill to advanced runner experiencing those moments of effortless transcendence doesn't happen overnight. Heck, it doesn't happen overmonth or overyear either. It takes many years of consistent stress. Perhaps scariest of all, a failure of consistency puts a massive wall right in front of the fitness snowball before it can gain steam. Stop-and-start running training is a surefire way to make running miserable.

Something has to drive that consistency, and that is where an overriding emphasis on process comes in. The problem with caring about results too much is that eventually with running, you reach those finish lines, and if you didn't dream past them, they will put a stop to your progression. There's even a term for it—"postrace blues," when an athlete goes into a funk because they finished a race (or didn't) and suddenly realize that nothing changes. Meanwhile, they often lose their compass of purpose because results drove their training. And while they are wandering, lost as a runner, they lose some of what they worked so hard to develop.

Process, though, keeps moving forward. It recognizes that there is only one finish line in life—death. Therefore, anything else that calls itself a finish line along the way, from getting the prestigious lawyer job to running a marathon PR, is merely a checkpoint.

Let's rewind back to Megan's medical school rotations. During that stressful period on her feet in the hospital, Megan had that puppy-like realization that process is where she found her running joy. I JUST WANT TO WAG MY TAIL AND FEEL THE WIND IN MY FUR. And it often looked like fur since she didn't always have enough time to wash her hair.

Although life was stressful, she cherished the process of running, even at 3 a.m. on the treadmill, because it made her a better runner long term. But more importantly, it made her a better person each day. She found her happiness in the daily grind, stressful 3 a.m. alarms and all.

But sometime in February 2016, it was 4:15 a.m., and she was still sleeping. David woke up first and glanced at the clock. His heart sank, like a sailor looking at a vicious storm on the horizon. "Oh crap," he thought. "Time to steer directly into the hurricane. Batten down the hatches!"

Slowly, carefully, he leaned over to Megan. With the dread of kissing Medusa, he put his lips on her forehead. Megan yawned sleepily. Then, suddenly, her eyes popped open. She saw the clock. And she screamed.

"Nooooooooooooooo!" she yelled. "Why? What? Noooooooooo!"

The yells quickly became sobs, as Addie dog emerged from her sleeping place under the bed, clearly thinking there was an earthquake. Instead of a run that morning, Megan got a five-minute cry before driving to work at the hospital.

What motivated those tears? Megan had set up a framework of thinking about running that viewed it as her daily salvation from stress, the rock in a stressful life that sometimes felt like quicksand. It made her better, it made her want to be better. She loved it, all of it, including the bad parts. And seeing the clock ticking past the point of no return, she knew she'd miss out on her daily dose of happiness.

Megan had started her running journey like most of us, thinking about results and prestige. "I can be the best! Times! Places! Wins!"

By 2016, her perspective had shifted. She didn't have much control over the stress of medical school at the time, and she definitely couldn't control the results she'd have at running races. So she let go and embraced the process.

"Daily joy! Long-term purpose! Lots of pizza! High fives all around because we're all in this together!"

Once you know how running development happens, it won't be surprising that she continued to progress as an athlete even in the face of stressful circumstances. And aside from one morning of earth-shaking sobs, because of a focus on the process, she smiled the whole time.

Actually, scratch that. She smiled most of the time. She isn't a puppy, unfortunately. There were times when she was miserable and despondent and hangry. She just got better at being mindful and living in the moment, rather than lamenting that she didn't live in an alternate universe where she was a happy puppy all the time.

The Pitfalls of Chasing Results

"Okay, wait just a minute," someone might say. "That's all well and good, but aren't results the whole point? Why try to become a better runner at all if not to get objectively faster?"

That is a valid question, and for some readers, the inquiry can end there. For some, it's plenty fulfilling to chase finish lines forever. For many others, though, it doesn't work that way.

From coaching many athletes at all phases of development, from 20-year-old professional runners to 70-year-old beginners, we have seen that caring a ton about results presents a risk of putting running on a self-serious pedestal that is always at risk of crumbling down.

Why? Zoom out. A bit more. Even further. What do you see? If you said "injury," you are on the right track. If you said "age-related decline," you're even hotter. If you said "time stretching to infinity, with only a small window to find our own personal meaning," ding, ding, ding. You are really starting to understand the happy runner perspective in this book.

Zooming out is a helpful tool for happiness no matter what situation you're in. It's what philosophers have done from the beginning of time, from Plato questioning the nature of reality in his metaphorical cave to Nietzsche probing what happens when you strip away preconceived notions of meaning. It's what most religions do too—asking followers to view their actions in the context of a universal force. It's even why therapy is so helpful. When you really think about it, many paths to personal enlightenment start at the end, zoomed out to the max—with death. To truly appreciate the process of life, maybe runners should start at the finish line and work backward.

In Western society, though, we are often insulated from death. That removal from life's finish line is by design. Atul Gawande's *Being Mortal* details how medicine and society created a system to sanitize the final phases of life, as much for family members as the person facing aging. As a consequence, the living don't have to face the stark reality of death all that often. At least most don't, except for doctors and health professionals.

In the United States, 80 percent of people die in acute care hospitals or nursing homes. Most people can view death with abstract removal. Doctors and nurses, meanwhile, see death firsthand.

So do medical students. Megan, like every first-year, got well-acquainted with a cadaver to learn anatomy. Every day at class, her team would dig a bit deeper into what makes up a human being, one scalpel stroke at a time.

Some scalpel strokes emphasized anatomical principles; other scalpel strokes emphasized mysteries of the soul. When you dissect the liver, it's easy to think about flash cards and physiology, but when you dissect the hand, you think about the person—their hopes, dreams, families, stories. You wonder whether that hand got to hold another in the final moments of life. You wonder when that hand last got to hold a big slice of cheesy pizza.

Anatomy class prepared her to diagnose and treat. But, as described by Gawande, it's different seeing death face-to-face.

When Megan was on rotations from 2015 to 2017, she got the real-world education on death. That seems dramatic, but it's strikingly common in hospitals, and the medical education is unsurpassed at preparing students for that moment. What struck Megan, though, was that even with all the teaching and preparation, the one thing she couldn't really be ready for was something simple: the deathbed.

In *The Top Five Regrets of the Dying*, palliative nurse Bronnie Ware describes what people think about as they approach the finish line. Megan saw the regrets firsthand—people wishing with their last breaths they hadn't worked so hard, that they were true to themselves and not expectations of others, that they expressed their feelings, that they had cherished relationships, and that they had let themselves be happier. Most of the points can be summarized thusly: the external validation of results and achievements doesn't mean much in the end.

The happiness research all backs that up. The process of life is everything, because as eloquently stated by country music singer Kristian Bush, "I've never seen a hearse with a trailer hitch."

As Gawande and Ware describe, and as Megan witnessed, dying is not a clean, poetic moment like in the movies. The last words often come weeks before a person's final breath, before the drugs to ease the suffering kick in and the sickness takes over. Most people don't have to think about death too much, and as a consequence some of the wisdom of the dying is lost. As people approach the end, they often don't care what they accomplished or how people view them—the results of a life are dust in the wind. They care about the hands held, the memories, and the emotions along the way—the process of a life endures until the very end.

Deathbed logic is almost cliché, but the cliché comes from the truth that people strive endlessly for finish lines that are impossible to reach, as if they're drawn by M.C. Escher. Accomplish one thing, and it's on to the next thing, and the next thing, without an end until the end. Remember how older people are the happiest of all, with well-being increasing well into a person's 80s and 90s? Maybe that is what happens when a person zooms out and realizes that maybe they're not in such a rush to reach finish lines.

Runners and everyone else face the same paradox. Strive and strive, only to reach where you wanted to go and realize nothing changes. Let's rewind our story to 2012, back before we had the wisdom given to us by SWAP athletes and Addie dog. That summer, David set all of his sights on a finish line, answering the age-old question, what happens when the dog actually catches the car it's chasing?

"I'll take 27 cents on pump five," David said to the gas station owner in Nederland, Colorado.

"Ummm . . . wait, what?" the owner responded. Helpfully adding, "Why?"

"It's all I found in the car cushions," David replied honestly.

At this point of his life, David joked that if someone stole his identity, they could have it. His education already left him $150,000 in the debt hole, and he interned for the summer at a nonprofit environmental organization in Colorado where his weekly pay would have made him a middle-class elementary student on allowance. That summer, he raced to put food on the table.

So he didn't put much food on the table. Each Wednesday, at a farmers' market sale, he'd buy a massive container of off-brand peanut butter and sweet potatoes that were four for a dollar. On weekends, he'd run in the mountains, hoping his beat-up Suzuki could make the trip back down on a quarter of gas.

The goal was the U.S. 10K Trail Championships, that August in North Carolina. He never really thought about why that was the goal, or what would happen after the race. He just ran. In retrospect, the training was stout—probably around 100 miles per week, all at altitude, living on scraps.

It makes sense that his relationship with Megan hit its rocky patch at the same time. He focused on running results at the expense of life process, skipping his future brother-in-law's wedding because his running (and bank account) couldn't afford it. He became a worse partner as Megan struggled to rehab from her first running injury. And he got really, really fast, chasing results, fueled by the dreams of the finish line (and peanut butter).

He won that championship. And after crossing the finish line, he was lost.

He went through a microcosm of all the deathbed regrets. He worked too hard for the external validation of results that didn't mean anything without thinking about why he was doing it, and what he would do next. Most importantly, he did not cherish relationships enough. As Megan struggled through her own dark times, he wasn't there with the unwavering support he should have provided, threatening their relationship entirely. The finish line triumph was actually a process failure.

In the days before the 10K, he realized his mistakes. With the only thing that truly mattered to him in danger, he wrote a note and delivered it to her the night before the race.

"I promise to be there for you, forever, unconditionally. You will never have to doubt my love or support, even for a second."

The 10K win didn't change anything in his life—in fact, his running got appreciably worse as his body rebelled against his overtraining. However, the brush with a regret that would have followed him to his own deathbed changed everything. Never would he let results get in the way of the broader life and running process ever again.

The funny thing in retrospect is that from the outside, that win must have seemed like a miraculous triumph of spirit. Here was this self-made runner, competing against the USA Cross Country Champion Bobby Mack, coming out on top against all odds. Lord knows that David's social media accounts probably made it seem like that. But the story—like all of our stories—is so much more complicated. Addie dog wasn't there to provide her wisdom until January of the next year, but we know what she'd say. WHY DWELL IN THE FUTURE OR THE PAST WHEN TODAY HAS SNUGGLES AND ZOOMIES AND SNOOZLES? David learned that he could be mindful like a self-loving puppy, or miserable like life was a series of tests of his self-worth.

This story plays out over and over again. Postrace blues and burnout are the deathbed regrets of runners, where they fall into a type of depression after reaching a finish line and realizing that it was about the process all along. A happy runner is like the happy old person (or puppy) who realizes it's all about cherishing the daily moments and relationships along the way. A running life can be freaking awesome . . . but only if you accept that the bad stuff is part of the awesome ride.

Using Affirmations and Long-Term Goals to Motivate the Daily Process

When you're reading this, you're at the moment where the initial conditions are set. You can't go back in time and change history, and if you can, please don't use your superpower to change your running background. The past is in the past, unless you're the Terminator or Bill and Ted.

But your future is just beginning. Now. And now. And again, right now.

All of these points are opportunities to start a new process as a happy runner. And the happiness research shows that orienting your perspective toward the present moment enhances well-being. So how do you set up a decision-making framework that leads from initial conditions to where you want to go without getting bogged down in results you don't control? For some people, it's as simple as writing down some affirmations and practicing the mantras. "I will accept myself unconditionally and enjoy every day I have." "I will love the journey and be present along the way."

Megan's, written on the to-do list whiteboard: "Be weird. Be you. Love what you do each day."

David's, written on the fridge (the place he visits most often): "I am going to love the process today."

Affirmations work. Develop yours, and write them down, emphasizing that no matter what, you are enough. Unconditional self-acceptance happens in the process of life, and it takes practice, like anything else worth doing.

But for a lot of runners (including us), these mantras only go so far. To support process-based self-acceptance, it might help to kick it up a notch by strategically weaponizing the potentially destructive power of results chasing.

So here are two steps, one involving daily affirmations and one involving long-term goals.

1. **Start by getting out a pen and a sticky note. First, write down three affirmations that describe the person and runner you strive to be.** For example, comedian Pete Holmes struggled with self-confidence for most of his career. His therapist had him try affirmations, and when they got to writing the last one, the therapist asked him to probe his deepest, darkest insecurities. The affirmation that resulted: "I am the real deal."

When recounting the story on his podcast, Holmes always laughs at how ridiculous it seemed in retrospect. That night, though, he tried it. Late at the comedy club, he took out his sheet of affirmations to give them one more look. After reading the final one silently to himself, a woman said his name.

"Pete?" she said. "Hi! I'm a friend of Conan O'Brien."

Then, she said the magic phrase. "Conan says you're the real deal."

Months later, Holmes signed a contract to star in his own late-night TV show, produced by O'Brien.

That seems surreal, and Holmes admits it's probably a cosmic coincidence. But affirmations seem to have a magical way of shaping the world around you. Plus, research shows they can work. So use them! They can't hurt, and learning to love yourself independent of results and achievements is a key step toward enjoying each day. At the very least, giving yourself some daily compliments can be a chance to laugh. As legendary NFL wide receiver Terrell Owens said, "I love me some me." Say that and try not to smile!

2. **Second, after the ooey-gooey, sweet-as-sugar affirmations, get a bit spicier. On another sticky note, write down your long-term running goals.** Dream really big. Putting your wildest aspirations out in the open is the first step to making them a reality.

The actual details of the time horizon (we like three or five years) or the goals (we like big, scary ones) are not all that important. Here is where the magic comes in—the time horizon keeps moving forward as you do. Every six months, reevaluate your goals, scrap the old sticky notes, and write new ones. In the meantime, after reading the affirmations to put your brain in the right place, make your daily decisions based on a simple question: What is the best course of action to achieve my long-term goals?

When you're tired in the middle of a work week and the process you desire the most is to sit on the couch, look at the goals and run. When it's snowy and you want nothing more than some hot chocolate and snuggles with your dog, look at the goals and run. And when your shin hurts just a bit, but you still want to run, look at those goals too. Now, however, the calculus shifts. Since injury is a big way to set yourself back, you don't run. You sit on the couch, sip hot chocolate, and snuggle with your dog until your shin heals. Big-picture thinking to motivate the small decisions adds purpose to the daily grind of being a runner, without taking away from the daily joy of the grind.

This method uses the human tendency to get motivated by results to add structure and meaning to the daily process, while staying grounded in process-focused self-acceptance through the affirmations. And here's the big secret—by staying focused on the purposeful process, you might just be able to make your biggest dreams come to life, all while not spending too much time worrying about things you can't control.

It all gets back to how running progression actually happens, through consistent stress and persistent belief. If you think about it, almost all big, scary dreams work the same way. Long-term dreams (results) motivate day-to-day decisions (process). It's the only way to put in the massive amount of work necessary to reach great heights without burning out along the way.

The Magic of the Long-Term Plan

Running development takes time, and multiple years is a good horizon to gaze at when charting your course. But it's not just running that works that way. Business, professional development, relationships—all follow a similar pattern. Let's look at an example from sports.

In 2012, the Houston Astros hit rock bottom. Their record was 55 wins, 107 losses, a record so putrid in a stretch of sustained putridity that some commentators even said they could be contracted, axed from Major League Baseball altogether. But the Astros' front office didn't see it that way. They viewed the failure as part of the process.

When Eduardo Pérez interviewed for a position as a bench coach after that stinker of a season, the general manager told him something crazy. "Our five-year plan is to win the World Series in 2017."

At the time, that seemed both naïve and idiotic, like the captain of the *Titanic* using the emergency radio to say that the ship would win the America's Cup in 1920. But the Astros organization dreamed big, got out their proverbial sticky notes, and charted a path to the impossible.

In 2013, they lost 111 games, one of the worst seasons in the last two decades. Then, things started to shift. In 2014, they lost 92. But *Sports Illustrated* got wind of their big plans and even put the Astros on the cover in June of that year, with the Nostradamus-like headline: "Your 2017 World Series Champs."

In 2015 and 2016, as their young prospects gained traction, they had a winning record. By 2017, their dreams didn't seem so crazy after all.

In October 2017, Pérez was now an analyst for ESPN relaying the story about the five-year plan the night the Astros won the first World Series title in team history. "I didn't think it was crazy," he said. "They believed in the process."

The Astros aren't totally unique—there are a number of teams that likely said something similar in 2012 after poor seasons. The difference is that the Astros committed to the process to reach those goals even when short-term results chasing may have had more immediate rewards. They held onto their prospects instead of trading them for higher-profile stars, they weathered the storm of poor season after poor season by believing in their sticky note dreams.

On top of that, they kept looking past 2017, reevaluating their goals as the goals got closer. By the time the 2017 season came around, the goal was not just to win the World Series (a result subject to chaotic unpredictability), it was to have a long-term dynasty. At the mid-season trade deadline, they took a risk to add star pitcher Justin Verlander, but because of that longer-term vision, they did it without mortgaging their future. They spent a bit more, but they didn't break the bank. The 2017 results were a checkpoint to evaluate the long-term process. A process-oriented approach motivated by a long-term vision turned a bottom dweller into the king of the baseball mountain.

Of course, that's baseball, not running. The only thing baseball players and runners have in common are funny clothes. But the same principles apply.

The Astros are like a runner that is relatively new to the sport, just starting to focus a bit more and having subpar results. Instead of selling out with 80-mile weeks immediately, and likely getting injured or burning out, the runner dreams big, setting her sights on a distant horizon, enjoying each day as it comes. She builds little by little, until all that consistent, day-to-day process adds up to something amazing. Years later, she is doing 80-mile weeks as if they are nothing, avoiding burnout because the focus remains on the horizon. The results come and go, the process keeps going. So she never loses sight of the process.

That's not just a hypothetical.

In 2016, Cat Bradley had just finished the U.S. 50K Trail Championships, and she was frustrated. For her, it was a poor race, out of the top 10. She was a 24-year-old who wanted to establish herself with a big result. But it had eluded her.

After the race, she came up to us. We hit it off, smiling and laughing. Cat wasn't frustrated anymore. She was driven.

But instead of chasing results, she was thinking about process. Cat joined the SWAP team with the sticky note goal of winning the Western States 100 in five years, and the sticky note affirmation of accepting herself and where she was no matter what. In the meantime, she got to work on the daily process. Suddenly, with nothing but a shift to thinking about the distant horizon and removing self-judgment, her results took off.

Miraculously, she won the lottery for entry into the 2017 Western States 100 with just 2.5 percent odds of being selected. As she built up for the big day, the goal of winning was still years away—her goal was to embrace the process of daily training and life. The 2017 race was a stepping stone, so she kept her mileage low to avoid injury. While some of her competitors were running 100+ miles per week, she averaged just 66 miles in the 12 weeks before the race.

In the prerace prediction contest hosted by the ultra-running website iRunFar, just 1 out of more than 1,100 entrants thought she'd win. And that one person? It was her boyfriend, Ryan. That seemed about right for the old results-driven Cat. But process-driven Cat was a different athlete entirely.

At mile 15 of Western States, she was more than 1 minute per mile behind the leader. If she was thinking about results, she might have gotten demoralized. Instead, she got motivated. "I just decided there would be no more negativity," she said. "There's nothing I can do about the people ahead."

She started moving up, one place at a time. By mile 60, she went into the lead—a lead she wouldn't give up the rest of the day. Cat came from nowhere to shock the running world and win the 2017 Western States 100. In a postrace text message, sent to David at 2 a.m. after crossing the finish line, she described what can happen when an athlete is liberated from results chasing and conditional self-acceptance.

"I have never raced like that. And I have never been that joyful."

Cat didn't control where she started, and she didn't control where she ended up. She only controlled what she did each day along the way. That's where she found her happiness, and with her happiness, her legs found a new gear.

Perhaps the most important comment, though, was not about the race at all. It was about her new long-term goal and affirmation.

"I want to be the healthiest, happiest runner I can."

After recovering from the race, she got back to work on her own happy runner project. Cat was back at it, chasing her biggest, scariest dreams, one day and one decision at a time. She and Ryan even got a puppy of their own named Shirley, partially motivated by a day spent with Addie dog. You can almost imagine Shirley giving her some of that puppy wisdom. EVEN THOUGH YOU ARE A CAT, I WILL LOVE YOU TODAY AND FOREVER.

The big question now, for Cat and every other runner, is a simple one: Why care about the running process at all? For that, we have to take a journey into the very psyche of what makes runners tick.

—2—
Know Your "Why?"

"Born to Run" can feel like a work of fiction. For some of us, it can feel more like we were born to sit in the shade and eat Fritos.

A lot of writing about running makes it seem like beautifully natural poetry in motion, when a good bit of the time it's more like a painful version of watching paint dry. Why subject yourself to a running life at all? Seriously . . . why? Okay, let's take a step back before we get to that question.

Have you ever watched the Westminster Dog Show and asked yourself, "Why the heck are they doing this?" As the Dachshunds dance across the stage and the Shepherds strut their stuff, it's easy to see the insanity and inanity of it all. Imagine if you went back in time and told the regal, untamed wolves that moving into the farmer's barn 10,000 years ago would end up here. "We'll take the unforgivingly harsh and desolate wilderness, just don't make us get makeovers and perms."

How about the beer mile? In a beer mile, runners compete to see who can finish four laps of the track, chugging a beer before each one. Watching the competitors swallowing juicy burps, it's easy to question the decisions that brought them to that point. Beer drinking is fun. Running is fun. Beer drinking and running seems like a misunderstanding of what happens when you combine carbonation and rapid up-and-down movement.

Those examples probably evoke similar reactions among most of the readers of this book: Huh? What? *Why?* Step outside of this audience, though, and most people would think the same thing of running training in the first place. "You're saying you run when you're not being punished or chased? You do realize that any sport that requires nipple guards and pooping in the woods is probably not a wise investment of your energy?"

Here's the point of this chapter: If you run long enough, eventually your own brain will start asking the same questions. Why do I do this? Why in the world would I wake up at 4 a.m. to run circles that go nowhere? Why does running define part of my identity at all?

If you don't grapple with those questions, you may be setting yourself up for a crisis. You might be like one of those dogs that realizes its wolf roots and stops listening to commands, or a beer miler whose digestive tract decides that it's basically a first-grade science fair experiment to demonstrate a volcano eruption. A crisis of self from lacking a "Why?" could cause you to lose motivation. You might start having less fun. You might even quit running altogether.

But the importance of knowing your "Why?" goes beyond simply having an answer. Anyone who has been in physics class, blissfully daydreaming, understands the concept that there are wrong answers. "Frolicking through a meadow at sunset!" you might say in response to a professor's question. "I asked you to tell me the first law of thermodynamics," the professor responds.

So it's not only important that you have an answer to "Why?" The type of answer matters too. Get out your shovels and we'll dig a little bit deeper into what that means.

Getting to "Why?"

Different people and personalities will have different "Why?" responses that work for them. Your approach may be completely different from ours, and that's okay. If that's the case, read our suggestions to identify what not to do, as if you're cheating off the test of the kid who day-dreams in physics class. "Oh, he chose true, so I know that one is extremely false."

For us, across all of the athletes we have coached over the years, we have found an approach to answering the question of "Why" that stands the test of time for some runners. We ask that their answers meet three criteria: they are internal, positive, and enduring.

Or, to put it another way, the answer is grounded in love. As Jack Johnson said, "Love is the answer, at least for most of the questions in my heart. Like why are we here? And where do we go? And how come it's so hard?" Love is sustainable, and as a recent 75-year study from Harvard showed, that one emotion is the biggest determinant of happiness over time. Hate and fear can be powerful, but burn your soul from the inside-out. As Addie dog would say, LOVE IS THE MOST SUSTAINABLE FUEL THAT DOESN'T INVOLVE PEANUT BUTTER FILLING.

As we'll discuss, that can mean you run for moments of effortless transcendence that come from time on the trails, that you find daily purpose from having a race on the calendar, or that running makes you a better, more patient person. The exact answer isn't all that important. What matters is that each response comes from within, and each is focused on bringing self-acceptance to your world no matter what.

That is admittedly so new-agey that if this book was scratch and sniff, it would definitely smell like incense and patchouli. But the big truth we have seen with all different types of athletes is that running is a sport that happens between the ears. Athletes who let external validation define their internal self-worth often face crises that can shake the very foundation of who they are as human beings.

So for our athletes, the only "Why?" answers that won't work are when the "Why?" is temporary, grounded in negative emotions, or based on comparison. As they say, "comparison is the thief of joy." And as we'll discuss, comparison can also be the thief of running progression and it can sabotage your running potential.

When you embrace the process of running, you're on the way to loving justifications for your running life. The next step is knowing your "Why?" for every running decision you make along the way. Do that, and you'll be able to stay consistent and reach your performance and happiness potentials. Fail to think long and hard about "Why?" now, and you may face a running midlife crisis later on.

Fire up your incense and soak in your patchouli, because the rest of the chapter dives into the philosophy behind an internal, enduring, positive "Why?" for your running life. For some readers, this might feel unnecessary. But for others, it might provide some insight into how you can avoid (or overcome) a midlife crisis with your running and stay joyful for the long haul.

Children and External vs. Internal Justifications

Now, slow down for a second. Take a few moments to ponder the central idea of this chapter (and book): unconditional self-acceptance. What does that even mean?

For us, unconditional self-acceptance means knowing that no matter what you have or do or achieve, you are enough. Wherever you are in life in this moment, it is enough. Say "I am enough" so often that it loses all meaning and it sounds like you are trying out a new rapper name. "I am DJ E-Nuff, and I spit mad rhymes about my self-worth."

Unconditional self-acceptance is easier said than done, especially in a sport like running that involves clocks, finish places, and disconcertingly short shorts. But fleshing out a "Why?" that stands up to all the external judgment inherent in a running life can help you avoid crises of self-confidence. Most importantly, it might help you avoid ever saying, "I don't love myself today because __" (the world's worst game of Mad Libs).

To see how this all unfolds in practice, it might be helpful to step outside running to start. So let's rewind to the very beginning, thinking about how we all develop our ideas about ourselves and the world. At some point, every unhappy adult was a child.

Based on the research (like the U-shaped happiness curve, showing children have higher well-being than adults), that child was likely happier. Why would happy children become unhappy adults, aside from the fact that daily naps are no longer a thing and Twitter is a thing?

In 2012, a group of researchers from England started a massive research project that may provide some answers. Their survey of

53,000 children across 15 countries on 4 continents yielded a not-so-surprising result: kids are pretty happy.

Across all of the countries, fewer than 1 in 10 children had low well-being and kids were significantly happier than adults. Close family and friends, unstructured time, and legal rights for children generally were associated with happiness. Perhaps most importantly, access to material things didn't substantially affect happiness. In fact, some of the richest countries, like South Korea and the UK, had the unhappiest, Eeyore-like children. The study authors theorized that it may be due (at least partially) to high-stress school environments.

Meanwhile, some of the countries where accomplishments and "stuff" mattered less were as happy and hopeful as Winnie the Pooh. The happiest and most hopeful of all? Romania and Colombia, where GDP was relatively low. It's not a perfect correlation, but it seems that the stress that comes with striving toward accomplishment can make even the happiest among us a little bit more Eeyore, and less Pooh.

The findings repeat themselves across the happiness literature. Once a certain threshold is met for access to basic necessities, more stuff and more accomplishment do not lead to more happiness. In fact, it may lead to more stress and self-judgment. For children and adults alike, the gap between life circumstances and well-being could get back to one of the simplest questions of all: "Why?"

That makes intuitive sense for kids, right? We have all been flummoxed by the four-year-old who asks "Why?" over and over until the conversation gets trippy and requires a philosophy degree to fully comprehend. You can probably imagine this hypothetical conversation with a stubborn kid at the dinner table:

"Eat your vegetables."

"Why?"

"Vegetables have nutrients that make you stronger."

"Why?"

"It's an evolutionary adaptation where living things co-evolved to create a food chain."

"Why?"

"Trillions of organisms live and die over millions of years, and advantageous adaptations are favored in a way commonly called 'survival of the fittest.' Energy acquisition is a trait that enhances the opportunity an organism has for survival and passing on its genetic code."

"Why?"

"Evolution ultimately has to do with sex . . . ummm . . . never mind. Have this ice cream instead."

That hypothetical conversation just illustrates that asking "Why?" is deeply ingrained in how we develop our perceptions of the world around us (and that you should probably not explain evolution in full detail to a four-year-old). You have probably ridden the "Why?" merry-go-round with a kid before. Kids ask "Why?" motivated by curiosity, genuinely trying to figure out how it all works and where they fit in. But it doesn't stop at vegetable eating. Many kids (and adults too) ask the same questions about what they do and who they are. And here is where the researchers theorized that there may be some explanation for the happiness gap.

"You have to get an A on this test."

"Why?"

"It will advance you to a higher math class, which will help you get into good colleges."

"Why?"

"Colleges are competitive, and your college determines the value of your education."

"Why?"

"Good colleges funnel graduates to the best jobs, like investment banking and corporate law."

"Why?"

"I guess it's really a design flaw in the system if we assume our societal goal is to make happy people, rather than churn out people with high-paying jobs . . . ummm . . . this is sad to think about. Here is some ice cream for both of us."

In some of the more Eeyore-like countries in the study, the "Why?" question leads children to more stressful answers focused on external validation, like test scores. An emphasis on internal validation—like the children finding their place in a complex world asking about vegetables and the universe—seems to lead to higher levels of well-being.

When you think about it, society is often structured in a way that incentivizes chasing external validation at the expense of internal contentedness. You may have read that piece of wisdom in a fortune cookie. Or possibly it's a quote from *The Big Lebowski*. But anyone who has gone through the societal grinder could probably identify with the general principle.

School gets more stressful by the year, as children strive for prestigious colleges (gotta get into Brown!). College stress is rising rapidly, as jobs get more difficult to come by (starting to feel blue!). Jobs are less fulfilling, as it's difficult to balance love of work with making enough money to afford a house and to have children (gotta make that green!). Parenthood gets harder as the lives of children get more complicated and competitive (now I'm seeing red!). And so it goes, like the world's most stressful, least joyful roller-coaster. There are mid-ride photos for sale, but they may involve crying in the fetal position.

A midlife crisis is when this comes to a head, and a person suddenly realizes they never thought enough about "Why?" along the way. The Talking Heads may have said it best in their song "Once in a Lifetime," which begins talking about a middle-aged person taking stock of their lives: "And you may find yourself in a beautiful house, with a beautiful wife. And you may ask yourself, well, how did I get here?"

In the next verse, the middle-aged person expresses discontent: "And you may tell yourself, this is not my beautiful house! And you may tell yourself, this is not my beautiful wife!" Even the sweetest fruits from an unexamined life can taste a bit sour, like biting into an orange and finding out it's a grapefruit.

If you don't ask yourself "Why?" along the way, you might even end up like the protagonist of that song, asking the question that is the endpoint of going from a relatively happy child to an unhappy adult: "My God, what have I done?"

You see this all the time in running too.

For some people, here is the brutal reality: Running like a stressed-out adult, with a "Why?" focused on external validation, can lead them to self-loathing. A runner may have started with a "Why?" focused on health, which morphed into chasing PRs, which transformed into winning races. Then, on a random January morning, they'll put on their shoes and realize none of it really mattered. Or even worse, maybe they'll think that they're not good enough, a failure even. So they don't get out the door that morning, or the morning after, or the next month. They lose the fitness worked so hard to gain. And they look back on their running career with regret and sadness, rather than fulfillment.

Or they get out there that January morning, not totally sure of their "Why?" They continue running, staying on the path even though they aren't sure why it's the path for them. And eventually, running becomes yet another stress, a box to check rather than an experience to cherish. And they ask themselves, "My God, what have I done?"

The sad running stories aren't talked about much. But if there's one thing coaching has showed us, it's that there are many runners who find self-criticism way more often than self-acceptance, including some of the best runners in the sport. We see it all the time in training logs, and we almost never see it in Instagram posts (including our own). And here's the scariest part—a lot of these runners think they're the only ones.

So here's the big takeaway: you are enough, and you are not alone. Take just a second to swirl that around your brain, like you're trying to look like you know what you're doing when sipping a glass of wine. Your value as a runner and person is independent of external judgment, and no matter where you are on the spectrum of self-acceptance now, there are tons of people right there with you.

How can we avoid feeling lonely as the sad star of our own running story? We can practice opting out of external validation and conditional self-acceptance altogether. It's all about having a "Why?" that is resilient against the realities of injury, aging, and all the other little things that can get in the way. Because the story doesn't need to be perfect to have a happy ending.

What happens if you don't make the leap to unconditional self-acceptance? It could work perfectly for you, in which case this chapter is much ado about nothing. But for some of you, if you're anything like us, you probably nodded your head pretty vigorously at the sentence talking about "self-loathing." You see the risk of your brain deciding your body isn't enough. This chapter is about a way of thinking about running that helps to turn the "enough" switch to *on* and have it stay there.

Burnout From An External, Comparison-Based "Why?"

Burnout is when a runner decides running is just not for them. It can be a long-term thing—an asteroid that hurtles in and wipes out all the progress you made. Or it can be short term—a temporary urge to say "fudge this stuff" and pick up another hobby that involves less mental investment, like watching TV news. No matter its duration, burnout is the ultimate running crisis, when the answer to the question of "Why?" returns nothing but silence and a tumbleweed blowing across the road. And for lots of runners, burnout happens way too early.

Pay attention to high school and college running, and you'll see the burnout story play out over and over, which could provide some insight into your own running journey no matter what your age. At its worst, the U.S. system for developing elite young runners works like a five- to eight-year assembly line. And all too often, when a young runner reaches the end of that line, their running careers end as well.

It begins in high school, where the cross-country team is often either focused on winning championships and sending kids to run at good schools, or it's a place for kids to hang out and run some, with little pressure. In the first group, the kids usually run lots, going from being nonrunners as freshman to doing tons of weekly miles as seniors. Since running provides short-term rewards to those willing to take risks, those kids find their potential sooner. With it, they find college scholarships.

Meanwhile, the other group usually steps off the assembly line early. The relaxed running programs only send their most talented runners to college teams. The rest might continue running, or they might not, but either way they are likely free of the baggage that comes from emotional burnout.

Fast forward to college. The kids are thrown into the full-body pressure cooker of academics and athletics, running more and more while often sleeping less and less. The performance goals are clear in the college system: make your conference championship, qualify for the national championship, excel in competition. Many coaches and teams try to reduce the performance pressure, but for motivated young runners, it's always chirping in the background, like an annoying, impossible-to-silence cricket.

"I can skip this workout with my shin hurting," they might think. "One day doesn't mean much. My health is more important."

Chirp chirp

"The Conference Championships are in four weeks, I should at least try to run."

Chirp chirp

"My competition is working out. I will too."

Then, a week later in a brightly lit room. "My shin has been hurting."

"You have a complete fracture of the tibia," the doctor says. "Crutches for four weeks, no running for two months."

Chirp chirp

"Everyone is better than me. I am useless."

And so the cycle of comparison-based incentives repeats. It's the same thing that contributes to one of the most heart-breaking phenomena on college track teams: eating disorders.

The stories are numerous, usually whispered in hushed tones to close friends or therapists later. One team we heard about required the athletes to eat together. The best runner was whippet-thin, subsisting on diet sodas and vegetables. Others compared, chasing her results. So the contagion was planted.

They started to have better results, temporarily. Races seemed easier, even as their strength melted away. So the contagion spread.

Then, the long-term symptoms became apparent. Almost everyone who competed in the comparison game got injured or slowed down, left with psychological scars that would follow them for years afterward.

Or, another story from the dinner table, this time at an Italian restaurant after a race. An athlete in a major conference program told us about their coach, a grisly veteran of the sport well-known for producing great teams. Even now, his words stick, like repeatedly walking through a hellish briar patch.

"Champions don't eat bread."

He removed the basket of bread from the table. The team just ate salad instead. And the athlete relaying the story is still learning to cope with the emotional scars.

We'll get into eating and body image in chapter 4, but for now, you can guess the big point—you are perfect and enough no matter what you look like. If your body runs, even if it's two steps many years ago, you have a runner's body. Plus, strong bodies last. Long-term success requires lots of fuel, so keep it coming!

Comparison is a slippery slope. Some comparison can make a person better, especially when it's kept in context. Wanting to improve relative to your past self or beat a rival can add purpose and meaning to the daily grind. But context has a way of slipping aside over time for some personalities. How can you beat your past self when your past self ran 100 miles per week and got lucky? Well, maybe you can lose some weight. Maybe you can remove bread from your diet. Maybe you can skip dinner. We both tried that at one point.

Or, one we all face—how can you beat your past self when you're now 10 or 20 years older, or raising a family, or working a stressful job? Maybe you can't. Maybe you burn out altogether. We both faced that, too.

The college system is so tough on runners not because of coaching or any bad actors—almost everyone wants the best for all of the runners. It's a systemic problem in any environment—whether it's the track or the classroom or the boardroom—that comes from a competitive setting focused on comparison and external validation. Enron and Goldman Sachs are basically runners who used performance-enhancing drugs, with just one of them getting caught and punished.

Megan learned firsthand what happens when a runner encounters the comparison dragon as it breathes *you-are-not-enough* fire. For her, an external "Why?" almost ended her running journey before it even really started.

Zoom back to January 2012, long before she'd have the happy runner epiphanies in medical school, and almost two years before SWAP formed. After finishing four years of field hockey at Duke, she wanted a new challenge. She ran periodically in high school, but she never trained in a focused way. Now, she was ready to get serious. She was ready to be a runner.

She e-mailed the track coach at Duke and asked about walking on to the team in her final semester of college. She started working out with the team. She excelled.

And she started comparing. "The top women are faster than me."

Chirp chirp

"I need to run harder."

Chirp chirp

"I need to run more."

Chirp chirp

At the Conference Championships, in one of her first races, she finished seventh in the 10K. But you can imagine what happened next. Megan came from field hockey, a sport that people don't usually play for life (unlike running). It has lower long-term risks to the body (unlike running). It is a team sport, where everyone shares successes and failures, with individual self-worth difficult to associate with success (unlike running).

Chirp chirp

"Six women beat me. I can do better. I can do more."

The whole time, she had felt a pressure on the top of her foot. It didn't exactly hurt, at least not in the way you usually think, like a papercut or sprained ankle. Instead, it just chirped every once in a while, softly and in the background.

Two weeks before the NCAA Regional Championships: "I can go faster on this interval."

Chirp chirp

"I can do one extra repetition."

Chirp chirp

At regionals, she lined up, ready to race herself into a spit-and-sweat puddle. Only now, the chirping had grown to a screech, a broken fire alarm in her cerebral cortex. After two miles, she hobbled off the track in pain.

A few days later, the doctor read the X-rays. "Stress fractures in the third and fourth metatarsals."

Chirp chirp

Megan responded like most motivated runners. She worked harder. She cross-trained for three hours a day, ready to come back to Duke while doing a master's degree and run faster than ever. Her body, though, had different plans.

"I'm tired," she told David. "I'm sad."

She didn't know it then, but what she was experiencing was overtraining syndrome. Months later, the blood tests would show a hormonal system that had grinded to a halt. "You can do all that," her hormones said as she cross-trained her butt off, "but we are out." In this visualization, the hormones drove off in a souped-up Cadillac, hydraulics bouncing, taking the party with them.

It took nearly nine months, but with a focus on bringing the party back to her running through lots of rest, Megan got healthy enough to run another track race. It was the final race of the regular season, run under the lights and in the rain at Duke's track at 9 p.m. To qualify for the NCAA Regional Championships, Megan needed to run 35 minutes and she had only been running for a few weeks.

But her mindset had shifted. She cared about the race because it was a manifestation of how much she loved the daily purpose and life-affirming moments of running. Overtraining is a lot like being trapped in a prison in your own brain, so she had a lot of time to think about "Why?" And her answer had gained clarity.

Most importantly, she learned the wrong answer for her. She was not trying to beat opponents or chase external validation. Her self-worth was independent of her running altogether.

Due to time constraints, the race under the lights mixed men and women. To run 35 minutes in the 10K after almost no training, Megan would need a pacer. So David joined her in the chase.

At first, there were six runners on the track, including another woman on the Duke team who was supposed to pace to 5K. The pacer went out too fast, splitting 10 seconds ahead of schedule in the first quarter-mile. The lap quickly caught up to the pacer's legs, and she stepped off the track just a half-mile in. One by one, the other runners fell off the pace. Until under the lights, in the rain, it was just us, matching steps, chasing 35 minutes.

The entire Duke team ringed the track and chanted her name with each lap. As Megan rounded the last turn, David stepped aside to let her sprint to the finish and own the moment. 34:54 . . . 55 . . . 56 . . . 57. She did it, 5:35 minutes per mile pace off of just a few miles in a few weeks. She'd get to return to the site of her downfall the year before, the NCAA Regional Championships.

At that race, she had no delusions of grandeur. She wasn't comparing anymore—her only goals were to race with joy and make memories. She finished 17th out of 48 in a race where only the top 12 qualify for the national championships. As David made his way to the infield where the racers were gathered, all he saw were people crying about races that didn't meet their goals. Then, he saw Megan.

And she was crying too—tears of joy. She did it. Her "Why?" was grounded in loving self-acceptance. So even though she was slower than the year before, she was smiling like she won. Because in some ways, when you think about it, she did.

O ne of Megan's Duke teammates, Ashley Brasovan, experienced a similar journey, but on a bigger stage. Ashley won the Foot Locker Nationals when she was in high school, beating future 18-time NCAA All-American Jordan Hasay. In other words, Ashley was set to be one of the best in the world.

Only, her body had other plans. She had stress fracture after stress fracture, barely competing while in college. As she described in an interview with *Citius Mag*: "The academic stress, the stress of being on the team, the stress of having a scholarship all compiled on top of each other and I put a lot of stress on myself." Coming into college, she said, "I was good, but everyone else was great, too. That was high pressure, and we probably pushed each other too much."

Ashley pushed herself so hard that her body pushed back. She had a great support system in the Duke coaching staff, but comparison to expectations and others was still too much. The pressure cooker of comparison can come from within, or from the outside, but either way, it can burn a runner.

After college, she recalibrated her "Why?" For her, balance and living a full life became more important than validating those high school results on bigger stages. "Running is still a big part of my life," she said in an interview with running website DyeStat. "The biggest difference is that I do have other things that make me really happy. And if for some reason, I got injured now—it's always devastating—but it wouldn't be the end of the world."

She slayed the insatiable results monster, found her "Why?" in a balanced running life, and got healthy. Less stress, more smiles, fewer tears (but still some).

And in 2017, a decade after her momentous win at Foot Locker, she showed the power of not caring as much about comparison. She won the U.S. Trail Half Marathon National Championship in only her second trail race.

Removing Comparison From Evaluation

You might be thinking the obvious retort to this hippie-dippie approach to "Why?"

"Well isn't it a catch-22?" you may think. "Progress requires evaluation. Evaluation requires external judgment."

The thesis of this chapter is that running progress is entirely internal; thus for some runners, external judgment can be a distraction, a red herring, an obstacle even. It's all about finding a framework that supports unconditional self-acceptance. Many runners can deeply care about external comparison and still check that box. For some, though, there's a risk of self-judgment (and even self-loathing) if comparison and racing are the be-all, end-all goals of the running journey.

All of this isn't to say you shouldn't race. You should (probably). Races provide opportunities to immerse yourself in the community, put yourself out there, and magnify all the good (and bad) that running can bring. But overemphasizing races or any comparison-based metric risks imposing a narrative that your value as a runner is defined by comparison. And it's not—or, at least, it doesn't have to be. Races and workouts can just be checkpoints in the process, providing structure and opportunities for reflection. They can be celebrations rather than evaluations.

Most importantly, athletes can learn to structure their "Why?" so that it is not conditional, an if-then statement that determines their fulfillment. For some athletes, this might seem ridiculous and unnecessary—the approach is not for them (and their endurance to read this far is impressive!). But it could help any runner who has struggled with the question, "Am I enough?" Let's look at some examples:

"If I run this workout under two hours, then it is a success." *No*

"If I am top three in this race, then it is a success." *No*

"If I finish this race, then it is a success." *Nope*, not even that

Instead, the "Why?" statements for these runners could be internal, independent of results, and support unconditional self-acceptance.

"I am a runner because I love it sometimes, I hate it other times, and no matter what it makes me a better person." *Yes*

"I run and I race because I never know when it will provide an unforgettable moment of enduring beauty, and I'm willing to wade through the stuff along the way to get there." *Yes*

"I run and I race because of community, health, fun, life, death, success, and failure. Being a runner is a part of my identity, even when

I can't run, even when I don't like running." *Heck* (clap) *to* (clap) *the* (clap) *yes*

Essentially, the goal is to remove grades from the running curriculum entirely. To understand why, think back to school. How are grades assigned, and what does that have to do with running happiness?

Before we even met—before we were even runners—we started to think about this question. One of David's happiest memories from college was at the registrar's office at the top of a tall building in New York City. His palms were sweaty from stress as he entered his petition to switch to pass/fail grading in the astrophysics class he took on a whim. "Approved," the clerk said. A weight lifted off David's shoulders. Doves emerged from the counter. Angels began singing Pharrell's song "Happy." It was glorious.

The phenomenon of grading systems correlating with life satisfaction is not just reserved for wannabe-astrophysicists who can barely distinguish Neil deGrasse Tyson from Neil Patrick Harris. A 2011 study from the journal *Academic Medicine* found that medical students in schools with 3+ levels of grades had higher levels of stress, more burnout, and lower well-being. Grading scale had more to do with happiness than curriculum or class schedule or any other variable. Dozens of medical schools have demonstrated these findings in real-world empirical studies. For example, the University of Virginia Medical School put pass/fail grading into practice, only to see massive increases in student well-being in just two years. Perhaps most importantly, student performance didn't decrease at all. In medical school, at least, grades are often a stress without a purpose.

Medical schools are at the front end of the changing approach to evaluation, with 18 of the top 20 schools using pass/fail grades during preclinical years. Law schools are lagging behind, with just a few using the system. For a hint at why, let's zoom back to 2013, when David was about to graduate from Duke Law and start SWAP.

The dean at the time, an amazing man named David Levi, was asked about pass/fail grading by a student leader. His response was astounding.

"The students would never accept it."

Huh? David thought. He raised his hand. "What do you mean?"

"Our surveys show that law students want grades. Most report extreme disagreement with going to a pass/fail system."

That blew David's mind. Some law students are so competitive that they choose against the opportunity to possibly enhance their own well-being. No wonder surveys show lawyers are a relatively unhappy, Eeyore-like bunch.

At least in medical school, with a stratified grading system, the "Why?" of education often becomes chasing better grades. Self-worth is tied to competition. Stress ensues.

With pass/fail, the "Why?" moves more toward engagement, learning, and community. Self-worth is tied to connection. Well-being ensues.

The pass/fail framework may not apply broadly outside of medical and graduate schools (the research is mixed). But the principle of competition versus connection applies across the life spectrum. Studies show connection and collaboration correlate with happiness, and both of those variables also improve productivity. Researchers from Harvard Business School showed that "givers" who "contribute to others without seeking anything in return" are more successful and happier than "takers" who "get other people to serve their ends while carefully guarding their own expertise and time." It's a lot harder to be a giver when your success is measured against the people you are giving to.

At the 2018 Winter Olympics, the Norwegians were a team of givers. Norway ran away with the overall medal count, crushing the rest of the world despite a population about the same size as the Detroit metropolitan area. An article in *USA Today* noted that many athletes credit their method for developing young athletes. "Unlike the U.S., where we keep score of everything all the time, Norway puts kids in sports but doesn't let them keep score until age 13. The idea is to make sports part of their social development so that the motivation to stay involved is to have fun with their friends, not winning."

Tore Ovrebo, the Norwegian Olympic Committee's director of elite sports, described the reasoning: "They can compete, but we don't make like No. 1, No. 2, No. 3 before they're in their 13th year. We think it's better to be a child in this way because then they can concentrate on having fun and be with their friends and develop. We think the biggest motivation for the kids to do sports is that they do it with their friends and they have fun while they're doing it and we want to keep that feeling throughout their whole career." Of course, Norway could be a juggernaut at the Winter Olympics because it's so cold that their refrigerators are heaters. But, at the very least, Norway shows that cutthroat competition isn't a prerequisite for success.

A landmark 2011 study in the journal *Child Development* on "Social and Emotional Learning" was even more striking. SEL is "the process through which children and adults acquire and effectively apply the knowledge, attitudes, and skills necessary to understand and manage emotions, set and achieve positive goals, feel and show empathy for others, establish and maintain positive relationships, and make responsible decisions." In many ways, it's the opposite of performance-based grading systems, because it cares about connectivity with others, not competitiveness with others. The study found that SEL teaching in a group of nearly 300,000 students from kindergarten to high school improved well-being and social skills. Perhaps most interesting—it improved performance by 11 percent. Frameworks that limit the emphasis on external evaluation and comparison seem to not only make happier people, but better human beings and (sometimes) stronger performers. Someone should tell the law students.

And someone should tell runners. Runners are all like those medical students grinding through graduate school. Running is hard, and none of us have to be here each day, just like medical school. Yet we keep coming back, again and again, like a hospital resident on their third overnight shift. So might changing evaluation work just as well for runners as it did for medical students (and Norwegians)?

Emphasizing competition and comparison is great if you are the fastest or at the top of your class. It's even great if you're simply improving over time. But what happens when you get injured? What happens when you slow down with age? And what happens when you simply have a bad day?

The answer is that all too often, the comparison-driven runner faces a running midlife crisis. Sometimes, when the "Why?" is focused on external factors, everything can go to crap in an instant.

It was mile 90 of the Western States 100, one of the biggest races in the world, and Clare Gallagher's knee locked up. She was running in third place at the time, a result that would establish her as one of the top trail runners in the world. And suddenly, she couldn't move.

David had scouts out on the course texting him updates for SWAP athletes. The text he got at 11 p.m. from mile 90 would be funny, if it weren't so heart-breaking. "Clare is trying to walk backwards now." Her knee failed her, she couldn't continue. While still in podium position, she had to drop out.

The race was the culmination of a long, winding road for Clare. It began in 2016, when she came from nowhere to win the Leadville Trail 100 Run. She became a professional runner, she set her goals high, and she gave her all to chase them. The biggest goal of all? The 2017 Western States 100-Mile Endurance Run, the World Series of U.S. trail running.

Things were going great in the build-up, until two weeks before the race. She stopped updating her training log, and she went off the grid. Later on, well after the race, Clare would explain what happened—she essentially faced a crisis of her running self. Her "Why?" was to perform at the top level, and she simultaneously wondered whether she was doing enough and if it even mattered at all.

When her goal eluded her, the crisis reached a boiling point. When your "Why?" is based on comparison and you fail, what happens next? The answer is that you burn out, you continue on an unsustainable path, or you grow as a runner and person. Clare chose the third option.

She went hiking in the mountains for three weeks, like a sojourn by a biblical prophet. When she came down, she gave David a call.

"I want to help others, use any platform I have to advocate for the environment, and love the process."

Clare had her "Why?" She had always been a delightful person, but her friends noticed a change. Now, she seemed fully content. Her running midlife crisis had resolved. She found a piece to a puzzle she didn't know was missing.

She trained well, but less, focused on long-term development. She engaged even more with the community and her friends. And if you followed the studies on medical school programs focused on connectivity, rather than competition, you can probably guess what happened next—a breakthrough.

At the September 2017 edition of CCC (the prestigious 100-kilometer race in the French Alps connecting Courmayeur, Champex-Lac, and Chamonix), never before won by an American woman, she won in dominant fashion. At the November 2017 North Face 50 Miler, the most competitive 50-mile race in the world, she finished second in one of the best races of the year. She did it all while running just 54 miles per week from July to December, around half of her previous total and that of some of her competitors. Knowing her "Why?" made her more content. It made her happier. It made her an even better person.

Oh yeah, it made her faster too.

Internal Motivation and Long-Term Growth

Knowing your "Why?" is essential if you want to combine happiness and performance in any endeavor that requires long-term commitment and consistency. On one side, don't think about your "Why?" and you may end up being good and miserable, like some partners at law firms who dread work each day. On the other side, if your "Why?" is external and comparison-based, you may have a crisis at some point, which will either stop your progress or crush your happiness. That's like the doctor who gets through medical school at the top of her class and goes through residency at a prestigious hospital to become a top-ranked internal medicine physician, only to realize that she doesn't like working with sick people.

The spot where performance and happiness meet is where the "Why?" aligns with your broader identity, life goals, and worldview. The "Why?" must come from within, or you'll eventually be left without.

We like to anthropomorphize Addie dog, partially because a dog that talks in all-caps is funny to us, and partially because her kindness makes us better people. But even Addie can face a running crisis.

You see, Addie is hairy. She is so hairy that when she gets wet, she gains 10 pounds. She is so hairy that we have hardwood floors, but it seems like we have a carpet. So for her, it must be a bit like long-distance running in a parka. There is a reason they don't run the Iditarod in the summer.

For her puppy years, she seemed to enjoy running. I GET TO BE IN NATURE WITH MY HOOMANS AND SQUIRRELS. She would occasionally be so quick that she'd actually catch squirrels, always releasing them immediately, seemingly horrified by her own talents.

But in 2016, around four years old, something changed. We were all running along the Continental Divide in Colorado, and David felt a tug on the leash. Addie had stopped like a stubborn mule, refusing to go another step. It had only been a few miles, and there was plentiful food and water. What happened? Was she sick?

I AM PERFECTLY HEALTHY, I JUST WANT TO SNIFF AND SNUGGLE.

That day, Addie decided that she wasn't a long-distance runner. She finished the run with a mile off leash, 20 meters behind us. Something clicked, and she decided she never wanted to run more than a few miles again.

We talked to a vet to make sure everything was okay, and the vet said it probably had to do with breed. Addie was likely a retriever mix, not exactly the long-distance runners of the animal kingdom. All those years, what seemed like the joy of running was probably just the joy of being with us. I AM NOT BORN TO RUN, I AM BORN TO LOVE. We never asked her to run long again, but boy will she sprint in circles and fetch like a total dog boss.

That is the "Why?" for a dog, which isn't analogous to what you are going through unless you are Air Bud (in which case, we really want your pawtograph). But all runners face the same questions, whether human or dog, and it all gets back to how running fits in the context of your life. And to understand that, you have to think about what makes you successful at anything you do. Do you enjoy your job or your hobby or anything? Chances are, your "Why?" is as strong as a superpuppy for those interests.

We can't tell you about your job or hobby, solely because we aren't the NSA and don't have access to your tax returns and Google search history. But we can tell you about our experiences with finding your "Why?" for running. SWAP itself is an example of the power of "Why?" We just had no idea at the time.

SWAP was formed in 2013 because we loved running and found deep fulfillment in helping others on their life journeys. In retrospect, the header of the SWAP website seems a bit presumptuous: "Running (and life) coaching from Megan & David Roche." But that was the "Why?"—to provide unconditional support on the whole life adventure.

So it had a well-defined "Why?" SWAP just lacked a few other things, like "Who?" "What?" "When?" and "Where?" Perhaps most importantly, it lacked "How?" SWAP was an experiment to see the power of "Why?" Could it answer all those other questions on its own?

Recounting the chronology of SWAP's start is cringe-inducing in retrospect. It began in 2013 with a ".blogspot" website, the type that were already an uncool way to use the Internet in 1996. Since the "Why?" was not financial, coaching began as a free offer. And, oh yeah, there were just three athletes on the team—the two of us and Addie. It was the comical, naïve business model that would be laughed off the *Shark Tank* set. "This is idiotic," you can imagine Mark Cuban saying. "Write up a business plan and invest in a website if you want to be taken seriously. And please, put on some pants." In our defense, we were working from home and the blinds were drawn.

The next day, a post went up on Facebook advertising the new "business" (very strong air quotes on that word). Miraculously, three intrepid souls reached out to be guinea pigs. It's possible that SWAP never would have survived if it weren't for them taking a chance.

SWAP proceeded to rapidly grow, begin to make money, and eventually have dozens of pros on the team because each decision was guided by an internal, loving "Why?" Because SWAP was all about supporting people, there was unlimited connection and daily check-ins with everyone. People paid what they could afford, anywhere from $110 a month to one athlete who didn't pay and would get gift cards from Megan for groceries during tough times for her family.

By 2018, SWAP had become successful beyond our wildest dreams, even if that was never the goal. Some people responded well to our "Why?" and we owe everything to them. And that is the point of the story—know your "Why?" and commit to your "Why?" and all the other questions have a way of answering themselves over time.

That "Why?" doesn't resonate with everyone. There are some people that look at SWAP (and read this book) with disdain. And we totally understand and accept that perspective. Everyone is different. As top triathlete and coach Siri Lindley says, the important thing is not having the right answer for other people, it's being fearlessly authentic to who you are.

Of course, as a business, SWAP is such small beans that Jack could be a munchkin and still climb our beanstalk. But fortunately, the story of an internal, enduring "Why?" repeats itself constantly when normal people follow big dreams. Almost any business has a similar origin story, and it provides insight into how to think about your running. One story that stands out is that of Spanx, a revolutionary approach to female undergarments. (I bet you didn't see that sentence coming.)

Sara Blakely first got the idea for Spanx when she was a door-to-door salesman for business appliances. She had no background, no professional pedigree, no reason to take a risk. In fact, after graduating from Florida State University, she thought she was going to be a lawyer, only to be saved by poor scores the two times she took the entrance test. So she searched for her "Why?" while selling fax machines in the hot Florida sun. The whole time, she was in some discomfort—the pantyhose she had to wear were uncomfortable and old-fashioned.

Then, the lightbulb turned on. She could do it better. Only, there was a small problem. She had no background in design, clothing manufacturing, or retail. And she only had $5,000 to her name.

While she had almost nothing, she had her "Why?" It wasn't external or comparison-based. She didn't seem to care about success as defined by others, or being ridiculed in the industry. She just wanted to solve the pantyhose problem and help women just like her.

So she moved to Atlanta, invested her $5,000 in her nonexistent business, and got to work. For two years, she researched design in the Georgia Tech library, connected with textile plants, and hustled day and night to keep the lights on. After months developing a prototype, she was ready to show it off.

But she got rejected again and again and again. Once, she showed up at a hosiery plant in North Carolina to try to enlist the help of the manager of the plant. He looked at the Spanx prototype, and like lots of men, he didn't get it. She left, frustrated but not discouraged, her "Why?" guiding her through the adversity. Two weeks later, her phone rang. The plant manager's daughters wouldn't let him pass up her invention. They saw the brilliance, the "Why?" coming through loud and clear.

It wasn't smooth sailing from there—the seas only got rougher for the one-woman show, like rogue waves battering a child's sailboat. She wrote her own patent to save $3,000 in legal fees, drafting it from a template in a textbook while at a table in Barnes & Noble. She camped out in department stores to try to get the attention of buyers. Eventually, her luck turned when Neiman Marcus took notice and made an initial order. There lies some of the magic of "Why?" Know it, internalize it, and live it, then you'll be ready to make the most of any luck you encounter along the way.

For Blakely, the rest, as they say, is history. She never paid for marketing and never sold a stake in the company. Her "Why?" guided her through adversity and criticism that would have crushed most others.

And oh yeah, it made her a billionaire too.

Developing Your "Why?"

So, how can a runner go about making sure their "Why?" fills them up, rather than deflates them? There's one final obstacle to look at.

Of all the developments in what it means to be a runner over the last few decades, the most prominent might be GPS watches and social networks. They can be tools for internal justifications for a running life—building community, setting goals, amplifying purpose. Or they can be tools for external justifications—comparison and negativity with each beep of the watch. It's a good analogy for developing your own "Why?" Usually, the same approach can be used for uplifting, long-term joy, or it can be a tool for self-destruction.

Take the GPS watch. Please, take it and bury it.

Just kidding. Kind of. GPS watches are a wonderful tool to track growth over time and to plan training. Used appropriately, they can be all reward with no risk, a running partner that fits on your wrist and doesn't smell like musty socks. However, quantifying running through a constant stream of numbers can also be a mix of a friend and an enemy. It might tell you a story you want to hear sometimes. Other times it says nasty stuff behind your back, like Regina George from *Mean Girls*. George says to the main character Cady Heron, played by Lindsay Lohan: "So you're, like, really pretty."

Heron responds, "Thank you."

"So you agree?"

"What?"

"You think you're really pretty."

Even while building Heron up, George was preparing to tear her down. Eventually, the subtext implies, George will sabotage Heron's self-esteem.

That philosophical analysis of *Mean Girls* aside, GPS watches are the ultimate frenemy. They're great when your growth chart is pointed up, the popular kid in class. They're terrible when you are aging, regressing, or otherwise prone to negative self-judgment, the loser that has fallen out of favor with the cool crowd. Combine external judgment of a GPS watch with the comparison of Strava, a social media app where runners share their activities, and disaster can strike. It's a story that replays countless times.

"I am useless," the athlete e-mails. "I am slower than I was."

Or, "I am slower than my neighbor."

Or, "I am slower than that pro athlete."

Or, "I am not the best pro athlete in the world."

Or even, "I may be among the best pro athletes in the world, but I won't stay there unless those numbers improve every day."

We have seen all those e-mails, from beginner runners to some top professionals. The frenemy whispers behind their back, "So you agree you're fast?" The whole time, it's implying they are actually not that fast at all.

The key is to restructure the "Why?" for running so that the answer is not comparison. Sure, if the goal is just to get faster than others and faster than your old self, that watch will have a tendency to become an enemy eventually. But if the "Why?" is community, joy and purpose in the process, the whole range of emotions that come with life, or anything internal and enduring, the watch can just become a tool to chase those aims.

Community? Strava is about cheering for others, not comparing to others. Joy and purpose in the process? The watch is about making sure you don't overdo it, while providing some fun structure to otherwise mundane runs. Emotional connection? GPS helps you remember each run, good and bad, a .gpx file that stores memories.

There are some simple methods to make the choice easier. Our athletes are instructed not to have the watch beep at mile markers, and to make sure the display screen doesn't show distance at all. Instead, it's just a tool to reflect on runs after the fact to make memories, engage with the broader community, and more strategically chase long-term goals. If that's impossible, we tell them to get off the GPS train altogether and settle down in analog-watch land.

The key is the question "Why?" Why do you run with a GPS watch in the first place? Know that answer, embrace the positive and internal option, and the frenemy will become a BFF.

So it goes with everything in your running life. Committing to the long-term process needed to meet your running and happiness potentials requires a long, hard examination of your own "Why?" Why run at all? Why race at all?

The Four Questions to Ask Yourself

Flow state is the Holy Grail of athletic endeavors. Mihály Csíkszentmihályi, the foremost positive psychologist and author of *Finding Flow*, defines it as an "optimal state of consciousness where we feel our best and perform our best." It goes deeper than that. Flow is "being completely involved in an activity for its own sake. The ego falls away. Time flies. Every action, movement, and thought follows inevitably from the previous one, like playing jazz. Your whole being is involved, and you're using your skills to the utmost." Find flow, and you find running nirvana.

Flow is a lot like buried treasure guarded by ancient spirits. You can try to find it, but you have to do a lot of work to get there.

There are 10 factors Csíkszentmihályi discusses, with the most important being a deep sense of meaning, lost sense of self-consciousness and doubt, and a high level of skill developed over time. Flow is a requirement for peak performance, and knowing your "Why?" is a requirement to find flow.

If your "Why?" isn't fully fleshed out, you'll never be able to put in the work to gain the proficiency to find flow. And if your "Why?" is based on comparison, it'll be hard to maintain meaning and lose self-doubt in a sport where failure is a constant presence along the way, whether it's through injury, aging, or simply having a bad training cycle.

You have probably found flow, perhaps without even realizing it. Maybe you were running down a slight hill, seemingly floating on air, when you threw your arms out and screamed at the top of your lungs. Maybe you were in a race, with a maxed-out heart rate and quiet mind, cresting the final hill of the day. Or maybe you finished a one-hour run and couldn't remember a second along the way, as if you were on autopilot. We call these experiences "moments of effortless transcendence," and it's a background reason to do this sport in the first place (along with post-run pizza).

But most of the time with running, you are not finding flow. One time, David pooped 11 times on a single run. Megan had to run around a one-third mile field at 3 a.m. during med school occasionally, and on one 12-mile run, on each lap she alternated saying to David, "I love you" (whoosh) "I hate this" (whoosh) "I love you" (whoosh) "I hate this."

We kept running, though. Everyone reading this probably has their own stories of comic relief from good running gone bad.

They say comedy is tragedy plus time. Well, one athlete we coached, Ryan Kaiser, was racing for the final time before he and his wife had twins when he starred in his own tragicomedy. He knew he'd be run-deprived while sleep-deprived, so he put all of his eggs in this race basket as a last hurrah (at least for the first month or two). At mile 78 of the Idaho Mountain Trail Ultra Festival 100 Miler, Ryan was leading by more than five miles, well ahead of record pace. Suddenly, in the dark of night, his feet hit pavement. He was on a road. The course didn't cross any roads.

Oh fudgeballs, that's not good. Ryan was miles off course, in the middle of nowhere, like a horror movie set in rural Idaho. If the *Deliverance* banjo started playing in the darkness, it wouldn't have been a surprise. Ryan survived to tell the tale, but he wasn't able to finish.

The heartbreak didn't deter him, though, even for a second. He said a few cuss words, had a hearty laugh, and gave his wife a kiss. Since his "Why?" was related to exploring his limits and not comparison-based metrics, the wrong turn was a chance to guffaw rather than give up. A few weeks later, he was back at it, more motivated than ever. Only this time, he was back as a dad runner.

Setting up your own framework to know your "Why?" is as simple as 1-2-3 (then 4). Get out a pen and paper, and do this at the same time you are penning your affirmations and evaluating your long-term goals to structure your process focus. The process of documenting your goals, and keeping track of your progress, has been shown to be a key factor in successfully changing your behaviors, just as Gretchen Rubin did in her *Happiness Project* and Ben Franklin did with his "Virtues Chart." So try to take these questions outside of your brain, whether that's with a checklist, a coach, a therapist, or anyone else you trust (EVEN YOUR DOG).

Make sure the "Why?" is authentic to you—not to the person you want to be, or the person others want you to be. In fact, make sure it's independent of external evaluation altogether. Making this list, and sticking to it, can change your running life forever. And if it doesn't reach that point, it can at least be a good exercise in thinking about what drives you.

1. **First, ask yourself: "Why do I run at all?"** This is the big one that drives your identity as a runner. It can be a multitude of reasons, as long as it's not "to beat others." Megan's is that it makes her a better person over time, just like that little girl who ran laps around the house to find contentedness. David's is that it takes away some of his self-doubt and allows him to find the person he truly is, just like that little boy who lived unhappily inside of his own head. Layered on top of that are some other reasons, big and small. "Purpose" for Megan. "Community" for David. Essentially, make sure your answer is grounded in positive emotions, like love, instead of negative emotions, like envy. And make sure your answer recognizes your ultimate fragility as a runner, and ultimate demise as a human being.

2. **Second, ask yourself: "Why do I run each day?"** This one is more granular, driving your decision to get out the door each day. It can be less meaningful and spiritual too. Megan's are endorphins and the power of running to instantly provide positive emotional input. David's are experiences and the power of running to make everything feel more real and less ephemeral. For both of us, well . . . we love eating. Runners have to eat a lot to stay healthy and improve. It's truly a glorious positive feedback cycle.

3. **Third, ask yourself: "Why am I racing at all?"** This one structures not whether you are a runner, but the choices you make in your running life. It's a question we ask of every athlete before

letting them race, because if racing does not have a "Why?" independent of comparison, it will eat you alive, eventually. Megan's is the satisfaction of giving her all to a task. David's is the motivation to push himself and stay the course over time. On the start line, we usually share a laugh and kiss. The training was the work to answer that question, the race is the celebration that the question is answered.

4. **Fourth, ask yourself: "Why do I have my long-term goals?"** This one does a lot of the work in driving the long-term process focus described in the previous chapter, with the other questions filling in the empty spaces. Now, since long-term goals are always in the future, the answer can involve some performance focus, like wanting to reach your ultimate potential. The key is for the answer to be enduring, so that it applies even after the initial goal has passed. For us, it's simply that it drives the process that we know we love, that we know makes us better people, that we know we want to do for the rest of our lives.

The coolest thing about "Why?" is that its power acts fast, like hemorrhoid cream for the soul. Jason Schlarb joined the SWAP team at the start of September 2017, after a year of poor races. Most distressingly, he had gotten down on himself and his running, losing the context that made him a previous champion of the Hardrock 100 and one of the most respected human beings in trail running.

So he thought a lot about "Why?" He wrote a poignant post on social media about his reasons for running, and how it fits into the person he wants to be. He wanted to help lift up others, he wanted to race not to be the best runner in the world, but to be the best person he could possibly be.

With his "Why?" clear, he jumped into a new system of training without a doubt. Every day, his training log practically let out a joyous yelp when it was opened. The pressure lifted, and it allowed his talent to shine.

Just three months later, he won one of the biggest races in China, against some of the top runners in the world. Little changed about his fitness—the new training approach just altered a few small things that wouldn't explain the massive improvement. Instead, Jason thought long and hard about his "Why?" He was suddenly more content as a runner and person.

And oh yeah, he was darn near unstoppable on the trails.

A big goal is a means to an end. Once the end gets there, you're left with a means that made you a happier person along the way.

You don't have to know all the answers. It would be crazy to know yourself like Ken Jennings knows all the daily doubles when playing *Jeopardy*. The answers can even change a bunch over time.

Yes, we hid the ball in this chapter. We got all this way just to tell you what you probably gathered while reading: It's all about asking the questions.

It's like a pump fake when playing fetch with Addie, only to see her sprint across the field in search of the ball. YOU GOT ME AGAIN, HOOMANS. YOU KNOW WHAT THEY SAY—FOOL ME 8,746 TIMES, SHAME ON YOU. FOOL ME 8,747 TIMES, SHAME ON ME.

So maybe the goal isn't to know your "Why?" at all. Instead, the goal is to think about your "Why?" Do that while lovingly embracing the process of a running life, and you might just stumble upon some principles that help you unconditionally accept yourself along the way.

—3—
Power Yourself With Kindness

Seventeenth-century philosopher Thomas Hobbes said that life outside society would be "nasty, brutish, and short." What Hobbes meant is that society is a necessary construct to quell humanity's worst instincts in relation to those outside their tribe. Cavepersons didn't duke it out for mammoth meat against a rival faction in a court of law. They fought for their right to live. It's kind of like the Whole Foods parking lot.

But society and community change everything. Align our natural instinct for self-interest with community goals, and our best natures come to the surface. Life isn't so nasty, brutish, and short anymore, unless you're in the Porta-Potty line 10 minutes before a race start. Most of the time, we cooperate with each other, and only then can we grow as individuals and communities beyond our species' more brutish nature.

Ironically, social media can turn back time to those mammoth fights and give weight to Hobbes's philosophy. Running life has changed rapidly with constant connectivity. That can be a bad thing—self-judgment on Strava, petty arguments on Twitter, curated lives on Instagram, gross toenail photos from people you barely know on Facebook. But with the bad comes nearly unlimited power for good. This chapter is about elevating your running life with community while avoiding getting dragged down into the prehistoric muck. Or, as Locke said, the ultimate truth for human society is "to love our neighbor as ourselves."

The book *Sapiens* goes into all of this further, chronicling humanity's development from the middle of the pack to the top of the food chain. The big breakthrough happened in the last 100,000 years when a weak ape called *homo sapiens* experienced the Cognitive Revolution—essentially, the ability to tell stories. Prior to that, communities couldn't cooperate beyond a handful of people, with most research indicating that strong social bonds can only be formed through direct contact with about 100 others. Add stories—like those of nations, shared goals, and education—and societies of cooperation can form. That rapidly let humanity become a juggernaut in the animal kingdom (for better or worse). Casting a wider net of community is a key reason that a few of those apes would eventually walk on the moon.

It's not only achievement that is best supported by community. Every synopsis of what makes people happy focuses on community and connection. Ruth Whippman traveled around the United States to write about happiness in her book *America the Anxious*, and her conclusion drove that point home simply: *happiness is other people.* That seems obvious, right? But Whippman found that seeking connection to others wasn't how people in the United States actually pursued happiness. Guided by the way society talks about these issues, embodied in "happiness apps" and self-help books, people had been taught that "happiness comes from within." While that is true to a certain extent, social relationships are the strongest predictor of happiness across time and cultures. After reviewing the research, Whippman summed it all up in *The New York Times*:

"Given all that, the next time you have the choice between meditating and sitting in a bar with your friends complaining about meditation class, you should probably seriously consider going to the bar, no matter what your happiness app says."

In running, you are presented with the same choice. How do you engage with the running community? That is an important question to answer for yourself in an effort to avoid a nasty, brutish, and short running life. Is it social media, group runs, a running team?

While it's important to think about how you engage, that is largely personality- and location- dependent. You probably can't have a big in-person running group if you live in Wyoming, unless you start a track club with some grizzly bears. Instead, there is a far more important, universal question: *Who is in your running community?*

Evolutionarily, we are hard-wired to care about people within our "family" or "tribe," to connect with them kindly and enthusiastically. And the research shows that type of connection is the main key to happiness. Thus, the answer about how wide we cast our net of community is not an idle one—it's the most important question of all.

So who is in the running community of a happy runner?

The answer is simple: Everyone.

If Everyone Is a Teammate, You Always Win

How big is your running family? Your answer could be the difference between long-term happiness, cheering on your extra-large squad, and jealous, bitter isolation in a running prison of your own making.

Megan came to this conclusion like Mike Campbell from Ernest Hemingway's *The Sun Also Rises*. "How did you go bankrupt?" he's asked. "Two ways," Mike said.

"Gradually and then suddenly."

But Megan's gradual progression to cheering on everyone didn't come until later in her story. Before that, there was just cutthroat competition.

Megan came out of the womb with a competitive fire that must have left a singed birth canal. Everything was an opportunity to excel, to be the strongest or fastest or smartest. Growing up, her favorite game was *Aggressive* Twister. It was a variation on the normal

Twister that involved complex yoga positions that became WWE wrestling moves that became punches and kicks in an effort to dominate her sibling rivals. After some bruises and tears, *Aggressive* Twister was banned. Soon after, *Actually* Sorry, Guess Who *Sucks*, and Poker *in the Eyeball* bit the dust too. No sport or game was safe.

Nor was any library reading competition. When Megan turned six, her parents signed her up for the elementary school book club over summer break. At the start of the next school year, she wrote about her experience in her summer journal project.

"Every three books you read, you would get a slip in a raffle."

If you know Megan, you probably know what happened next.

"The first day, I ready twenty-eight books! I did that practically every day and in one summer I read six hundred and fifty-four."

In retrospect, that seems like too much of a good thing, like eating 15 pounds of brussels sprouts a day because you read a news story that said they were healthy. But it wasn't just external competition—Megan was also fiercely competitive with herself. If she missed a goal in soccer, she would come home and practice the same shot until past dark. If she missed her mile PR in gym class, she would run quarter-mile repeats until the bottoms of her feet rubbed raw. It was an equal-opportunity competitive fire, as if a canister of napalm was perpetually awaiting a spark, taking her self-acceptance along with it.

Over time, though, the fire started to burn itself out bit by bit. College field hockey made her more reliant on teammates, more comfortable with failure, and more focused on long-term process. College track, overtraining, and injury showed her that she couldn't evaluate her self-worth in relation to external validation. But in 2014, even though it had diminished, there was still some competitive napalm simmering within her. All it needed was one final spark for the whole house to go up in flames.

In July 2014, we were sitting at our computers late one night when the spark ignited. Megan was flipping through a dermatology Power-Point on her computer, while David was purposefully facing the opposite direction to guard himself from the grotesque horrors that medical students look at in PowerPoint slides. He was checking his coaching e-mails, when all of a sudden he gasped. It was an e-mail from Corrine Malcom, a world-class biathlete.

"Megan!" David exclaimed. "An elite athlete is interested in SWAP! I think she has the potential to be a national champion at longer ultras."

It was a momentous occasion as the SWAP team grew. Up until that point, SWAP consisted largely of runners who wouldn't be winning national championships in anything but smiling competitions (the only results that really matter!). The team members at that embryonic stage of SWAP were a group of intrepid souls, some who probably joined for the "unique" coaching philosophy, others who probably joined for the $30 a month coaching fee. So that e-mail made David's heart soar.

Unfortunately, it soared about two feet before being shot down. Megan was furious.

"So let me get this straight. You are going to train elite female runners? And by the nature of your coaching you will turn them into champions. Then those same elite female runners are going to be my competition. And maybe they'll beat me?"

In retrospect, two things jump out. First, it shows Megan truly believed in the SWAP approach (cue the "aww" from the studio audience). Second . . . wow, that is an unsustainable approach to competition (as the audience sighs sadly).

Megan's response segued into an argument, a heated one, fueled by competitive fire. It was shocking for both of them. The only time they argued was when Megan insisted on using Apple Maps for driving directions, which is like navigation by process of elimination. ("It says turn right, so we should either turn left or give up.")

But this argument lasted all night with no resolution. They went to sleep angry and unsatisfied, like an emotional journey guided by Apple.

The next day, Megan apologized. Overnight, her gradual realization that she was a bit too competitive morphed into an epiphany all at once. Viewing others as competitors rather than teammates was self-defeating. Being competitive with herself and others was requiring a lot of energy, making her a worse person. She was constantly trying to beat her own times on hill climb segments and constantly researching competitors at top races. All of a sudden, it became too much. She didn't care anymore. It was not sustainable.

Perhaps it was caused by getting little sleep in medical school or seeing the end-of-life process in the hospital, but competition and winning didn't seem like the most important things anymore. Instead, Megan wanted to challenge herself and cheer for others at the same time. Corrine spurred the philosophy that would become a central principle of SWAP: *If everyone is a teammate, you always win.*

Since then, SWAP has grown to include a bunch of top athletes Megan would have formerly called competitors. Corrine herself became the U.S. 50 Mile Trail Champion two years later. The team won 10 female national championships. But Megan's philosophy was never truly put under the microscope until the 2017 North Face 50 Miler. It's easy to say everyone is a teammate when you're always winning. But what happens when you lose?

North Face was Megan's first race over 50K. It was entirely out of her comfort zone in shorter distances, where she loved the old friend *continuous pain* and the good buddy *crushing intensity*. So she was nervous about even finishing, let alone competing at the front of the race. She lined up next to Clare Gallagher (from chapter 2), a long-time SWAP athlete and winner of major international races like the Leadville Trail 100 and CCC. David had instructed Megan to hang with Clare for the early miles of the race.

Megan and Clare yo-yoed for the first 15 miles. In between, they talked about life and the universe and watched the sunrise peer over the Bay Area mountains. Around mile 15, Clare started to roll. It was obvious she was having a good day. She was effortlessly bouncing around on the trails while telling jokes and snacking on Sour Patch Kids. (Side note: Yes, you can eat candy in ultramarathons! Never has there been a better selling point for a physical activity.)

Megan let Clare go. She wasn't sure it was a comfortable enough pace for a 50-mile race. She was afraid of the unknown. She was afraid of blowing up on her favorite Bay Area trails.

As Clare powered ahead, Megan's competitive fire faced its big test.

"DAVVIIDDDDDDD!" She screamed in her head. What would come next? Would she be angry?

She finished the thought. "Wow, he's a gosh darn good coach!" She laughed and cheered her head off for her teammate. She asked about Clare at every aid station.

"She's crushing. She's closing in on first."

"She looks so strong and happy. She's all smiles and grit."

This feedback was a stronger fuel than caffeinated gels. Megan crossed the finish line in fourth. Clare was waiting at the finish for a hug, having run a brilliant race to finish second. But perhaps even more importantly, the other female finishers were there too. Megan hugged the winner, Ida Nilsson. She hugged third place, Megan Kimmel. She hugged every woman and man she could get her sweaty, gel-covered hands on. She would have given herself hugs if she could.

Prior to 2014, Megan would have viewed this moment as a nightmare. An athlete from within her personal running community had beat her to the finish. Not only that, two other women beat her too. Megan was fourth—one place off the podium. Old Megan would have thought it was a personal failure.

But new Megan viewed this moment as a community success, a dream in the making. A SWAP teammate and friend had a heck of a day and Megan had run a smart and strong 50-mile debut. What amazing women were out there! What a community! What hugs! What candy!

Megan left TNF50 ready for more ultra-experiences. She also left with a full heart. By cheering on the whole community, rather than living in her own head, she had quintupled her dopamine stock. She had found self-acceptance by letting go of the need to prove herself. It was rewarding and fun to root for others.

But that isn't all. By lifting others up, she lifted herself up too.

Developing the Kindness Habit

When fellow runners are all a part of your big running family, some things fall into place. Results matter less because you care less about beating people. When results matter less, you won't beat yourself up as much since success and failure aren't defined by finish lines, but by the process along the way. Your "Why?" will trend toward internal, positive justifications for your running life, rather than measuring yourself in relation to others. In sum, you'll set up a happy runner foundation, stabilized by your happy runner family.

But even if you don't care about all that, there is something else a bit more selfish at play.

You get faster, too.

Before you get faster, though, you have to learn what it means to be a kind runner in practice.

Lauren Welton, a 26-year-old from Texas, embodies what it means to be driven and strong while also viewing other runners as members of her big running family. Lauren is the type of athlete who without question and without complaint would attempt any workout in her training log. Because of this motivated focus, we go through and reread her training plan each week, skimming for typos. One stray tap of the "zero" key could make a 10-mile run last a couple days.

In one of her first races as a SWAP athlete, Lauren raced the Habanero 100K in the Texas hill country. Around halfway through the race, Lauren developed unbearable blisters, the type that would even make a medical student blush if a photo showed up on a PowerPoint slide. Without question and without complaint, she switched into the only pair of additional shoes she had with her—a pair of Birkenstock sandals with just two straps. Lots of people swear by 'Stocks, but this would be the ultimate test of both runner and sandal. Could she lift herself up by her sandal straps? If you know Lauren, you know how this ends.

She went on to run 23 miles in two-strap sandals and ravaged feet, securing a fourth-place finish. Her own dilemma was an opportunity to laugh, not to despair. In the midst of adversity that would cause almost anyone else to drop out, she was living the kind runner mantra: You can take your running seriously without taking yourself seriously.

That point is an essential place to start. Taking yourself super seriously rarely works because eventually the universe will show you that it disagrees wholeheartedly.

That doesn't mean you can't view what you do seriously, though. Passion for the long-term process requires deeply caring. Just remember that while running (or any passion you have) is beautiful and meaningful, you are the same person who occasionally faceplants while jogging on a smooth sidewalk.

Lauren's story also shows the next principle of a runner focused outside themselves: By not being overly self-serious, you can be a competitor who still truly roots for others. The Last Man Standing Race in East Texas involves running a 5K loop every 45 minutes until there is only one runner left. It seems like the race director got the idea after reading Dante's *Inferno*, or a book on medieval torture techniques. It suited Lauren perfectly.

We waited and waited for a race update, knowing that Lauren was enduring hellish, medieval, Iowa Caucus–style suffering with each hour that passed. But in community, the suffering found extra meaning.

Lauren wrote post-race: "After 15 hours, there were two left standing: a badass female ultrarunner who told me she has kids and was going to use the $600 prize money to make their Christmas special, and me. After the 20th lap I knew she was tired, but this woman was going to move mountains to win this prize money. It was so inspiring."

"So I felt good about my next decision, which was not a pity move, but a 'I know this woman is going to grind it out for two days to make this happen' move. The winner of the race has to do a final uncontested lap to claim their victory. So when we started our 21st lap, I followed up a hill behind her and when I knew she was far enough ahead, I went back and dropped out so she'd be surprised with the win and didn't have to run anymore."

As soon as it became clear that Lauren's internal, process-driven thirst had been satisfied, she chose to win through kindness. It wasn't surprising that she experienced genuine happiness and a deluge of dopamine.

That night in the same e-mail to Megan, she highlighted her joy. "Throughout the day, I was all smiles and encouraged every runner. Having never met any of these people, I left this race with my heart feeling so incredibly full. Could not have found more joy today!"

Lauren didn't know anyone at this race, but they were members of her running family. It's easy to have benevolence for those who you know personally, but it's harder to have benevolence for strangers. It wasn't surprising that Lauren chose the harder, kinder option. As a result, whether she finished first or last, she would have won.

The science of kindness demonstrates the quick-acting power of elevating those around you. Sonja Lyubomirsky, a psychology professor and happiness expert, conducted a study at Stanford University where she asked students to carry out five weekly "random acts of kindness." Her study consisted of three groups—one where students did all of their acts in one day, another where the acts were spread across the week, and a control group. The acts of kindness ranged from "buying a homeless man a Whopper" to "being a designated driver at a party."

Kindness created happier students rapidly—but only in the group where students performed all of their acts in one day each week. It seems that thinking about these acts and deliberately performing them in one day enabled students to perceive themselves as generous people and expand their social networks, rather than as people that are just occasionally kind. In other words, kindness needs to be a worldview applied broadly, not something to do just when it's convenient or out of obligation.

In SWAP, we talk incessantly of kindness, like a CD player skipping over the same line. We even program it into training. Traditionally, we characterized athletes' full rest days as "treat yo' self days," when they would eat their favorite foods and indulge without hesitation in the finer things in life (like naps). We hoped that sleeping in and consuming chocolate chip pancakes could help ease the rest day blues and bring a small shot of dopamine.

After reading some of the research, we converted SWAP's "treat yo' self days" to "treat yo' friendz days." The hope was to strategically boost kindness and generosity on rest days, boosting happiness in the process. We also hoped to emphasize a culture of unconditional support in the running community. Little by little, kindness can become a habit, like brushing your teeth. You just have to work at it, one little act at a time.

That's so freaking hard in practice, though. We screw up our kindness goals all the time. The goal isn't to exude an infallible aura of kindness, but to accept yourself and others as much as you can given the constraints of your background, brain chemistry, and perspective. To put it another way—the key isn't to do everything right all the time; it's to practice being a bit better most of the time.

Giving unconditional support is an end in itself. But it also can reflect oodles of goodness back onto you. Sonja Lyubomirsky writes, "There are a lot of positive social consequences to being kind—other people appreciate you, they're grateful and they might reciprocate." All of the happiness research indicates that kindness gives you more than you put out. Negativity hurts everyone, but you most of all.

Some people call this karma. We believe in probability. If you help someone, there's a chance you will benefit—and at the very least you will be a happier and kinder person. It's easier to think you are enough when you aren't constantly feeling negativity toward those around you. That in turn supports consistency, which supports development over time.

Let's rewind to the conclusion of Lauren's story. After The Last Man Standing race, the badass ultra-runner that beat her out was able to buy her kids new shoes for Christmas. For Lauren, people at the race told her story, leading to her drop-out getting her more acknowledgment and satisfaction than any win ever would. Not only that, she got some shoes too—Birkenstocks heard her stories, and sent her a brand-new pair of sandals. Now that's a kickass circle of kindness.

Kindness Can Be a Performance Enhancer

Kindness is just like training, but with less nipple chafing. Lots of little actions over time can change everything in the long run. But developing the kindness habit is not just about being a happier runner. Since it feeds into positive emotions that fuel daily training, kindness actually makes you a stronger, faster runner over time too. It can even make faster running take less energy! Before getting to that, though, we need to take a step back to better understand the philosophical underpinnings of a kindness-oriented worldview.

To avoid writing a whole book on kindness (title: *Harnessing Your Puppy Power*), we'll hone in on the philosophy of Confucius. *Jen* (pronounced "wren" in case you ever appear on a podcast) is the virtue that serves as the foundation for Confucianism. In English, jen translates to "humanity," "humaneness," "goodness," "benevolence," or "love."

Confucius himself describes jen best: "A man of humanity, wishing to establish his own character, also establishes the character of others, and wishing to be prominent himself, also helps others to be prominent." A person who embodies jen works toward the ideal of what humanity should be and encourages others to strive for benevolence along the way.

Dacher Keltner, in his book *Born to Be Good: The Science of a Meaningful Life*, defines a concept called the jen ratio. He writes, "The jen ratio is a lens onto the balance of good and bad in your life. In the denominator of the jen ratio place recent actions in which someone has brought the bad in others to completion. . . . Above this, in the numerator of the ratio, tally up the actions that bring the good in others to completion. . . . As the value of your jen ratio rises, so too does the humanity of your world."

"It was my understanding that there would be no math," an irked reader might say. But this is math that even Addie dog can understand. Essentially, the jen ratio is the positive observations in our lives divided by the negative observations. For our runner-focused framework, think of it as community-oriented kindness over self-indulgent ego: the Golden Rule with a calculator.

Let's break down each component. When you do that math on the jen ratio as a runner, you cannot simply put zero in the denominator. In order to run at all in a sport that is mostly individual, we are required to have some element of self-interest and competitive nature. These survival skills are coded into our neural circuitry, and denying them is denying our humanity altogether.

However, ego just has to meet a bare minimum threshold. Once we achieve the minimal denominator needed for survival as a runner, our jen ratio and our connection to community matter most for happiness. Keltner summarizes: "Literature reveals time and time again that what makes us happy is the quality of our romantic bonds, the health of our families, the time we spend with good friends, the connections we feel to communities. When our jen ratios are high in our close relations, so are we."

If your close relations include the whole running community, then there is almost no limit to the positivity that can come from a jen ratio focused on kindness. The beauty of this concept is that while the jen ratio could make us happier runners, it could also improve running performance.

Think about the negative emotions that you generate when you root against a competitor. Eventually those emotions culminate in fatigue and desperation and burnout. As Darth Vader would attest, hate and ego are powerful, but they eat away at what makes us human and happy.

Sports performance research supports Lord Vader's findings. Countless studies have shown that negative emotions lead to higher levels of muscle tension, breathing difficulties, and loss of concentration. Further, negative emotions lead to a spiral of negative thoughts about performance and can cause existential crises in the middle of a race or a training cycle. The dark side is exhausting.

It goes beyond racing. In the daily act of training, a little bit of kindness to yourself and others can support consistency. On intervals, a bit of joyous belief might let you go a second faster. Add up the major gains from consistency and the marginal gains from joy in the process, and a kind runner becomes a far faster runner.

Neuroscience confirms that positive emotions and benevolence can be performance enhancing. When we act cooperatively and root for others, the nucleus accumbens, the reward center in the brain, lights up with activity. The nucleus accumbens is filthy rich with dopamine receptors. And there are few things that make runners faster than making it rain with dopamine (and none of them are legal).

On top of that, studies have shown that positive attitude makes for faster runners. Even smiling can improve running economy, making faster paces feel easier. Being easy with a smile or laugh is not only the best trait in a friend, it might be the best little thing you can do to make a big difference in your running training.

One way to do this in your everyday life: challenge yourself to a laughing contest. A fun exercise for an adult is to see how many times you actually laugh in a day. For a lot of people, it's way lower than you might think. Meanwhile, there are tons of chances to laugh. So let's do it!

Watching TV? Laugh! Bad joke from a friend? Laugh! Bonk on a run? Laugh! Poop yourself? Laugh!

Basically, search for chances to practice laughing and smiling. The research is incontrovertible—positivity correlates with well-being and sustainable performance. And it lifts up everyone around you, too.

Case in point—this was a challenge we actually gave our athletes inspired by Margaret Link, the director of marketing at Sufferfest Beer Company. We met her and something immediately jumped out—her laugh. In a one-hour conversation, she probably laughed 60 times. A stuffy meeting slowly morphed into a joyous celebration, with everyone reflecting Margaret's smile. It's no wonder that she rose to such a prominent position at 28 years old, all while being a kickass athlete too. Her jen ratio tipped the scales at *Puppy*. That gave her the strength to overcome all the crap life threw at her along the way.

Yet again, Confucius sums up this concept best: "One who is not a man of humanity cannot endure adversity for very long, nor can he enjoy prosperity for long. The man of humanity is naturally at ease with humanity. The man of wisdom cultivates humanity for its advantage."

In order to be a successful runner, you have to endure. It's much easier to endure when you are benevolent, genuinely rooting for others, and making it rain with dopamine.

Enthusiasm Is the Greatest Thing Ever

Events and circumstances in life are not always a choice. But our perspective on them often is. Make the choice to be kind, then make the choice to be enthusiastic, and a lot of things can sort themselves out. A rainy day becomes nature doing the sweating job for you, a burned roast means you get to order the best pizza ever, and a bad run becomes a delightful learning experience.

It isn't always easy, but it's usually true: An enthusiastic runner is a happier and faster runner.

A 2011 article by the founder of essay website Semi-Rad, Brendan Leonard, summed it up eloquently. "Your life, even the bad parts, is [&*^$#@!] amazing. And most of the small things that make up your life are amazing, too—mountain bike rides, rock climbs, ski runs, sunsets, stars, friends, people, girlfriends and boyfriends, dogs, songs, movies, jokes, smiles . . . hell, even that burrito you ate for lunch today was pretty phenomenal, wasn't it?"

That mindset isn't for everyone. There are probably some people reading this right now who think that's a steaming pile of something crazy smelly. For everyone else, there could be a massive reserve of untapped power in fully accepting that it's okay to be enthusiastic. We call it embracing the power of awesome.

Things are awesome. People are awesome. Heck, multiple slices of pizza or sunrises can be the greatest and most awesome pizzas and sunrises ever. As Leonard says, "Enthusiasm doesn't have to stand up to criticism. It doesn't even have to really make sense. If you finish a run, MTB trail, or sport climbing route, and you ~~like~~ love it, I encourage you to try out new superlatives when describing it to someone else." *Heck, yes! Awesome!*

You know what's the best way to be kind to people? To tell them they are freaking awesome, because they are. You know what's the best way to love running? To scream like you're on a roller-coaster and laugh at your stumbles. You know what's the best way to get fast? To channel Addie dog's enthusiasm and all-caps LOVE the running process, even when you don't.

If there's one thing that wisdom teaches us, it's that most wise men spent a long time faking it before they were making it. Behavioral psychology supports the principle that acting a certain way can make us more like that over time (smiling makes you happier, acting energetic makes you more energetic). It goes for school, your job, being a parent, and being a happy runner too.

Part of the SWAP experiment initially was replacing the niceties "Thank you" and "You're welcome" with "YOU ARE AWESOME!" and "YOU ROCK!!!" It may sound a bit childish. Actually, scratch that, it's extremely childish, and even more puppyish. And that's the whole freaking point.

It Takes Enthusiastic Practice

Some people exit the womb more kind and enthusiastic than others. And that is okay—we all are different. Plus, our brain chemistries vary in spiciness, from ghost pepper to mayonnaise. David came out of the womb as a packet of mayo, nice but reserved and boring to a fault. That all changed one day at his locker in sixth grade.

As he was standing there, one of his classmates, Stephanie, whom he didn't know particularly well, dropped a pencil on the ground across the hall. David quickly played a game of hallway Frogger to retrieve it. As soon as he delivered the pencil to Stephanie, he broke out in a big, snaggle-toothed smile. She immediately smiled right back. In retrospect, there was no particularly good reason for that smile—it just happened. And it changed his life.

Stephanie's response caught him off guard. "You are such a nice person!" she exclaimed.

David absorbed Stephanie's response as if it was the last drop of water in the desert. Her words made him feel good and made him ponder, finally putting that time he spent in his own head to good use. Other than the day he met Megan, it was the most important in his life.

Because on that day, David made a choice. He would try his best to be relentlessly kind and enthusiastic. Ten years later, by the time that he met Megan for their first frozen yogurt date, he was well-practiced. As a behavioral psychologist would guess, kindness and enthusiasm had become a habit.

At first, Megan didn't think it was real. She called her mom after the first date and recounted her experience.

"He's very charming, extremely enthusiastic, and *very* weird. He also ordered potato chips on his frozen yogurt. The thing is, I don't know if his enthusiasm is sustainable."

Megan continued to be an "enthusiasm skeptic" in the early days of their relationship. She even brought up enthusiasm on one of their long hikes in North Carolina.

"Do you think that your exclamation points ever lose their meaning? Do you think that by constantly telling people they are amazing, that you lower the standard of amazing?"

David's response was simple: "Nope. I think great things don't require bad things to offset them. You can be both enthusiastic and honest."

Four years after they started dating, Megan had surpassed her enthusiasm teacher. It helped that she had the best mentor during that time—Addie dog. Addie is the ultimate enthusiasm test case. Is enthusiasm a depletable resource, to be dispensed with precious care? HECK NO, ENTHUSIASM IS RENEWABLE AND YOU ARE PERFECT AND I LOVE YOU AND I SEEM TO HAVE LOST MY TRAIN OF THOUGHT.

When we moved to California back in 2013, Addie flew across the country in the pet-cargo hold of a United flight (hey, it can't be worse than their economy class). Twelve hours after dropping her off on the East Coast, we picked her up in San Francisco. Only now, she had some friends with her. Four airline employees were mid-cuddle as Addie squealed joyously.

Eventually, we pried Addie from their snuggles and brought her home to our brand-spanking-new 340-square-foot studio apartment. Luxury! If you are reading this during a cold winter or humid summer and ever want to feel better about where you live, look up the Bay Area on real-estate website Zillow. The $2.4 million condos that are 30 minutes from anything will help explain why we tried to fit three smelly creatures in an oversized shoebox.

But Addie loved her smelly shoebox. Every day while David worked, she camped out by the window. Her favorite spectator sport was watching people go by.

Every few minutes, her tail started wagging, almost sending her airborne like a furry helicopter. The hairycopter would always be started by a person ambling past. At first, people would look through the window at her with detached curiosity. Over time, though, her relentless enthusiasm would wear people down. First, it'd be a child that waved, inviting her out. We'd open the door, and Addie sprinted to their feet, rolling over and making one thing clear. YOU ARE THE GREATEST PERSON IN THE WORLD. I WILL LOVE YOU FOREVER. After that, it'd be an adult that saw Addie's joy. Then another neighbor. Then another.

After a few months, people would walk by just to say hi to Addie. She'd have standing appointments with kids in the neighborhood. Addie loved one frequent visitor so much that she started squealing preemptively when the woman rounded the corner a block away.

Addie did that every day for the next few years, only getting more enthusiastic with age. In her head, every time she got to see someone, Whitney Houston started playing. IIIIIIIIIIIIIIIII WILLL ALWAYS LOVE YOUUUUUUUUUUUUUUU. Addie helped both of us learn a universal truth for puppies and humans alike. Love, it turns out, doesn't get depleted. You just get more to give out.

Over those few years, spurred by her smelly family, Megan saw how enthusiasm and love helped people around her. But it took medical school rotations to see how it might help herself.

In 2016, Megan's first clinical rotation was surgery—a six-day-a-week, eight-week-long intensive rotation that involved arriving at the hospital at 5 a.m., rounding on patients, and then spending all day standing in the operating room.

On the second day of the rotation, Megan spent the entire morning "retracting," a medical student job that involves using tools to anchor tissues and organs so that the surgeon can have a better field of work. Retracting involves hours of standing in one position while accumulating neck kinks and shoulder cramps. Depending on what you're retracting, it doesn't always smell great either.

Megan spent that morning worrying about having to leave early for an orientation activity. How were the surgeons going to keep operating if they didn't have a clear field of view? She was indispensable, right?

Wrong. In about 45 seconds, they had set up a circular clamp contraption with five different tools. They had easily established a beautiful and effective surgical field.

Megan was furious. She had spent hours laboring in uncomfortable positions just to have her place taken by a far more effective circular clamp? Was she even needed on this rotation?

That moment set the tone for the entire experience. Over the course of the rotation, Megan actively worked to avoid having to stand in the OR. Her feet were already exhausted from trying to run 80 miles a week on the treadmill at 3 a.m. and she didn't feel like being a surgical tool. She knew that surgeons were busy people and weren't always thinking about the whereabouts of medical students. So a couple times in the last week of the rotation, she escaped.

Once, she made it as far as the woodchipped trails on Stanford's campus, and another time she escaped down the hall to the storage closet, where she could sit and close her eyes in peace. She sat there for five minutes, laughing at her exhaustion.

Megan was miserable, and it showed in her interactions with doctors and patients. It also showed in her grades. At the end of the rotation, she was frustrated with herself and wondered how she was going to survive two years of clinical rotations.

On the last day of the rotation, she decided she had enough. She wasn't thinking about surgery specifically, but her approach to life generally. Her goals for the rest of medical school were simple: commit to daily enthusiasm and kindness. HECK YES, SOUL SISTA, SHAKE THAT TAIL LIKE A HELICOPTER.

Her commitment was part out of self-preservation and part out of curiosity. Being miserable spurred some pretty comical sarcasm in storage closets, but it wasn't helping her learning or her daily enjoyment. And it sure as heck wasn't helping the people around her.

Megan went to internal medicine next. She spent extra time each day getting to know patients and their families. She was always there for the residents and doctors she was working with—aiming to get to know them as people and bring a little joy and entertainment to their days. With each day, the commitment to enthusiasm got easier and easier, like Addie sitting at the window and becoming the star of the neighborhood. Megan often didn't have answers, but she had smiles.

And she started to realize that a lot of the time, the combo of a smile and a genuine laugh was the right answer (at least when the question wasn't "Why am I uncontrollably vomiting?").

Over time, Megan's outlook on clinical rotations started to improve. After each rotation, she wanted to specialize in whatever she had just practiced. David always laughed as Megan professed that she wanted to go into internal medicine, obstetrics and gynecology, pediatrics, and family medicine.

With this new outlook came drastically better grades. Megan improved in the "clinical interaction" component of grading, but she also improved in raw test scores. Being engaged, enthusiastic, and present meant that it was easier to connect medical knowledge to a meaningful patient.

Megan hasn't looked back. It turns out that replacing periods with exclamation points in the way you think about life can make some people kinder and happier. And it may improve performance too.

Harnessing the Awesomely Infinite Power of Enthusiasm

Sixth-grade David and 20th-grade Megan and all-the-time Addie may have been on to something with their commitment to enthusiasm. Recent research performed by Dylan Minor out of Northwestern's Kellogg School of Business showed that being within a 25-square-foot radius of a high-performer boosted performance in coworkers by 15 percent. On the flipside, being within a 25-square-foot radius of a "toxic" performer dropped performance in coworkers by 30 percent.

Where this research gets really interesting is the question of "Why?" Why do high performers help those around them? Is it objective skills or contagious enthusiasm?

You probably answered the leading question correctly—task-oriented enthusiasm makes everyone better. Performance gains did not persist if the high-performer left. Theoretically, if the gains were due to better productivity or technical skills, they should persist or even improve independent of the long-term presence of the high performer. Minor himself concluded that these gains were likely the result of inspiration and social pressure.

To put it in SWAP language, if you're around an awesome "F#%& yes!" person, you improve. If you're around an unenthusiastic "No" person, everyone suffers.

In running, the best example is the "Shalane Flanagan Effect" described by the *New York Times* in November 2017. The article summarizes it: "Every single one of her training partners—11 women in total—has made it to the Olympics while training with her, an extraordinary feat. Call it the Shalane Effect: You serve as a rocket booster for the careers of the women who work alongside you, while catapulting forward yourself."

Flanagan did it by replacing cutthroat competition with kindness, by drawing the lines of who she considered her running family widely. "Instead of being threatened by her teammates' growing accomplishments, Flanagan embraced them, and brought in more women, elevating them to her level until they become the most formidable group of distance athletes in the nation." The article credits her passion, being team-oriented rather than selfish.

Perhaps most interesting of all—Flanagan thrived too. Kindness and enthusiasm to those around you builds up a support system that elevates you as well. When she won the New York City Marathon in 2017, the first American woman to win in decades, she famously screamed in full view of the cameras. While the sound didn't come through, you could read her lips clearly. And you could imagine all those training partners saying the same thing.

"YES! F#%& YES!"

Des Linden returned the favor at the 2018 Boston Marathon. The weather was historically brutal—30 mph headwinds and torrential rain. Those are conditions made for hot cocoa and Netflix, not running. And, as you'd expect, the results were not great.

Woman after woman dropped off the pace. In the first few miles, Linden decided she might drop out. As she recounted in an article in *USA Today*: "It was pretty nasty out there in all honesty, with pretty tough conditions . . . I thought early on that I might be pulling the plug. So I just nudged [Shalane Flanagan] and said, 'Hey if I can block the wind or help at all let me know.'"

Linden meant it. Pre-race favorite Flanagan had stomach trouble and had to stop at a Porta-Potty. In one of the biggest races in the world, which an American woman hadn't won in decades, Linden forgot about her own race and dropped back to help pace Flanagan back to the lead pack.

Only, when they got back to the lead pack, something had changed. Linden's fatigued legs were replaced by kindness and enthusiasm rocket boosters. Somehow, she won, and she did so in emphatic fashion. From nearly dropping out to dominating one of the world's most competitive marathons . . . maybe the best superpower is inside all of us. Maybe if we harness our kindness and enthusiasm potential, we all can become Linden-like superheroes.

When it comes to running, what is the basis for enthusiasm and kindness performance gains? It all gets back to emotions and neurobiology. For example, a study published in the *Psychology of Sport and Science* journal showed that simply smiling can improve running economy by 2 percent. In a three-hour marathon, that could equate to a few-minute improvement (and some fantastic-looking race photography). More studies come out all the time showing that positivity is the ultimate performance enhancer.

Perhaps emotional state can even change the way we respond to stress in the first place. John Kiely, a researcher and successful coach in England, discussed in a 2017 *Sports Medicine* paper that fitness adaptations are influenced by an athlete's neurobiology. In turn, both emotional stress and emotional state influence neurobiology. So two runners who do the same training session can adapt totally differently depending on their state of mind.

More and more, performance psychology is showing us the key to breakthroughs. It truly is not all about the miles. It's about the smiles. F#%& yes, indeed.

The Magical Power of Persistent Belief

Kindness and enthusiasm form a rising tide, lifting up all the boats around you. It lifts up your boat too. But what happens when you've done everything right, with your ship sitting beautifully on the sea, and the air is knocked out of your sails entirely?

You can probably tell we don't know much about boats. But we do know about failure.

In life, you'll fail and you'll screw up no matter what you do. There is only one antidote to the virus of failure: persistent, resilient, stubborn belief.

Runners fail more than most. If you're lucky enough to have the genetics and life circumstances to be really good, you'll fail publicly, in glorious fashion.

In 2017, Sarah Keyes learned firsthand about what happens when kindness and enthusiasm run headfirst into failure.

Six months before the 2017 Western States 100, she got a surprise—a rare, coveted sponsor invitation to run the most prestigious ultramarathon in the United States. With that sponsor invitation came the duty to blog about her journey to Western States. Starting in the thick of winter, she trained hard and she wrote often.

Training hard in December in Saranac Lake, New York, meant running in single-digit temperatures and trudging through epic quantities of snow and ice as a human snot-sicle. Sarah would do her training runs at 4 a.m. before she worked long hospital shifts as a nurse, giving her all for this opportunity. Despite the early morning wakeups, Sarah had stability in this life. She had no pressure to perform and no one watching her results.

That all changed when Sarah started to plan a two-month running tour of the United States to meet her sponsor obligations. She planned to live out of her truck with her dog, Mocha Pebbles, writing for a large audience along the way.

She was dreaming big. In April, she wrote in her blog, "Being offered an opportunity to participate for the first time in Western States is not to be taken lightly and I intend to make the most of it."

Sarah planned to stop in key running cities such as Jackson Hole, Park City, and Tahoe to organize group runs, and then finish her cross-country trek at the Western States starting line. She also hoped to go for a fastest known time (FKT) on the Zion Traverse as a key long run.

Her journey seemed idyllic, but she was honest in her approach. Sarah wrote, "I drove away from my town, a town where I felt like I belonged more than ever before. Away from a wonderful man that supported my decision to take this trip and a job where I finally feel comfortable. I drove away from stability and into uncertainty."

She was also honest with herself about her "Why?" (she should really coauthor this book). Sarah chronicled, "I've thought a lot about why I was taking this trip and besides the 'life is short' motto, I now know I want to inspire others to follow their heart. Even to my own ears, that sounds a little mushy and is a tad selfish, but I do hope what I do shows others they can pursue their goals too. In some ways, running ultras could make the world a better place."

On May 13, Sarah went for the Zion Traverse FKT. She finished in 8 hours 27 minutes and 36 seconds, only 67 seconds behind the FKT held by Joelle Vaught. On an eight-hour journey, 67 seconds is the difference between a very fast bathroom break, or a quick stop to take a photo—something that David suggested to her that morning.

That was a failure, sure, but failures can be fun too and her eyes were still on the race on the horizon, Western States. She had called her shot, now it was time to take it.

On June 24, Sarah's road trip ended as she toed the starting line at the Western States 100. Sarah was having the race of her life and sat in the top 10 coming through Michigan Bluff at mile 55, when something went horribly wrong. Her feet were rubbed raw. It was essentially rapid-onset trenchfoot, caused by the extra-wet conditions.

But Sarah was committed to finishing. She walked most of the rest of the way, all 45 miles to the finish. And it couldn't help but feel like a failure. A depressing failure, not a fun one.

"I've read other runners' accounts of how running had saved them from their demons of depression, but I felt like running had caused mine . . . [Before Western States,] my glasses weren't only rosy, they were bedazzled. It got so bad I think I claimed that unicorns were real at one point. As those little gems began to fall off one by one, I realized that the glue holding those sparkles on wasn't as strong as I thought."

But she believed. Even when things were at their worst, and the cloud of depression settled on top of her, she held onto a persistent belief that she had unlimited adventures ahead. In a phone call with David in July, she put it succinctly. "I'm sad. But I'm hungry."

On October 17, Sarah hungrily toed the starting line at the Ultra Trail Harricana, a competitive 125K race in Quebec, with the goal of finishing, adventuring, and accumulating points to qualify for Ultra World Tour Mt. Blanc. She went for it, again. This time, she won in a massive course record. But most importantly, her belief let her find her "sparkle" again.

Sarah wrote after the race, "What felt like a step back four months ago is now a leap forward. I've found growth even in dark times; part of the balance of life. I still define myself as a runner, but my definition of runner has changed, and on the right day, unicorns still do exist."

During the process, she owned the good, the bad, and the ugly. She was honest with herself and with others. Throughout her journey, she allowed her whole, raw story to be shared, lifting others up even as she was down.

The incredible thing about owning everything in your running life is that you can't go wrong. All of life's emotions add flavor to a story. The good, the bad, and the ugly are all part of being human, life's version of Neapolitan ice cream. The bad and the ugly aren't always fun in the moment, but they often provide inspiring stories and some comedic entertainment. Belief turns tragedy into stories, failures into bumps in the road, and ultimately the lowest lows into the highest highs.

Running is inherently a process that produces cycles of good, bad, and ugly. It's okay to care about running and own those dreams, but it's always helpful to remember that at the end of the day, we are all here for the stories. Self-acceptance can be independent of outcomes—as discussed in the next chapter, you are perfect no matter what. So belief in yourself doesn't mean thinking you will win the gold medal, it means thinking you can continue to grow, even when handed evidence to the contrary. You are enough, unconditionally.

The lesson from Sarah's fairy tale? Unicorns do exist. You just gotta believe.

Feeling Small and Dreaming Big

Kindness, enthusiasm, and belief make your dreams possible. Actually, scratch that. They make possible the dreams you don't even know you have yet.

Nearly every entrepreneur is a case study in the power of enthusiasm and belief (the happy ones usually have kindness, too). Cathy Hughes embodies all three, and her story shows how you can develop as a runner while holding tightly to just a few main principles.

Hughes is the founder of Radio One, a massive media enterprise, and the first African American woman to head a publicly traded company. But before all that, she was just a poor kid with a dream and a toothbrush microphone.

Hughes grew up in Omaha, Nebraska, in the segregated 1950s. As a kid, she developed her own practice radio show in the bathroom, using a mirror and a toothbrush to grow her personality and broadcast to her four siblings. She knew that she would go on to develop her own radio show someday. She would find a way to make it happen.

On the other hand, the nuns at her grade school were not convinced. Hughes recounted the story on the "How I Built This" podcast.

"Everyone at that time thought there was something wrong with me. There were no black people in radio, particularly no black women. . . . They thought I had a pipedream. I had nuns at my school describe it as delusions of grandeur. They told my mother that she should seek counseling for me because I had these visions of being on the radio."

That didn't stop her.

In the late 1960s, she seized an opportunity and started working at Howard University's radio station in Washington, D.C. Shortly thereafter, she became interested in an AM station, WOL 1450, which was up for sale. In order to buy it, she only needed $1 million and the ability to outbid Muhammad Ali, who was also interested. The only problem? She was short $990,000.

That didn't stop her.

Hughes went in search of a loan. She tried 32 lending institutions, all of whom said no.

That didn't stop her.

A yes finally came from a lender in her first week on the job at the Chemical Bank of New York, who was enamored with Hughes' enthusiasm. With the loan secured, Cathy owned WOL 1450 and moved into the radio station as a home for three years with her young son because she couldn't afford to pay rent.

Hughes changed WOL 1450's format immediately. She converted WOL 1450 from a station that focused on playing all music, to a station that discussed politics and cultural events from an African American standpoint. She dubbed this station Radio One. She was told it was stupid and reckless, that it would bankrupt her due to the high cost of original programming.

That didn't stop her.

The station thrived. Hughes went on to purchase underperforming stations through Radio One, improving radio reviews by incorporating talk shows centered around local demographics. By 2001, Radio One (now Urban One) was the largest urban-market broadcast company in the United States, with 18 million listeners and Hughes' son as the CEO.

Why couldn't Hughes be stopped? She never lost her passion and kindness. Her big advice: "If you allow yourself to be bogged down and lose your enthusiasm, then you are dead in the water. If you remain optimistic, cheerful, and committed to your goals there is nothing that can stop you."

But where did that belief come from in the first place? Why not just curl up into a ball and give up? For Hughes, it was understanding her place in the context of the universe.

"When you really believe in God, you can believe in yourself. . . . People used to say that nobody is interested in all that religion, and I say that's not religion, that's spirituality. There's a big difference between being loyal, and understanding yourself in relation to creation."

Understanding yourself in relation to creation. Take a few seconds to ponder that. Preferably, it's nighttime and you can go look at the stars above your head, gazing a few billion light years into the past. The key that Hughes described is to zoom out and escape the universe between your two ears in order to understand how the person between your two ears fits into the universe.

She emphasized that it wasn't dogmatic religion, but a spiritual perspective and grounding. For some, spirituality can mean a practiced religion such as Christianity, Judaism, Islam, or Buddhism. For others, spirituality can mean a deep connection to nature or developing a communion with others. Even atheism can be a form of spirituality.

Spirituality can help us feel small. The next time that you are running through a forest or standing on top of a mountain, think about your physical size in relation to the world. We are ants in comparison to redwoods. Next, think about your running dreams in comparison to the development of the world. Our running PRs are tiny etches in the milestones of the world, and likely in the milestones of our own lives. There's a reason we started the book talking about death. It's something we all share as a human community, and it's something to think about deeply to gain a zoomed-out, spiritual perspective on the world.

There is something powerful about feeling small. When you are small, it's okay to mess up (as long as you have positive intentions and are not wielding nuclear codes). It's okay to really go for it and believe in yourself. And it's okay to try a made-up, radio broadcast in the bathroom at peak shower hour.

Spirituality—whatever that means to you—can enable us to feel small and dream big, accepting ourselves even when faced with the crap and complexity of life. That is a powerful tool for running (and for life).

So, why believe? Because, ahem . . . why the heck not?

Make a List and Check It Twice

For learning new behaviors, there are three interweaving techniques that work like a charm. We call those three techniques the 3 Rs—repetition, reinforcement, reflection. They all start with the same letter, so it must work! It's not a unique approach, but the basic idea is to develop tools that allow you to split up your actions into manageable chunks.

When practicing kindness, enthusiasm, and belief, it's helpful to think of yourself as a little puppy learning not to poop on the carpet. The carpet is easy to poop on—it's right there!—and it's satisfying as heck in the moment. But do that a lot (in this analogy, be mean or resentful), and you'll end up getting in trouble and eventually having to sleep in your own mess. The exact techniques aren't all that important—there could be more or fewer, and they could even start with different letters (blasphemy!). All that matters is supporting a framework to think a bit more deeply about your actions.

1. **The first (and most obvious) technique is repetition.** Do something lots, and it becomes something you do, until it becomes part of who you are. Character is just habit plus time. So when it comes to developing your kindness, enthusiasm, and belief habits, the key is to support repetition over time.

That's easier said than done. It's fun to be kind when your tail is wagging; it's hard when you missed breakfast. As comedian Pete Holmes said, "I am a great person as long as all of my basic needs and wants are satisfied." If only we were truly like dogs, and the promise of a belly rub would make everything easy. How do we support repetition without the magical power of belly rubs?

2. **We ask athletes to use the second technique, reinforcement.** Unlike dogs, human reinforcement has to come from within, because no one will give you a Milk-Bone for being kind. Meditation faces the same problem of internal incentive structures, and it relies on mindfulness, usually meaning accepting and acknowledging your thoughts and feelings. Here, it's about practicing mindfulness of your actions and energy.

Bring light into the world with your spirit? Boom! Give yourself two mental points (don't actually count the points). Snap at your partner or honk your car horn for no good reason? Crap! Think about how to handle the situation differently next time, but give yourself grace in the meantime. Kindness, enthusiasm, and belief all release happy brain chemicals, so making yourself aware of what is releasing them (or not releasing them) can give you the same good mojo as a belly rub.

3. **But the final technique is the most important—reflection.** In *The Happiness Project*, Gretchen Rubin describes the seemingly magical power of measurement for changing behavior. It's a problem psychology research studies grapple with all the time—often, actions of study participants change just by being in the study (called the Hawthorne effect). For drug trials, the placebo effect is sometimes stronger than treatments. The Heisenberg uncertainty principle outlines how this works on the quantum level, articulating that the position and velocity of a particle cannot both be known at the same time, and it's often used to illustrate the idea that measuring something precisely can alter its fundamental properties (though quantum mechanics is rather different than human behavior). In other words, the act of measurement is powerful. And for us, it can be a science-supported belly rub to support your behaviors.

Kindergarten teachers understand this concept. What is better motivation than a happy-face sticker on the class Chore Chart for cleaning up the sandbox? You can sticker-ize your life to support reflection too.

Start with the behaviors you want to support. For our athletes, it's kindness (both to yourself and others), enthusiasm, and belief. Each night or week, reflect on how your behaviors aligned with those goals. Smiley stickers are the best positive reinforcement, but you can also use numbers from 1 to 10, or you can just have an imaginary spreadsheet in your head. The key is just to spend time thinking about your actions. Repeat, reinforce, then reflect, and eventually you might find yourself being (and running) a bit more like a puppy. And puppies almost never get tired.

So if you're keeping score at home, we suggest you have a few different tools in your happy runner toolbox, all of which you can start right now. First, a list of three positive affirmations about the type of person and runner you want to be, which you look at and think about each morning (chapter 1). Second, an outline of your long-term goals, dreaming your biggest and scariest dreams to motivate love of the daily process (chapter 1). Third, a four-point answer to the key "Why?" questions, laying out what drives you, then you stick to those answers even on days it's not so easy (chapter 2). Finally, a checklist of the habits you want to build into character traits, and you repeat, reinforce, and reflect on those habits each day (chapter 3).

Or, possibly even better, you can just spend some time under the stars or in the trees every once in a while. You can zoom out. AND YOU CAN THINK ABOUT THE AMAZINGNESS OF YOURSELF AND PERFECTION OF OTHERS AND AWESOMENESS OF EXISTENCE.

In some cases, a dose of that puppy wisdom might be all you really need.

Enthusiastically, Kindly Forget the Haters

The final obstacle to your happy runner life is the unfortunate flipside of being a part of a community. Usually, community and connection bring joy. But sometimes, you can't avoid the sad truth. If you live like a puppy, sooner or later, you will find out that lots of people don't like dogs. But don't become a cat, or a walrus, or a flamingo in response. Haters gonna hate whatever animal you decide to be. So embrace your inner puppy, even around puppy-haters.

And try to laugh at them. A prime example of a hater's nihilism at work happened in St. Petersburg, Florida, in 2014. On two random, unplanned days, more than 750 strangers participated in a Starbucks coffee pay-it-forward chain. The chain was started by a woman in her 60s who offered to pay for the customer behind her. The chain propagated from there. According to CNN reports, it brought smiles to customers' faces and joy to busy baristas.

A puppy-hater was bound to show up eventually. The chain was ended by a man who clearly thought the Starbucks experience should be Hobbesian—nasty, brutish, and short. He wrote on his blog, "In case any of you are caught up in the Pay It Forward baloney at Starbucks, I just drove through the line, bought a venti mocha frap AND DID NOT PAY IT FORWARD. The chain is broken and the silliness should stop."

Yes, he used Addie dog's all-caps for a hateful message. NOT COOL, BUT I STILL LOVE YOU.

Haters love one thing most of all: sabotaging enthusiasm and kindness that they don't share. Everyone reading this has their own stories about haters, and they are surely infuriating. But perhaps nowhere is it more clear than in Internet comments sections. Here are a few entertaining examples from the comments section of David's *Trail Runner Magazine* articles:

"What a bunch of 1980s era bro science. I don't need a side of diabetes with my 10K PR." (an article outlining the scientific studies on glycogen)

"This is Trail Runner Mag . . . not 'David Roche's forum to sell silver bullets and unicorn crap.'" (an article on perceived exertion)

And there are many others we can't publish due to the sheer mean-spiritedness. Sometimes, these comments are so ludicrous that they are entertaining. Often times, we learn things from them (like what the term "bro science" means). Other times, they hurt a bit.

Tim Ferriss, a top entrepreneur and author, published "7 Great Principles for Dealing With Haters" as a response to the incessant hate. One of his principles seems awfully true: "10% of people will find a way to take things personally. Expect it." The 10 percent rule is especially important if you view your running team as the whole community—a larger denominator means a few more haters in the mix. Thinking about it this way softens the blow and also enables you to do great things. If you try to cater to that 10 percent, you'll produce self-conscious crap instead (and not of the unicorn variety).

Another one of his principles is a quote from 17th-century poet-philosopher George Herbert, getting at how you respond: "Living well is the best revenge." Ferriss adds, "The best way to counter-attack a hater is to make it blatantly obvious that their attack has had no impact on you."

So David responded to these *Trail Runner Magazine* comments with kindness and enthusiasm. "Thank you so much for your engagement!" is the go-to puppy response. Whatever you do, don't "Pay It Backward" by responding with something less than enthusiastic kindness. As an added bonus, enthusiasm is exactly what bothers haters the most.

Your running life will come with tons of haters. There may be people that think running is stupid, other runners that think your training is stupid, or really anything else you can imagine. Hate is a creative emotion, it turns out. The key is not letting that impact your unconditional self-acceptance. So, in the face of a creative, destructive emotion, remember the rules:

Forget 'em. Laugh. Be enthusiastically kind.

Running requires consistency over time. If you give energy to haters, your running consistency can be compromised. Thank the haters and move on.

Remember that hater who commented about the happy runner approach being full of "unicorn crap"? We just want to use this time to let them know we understand what they are saying. We see how some things we say (like this book) could seem like total unicorn crap. We want you to like us and it sucks that you don't. But you know what? We don't like us all the time either.

But, we're getting better at it, partially because haters have provided a needed stress-test to our happy runner worldview.

So, in conclusion, we'd like to give them a joyous thank-you for associating us with unicorns, possibly the only animal on par with a puppy. We are waiting for you with open arms, a wagging tail, and a hug.

Or, at the very least, we'll buy you a coffee to thank you for your engagement.

—4—

It's Not All Puppies and Unicorns

If happiness were truly a choice all the time, this book could be a lot shorter. It'd not only be pocket sized, it'd be one sentence. We'd read you the chorus of the song "Don't Worry, Be Happy," and then we'd all celebrate. We got it! Yes, it seems like a good plan to not worry and to be happy! Then, we'd all share high fives and ride off on our pet unicorns.

Oh crap. There's a problem. The only unicorns are horses with paper towel dispensers strapped to their heads. This isn't a fantasy land. In fairy tales, all the endings are happy. In the real world, that only applies to Addie dog at dinnertime.

This book is all about zooming out and finding a framework for unconditional self-acceptance in your running life. Sometimes, though, that is impossible.

Have you ever been depressed? Had an anxiety attack? Felt like the whole world was collapsing in on itself and that your heart wanted to leap from your chest? We both have. Chances are that most of you have had experiences like that too.

For the first couple years, our coaching focused on the first few chapters of this book—supporting people in their happy runner journey, mostly by telling them they were awesome and perfect and their dirty running clothes smelled like a field of wildflowers in springtime. That all changed when a pro athlete joined the team in 2015. She was a mental health expert, and she said the questions we provided were incomplete.

She changed everything. And she did it with just two words.

The final question we ask used to be a catch-all designed to probe what makes an athlete tick: "Is there anything else a coach/friend/confidant should know? Nothing is off-limits, and all is confidential."

Through that question, we heard about running stuff like fear of racing, self-loathing from slow runs, dreams of one day being the best in the world. Sometimes, we heard about more personal stuff, like childhood trauma and miscarriages. But that question only elicited deeply personal responses about 20 percent of the time. "Alright," we thought. "That seems about right . . . maybe?"

Actually, we'd soon learn, it wasn't right. That question wasn't enough. The pro athlete asked us to add two words at the end. "Any demons?"

The floodgates opened. Nearly everyone had their struggles to share. The people that seemed the happiest sometimes had the scariest pasts haunting them with each step in the present. Almost everyone could have written a book about what they had overcome. Fear of death, difficult marriages, sexual anxiety, insomnia, not liking dogs—the answers flowed in, often accompanied by heaps of insecurity. And so many of the athletes thought they were the only ones that had these feelings.

We aren't mental health professionals, so we couldn't provide expert assistance on most of the topics. But what we could provide is a listening ear. We could try to destigmatize it all in their own heads, talking to them about therapy or medical help or other support when needed.

Author Wendy Mass is attributed with a quote that you may have seen on a poster or on social media: "Be kind, for everyone you meet is fighting a battle you know nothing about." That's an essential point. The topic of this chapter, though, is slightly different than that poster quote. *You* may be fighting a battle that *others* know nothing about. And that's okay too—you are enough no matter what.

You are enough if you are depressed, if you suffer from anxiety, if you have a crippling fear of trees, and even if you don't like dogs. It's all part of the human condition. And over the last few years, we have seen that it's all part of the happy runner journey.

You probably can't zoom out to overcome depression. You might not be able to accept yourself unconditionally when suffering from an anxiety attack or an eating disorder. Maybe, though, over time, you can do something else. You can shift the internal monologue about all these things that sometimes get in the way of being a happy runner.

To the rest of the world, they might be called demons. But to you, they're just part of what makes you who you are. And as the happy runner mantra goes, "I love me some me."

The first step can sometimes be the hardest, just like on a run. This chapter is designed to help you with that first step, thinking about depression, anxiety, and other potential obstacles on your happy runner journey.

It's not all puppies and unicorns. Actually, scratch that. Maybe it all can be puppies and unicorns. But first, we have to acknowledge that puppies and unicorns can be depressed, or anxious, or sad, or anything else too.

The Mental Health Spectrums

Based on recent statistics, around 20 percent (and possibly more) of the U.S. population age 18 and up suffers from anxiety or depression. Gosh, given the prevalence of anxiety and depression, they are basically side effects of being human. It makes sense intuitively. Thirty thousand years ago, someone with the same exact brain structure as you would have been gathering nuts and berries, watching for predators, and spending time with family. That same person today is on a smart phone, imagining predators, and spending time with their own thoughts. If nothing else, it's certainly an interesting evolutionary experiment.

The millions of people dealing with mental health issues are not choosing it, raising their hands with vigorous enthusiasm during the mental health draft. "Oooh, me me! I want the anguish and difficulty!" That type of draft pick would only be made by the Cleveland Browns.

There are no statistics on the prevalence among runners, but it's almost certainly pretty high. What is running but a lot of time spent in your own head, getting acquainted with your thoughts, feelings, dreams, and everything else, with tons of chances for self-judgment along the way? We see anxiety and depression constantly among athletes of all types, and we've suffered from it too.

The big message of this chapter? In a world where these issues are so common, it's essential to give yourself grace about your mental health, viewing it alongside other parts of your physical health. It's not a choice, something that defines you, or something that makes you less worthy as a person, runner, parent, friend, dog cuddler, or anything else.

Here, we lump depression and anxiety under the general heading for mental health. They're like Shaq and Kobe—not together all the time, but often paired, and always kind of annoying to live with.

The first few chapters of this book talked about happy runner tools. But happiness and depression fall on separate spectrums. Talking about one without the other is incomplete. Gretchen Rubin explains beautifully, "I came to another important conclusion about defining happiness: that the opposite of *happiness* is *unhappiness*, not depression." So you usually can't happy your way out of a depressive state.

Sometimes, no amount of self-help (OR PUPPY LOVE) can lead to a happier outcome without medical intervention or therapy or the passage of enough time so that a depressive episode or an anxiety attack runs its course. All of this stuff falls on a spectrum. And wherever you are on the mental health and happiness spectrums is okay.

We aren't experts in this field. Megan could write about the neurobiology, but as we'll talk about, most medical training doesn't even confront these issues head on. So why are we talking about it at all? *Because* we aren't experts. Removing stigma in athletes requires an openness to starting the conversation. So let's break down the mental health spectrum in a conversational way.

Depression can be used conversationally to represent feeling down or blue, unable to see the dessert coming after the asparagus is finished. It can also be used in a clinical way to represent a period of hopelessness or despair that impairs ability to function in daily life. *I don't deserve dessert, and it tastes bad anyway.*

Think about a light rain storm. Perhaps it's disappointing and less pleasant than a bluebird day. But maybe you can still put on a favorite pair of rainboots, sing Rhianna's "Umbrella," and splash through puddles until you put a smile on your face. Your smile will get even bigger when you Google the meaning of "Umbrella."

Now think about a hurricane. If you try to fight a hurricane with rainboots, Rhianna, and puddle splashing, you are going to get blown halfway across town. You flying past the bus stop might make for a solid segment on the local news (*Local man impersonates cow in* Twister, *more at 11"*), but it's probably not good for your health. Hurricanes require expert meteorologists and disaster management specialists.

That light rain storm is feeling blue. The hurricane is clinical depression. Often, it takes therapy and/or medication before singing like Rhianna is even a consideration. Other times, it's still impossible. Anxiety presents similarly, varying from healthy nerves before a big presentation to panic attacks that can consume your sense of self entirely, like a snake swallowing a Kia Sorrento.

And no matter what you're going through, it's okay. There is nothing wrong with having mental health issues, whether you're a runner or not.

Lifting the Stigma

Grab the remote and let's press pause. There's such a stigma at times that depression and anxiety are swept under the rug, away from sight. So let's stop for a second and repeat that last statement: "There is nothing wrong with having mental health issues."

That's important for people who deal with them. It might be even more important for people who don't, to gain empathy and act as effective partners, friends, and members of society. Depression and anxiety are manifestations of complex neurobiological processes. It's not something that you choose. And it's not a weakness. You are enough no matter what your brain might tell you in the moment (and others are enough no matter what their brains might be telling them).

Runners deal with these issues a bunch. We've seen tons of athletes struggling with it silently, out of sight, practically under the rug. It makes sense that athletes might be less open about it. After all, sports can be about winners and losers, anointing champions, giving heroes auras of invincibility. Combine that with the stigma about talking openly on mental health, stir it all together, and it can be darn near impossible for some athletes to be open about mental health.

Kevin Love, an all-star forward for the Cleveland Cavaliers, had a mental health crisis in 2017. He had a panic attack. As he wrote in the *Players' Tribune:* "It came out of nowhere. I never had one before. I didn't even know they were real. But it was real—as real as a broken hand or a sprained ankle."

It happened in the middle of a game, when all of a sudden his heart beat got out of control. Love's breath quickened and he began to hyperventilate. As the world started spinning, his mouth went dry and the air felt oppressively heavy.

At the next timeout, the attack hit a crescendo. "I was running from room to room, like I was looking for something I couldn't find. Really I was just hoping my heart would stop racing. It was like my body was trying to say to me, *You're about to die.*"

Most likely, a lot of people reading this are nodding their heads right now. Now that we have a better understanding of these issues from coaching and medicine, we see that we have felt something a bit like that, too. And Love's struggle was just beginning. He found himself questioning why it happened. Perhaps most difficult—he didn't yet feel comfortable opening up about it.

"Call it a stigma or call it fear or insecurity—you can call it a number of things—but what I was worried about wasn't just my own inner struggles but how difficult it was to talk about them."

He started seeing a therapist, and he had breakthroughs. Opening up let him grow. His takeaway? Mental health is something that almost everyone struggles with at one time or another. And it's okay to share what you are going through. Not only that, Love said, "It could be the most important thing you do. It was for me."

After Love and fellow NBA star DeMar DeRozan opened up about mental health issues, a bunch more basketball players began speaking openly about their struggles. The same story could be told for runners, with some top athletes like Western States 100 winner Rob Krar opening up about their struggles and making it easier for others to do the same. It turns out that confronting stigma can remove its power.

But mental health stigma is a tough nut to crack. To see just how hard it is, let's look at another example of a high-pressure, results-oriented field: medicine. You would think complex neurobiological processes are easy for doctors to grasp, like an NBA player palming a basketball as if it's an orange. But the medical field is fighting through its own mental health crisis.

According to the *Journal of the American Medical Association* (JAMA), close to 30 percent of medical students suffer from symptoms of depression and 10 percent of medical students experience suicidal thoughts. Anxiety is likely even higher. Of those 30 percent of students with depression, only 15 percent will go on to seek professional help.

For context, these numbers indicate that medical students are around five times more likely to suffer from depression than the general population. We all know that medical students are overachievers when it comes to beating the numbers, but this is a dangerous statistic.

In part, the prevalence of mental health issues in medicine can be attributed to the expectations and demands of the field. Medical students are supposed to embrace the rigors of training in the same way that runners are supposed to embrace mile 23 of a marathon. They underperform in tests just like runners underperform in workouts. The opportunities for self-judgment are endless. And like runners, it's sometimes easy to hesitate when asking yourself the big question: "Am I enough?"

A large part of medical student depression seems to be related to the stigma of asking for help. Just like athletes, those auras of invincibility can sometimes be part of the culture. Admitting depression is often characterized as a weakness that could influence professional outcomes and career advancement.

Rahael Gupta, a University of Michigan medical student, wrote about her personal experience with depression in a JAMA essay titled, "I Solemnly Share." It took courage to share her story. And it wasn't just personal courage, but professional courage too. In fact, she was encouraged not to be courageous—not to write about these experiences on her residency application.

A University of Michigan article on Gupta captured the story. "I spoke with a surgeon who is absolutely wonderful," Gupta recalls. "But he told me: 'As someone who values wellness I think what you're doing is great, but I have to be honest—if a student on their residency application said they were depressed, I would think twice about giving them an interview.'"

This statement would have deterred most people. But Gupta was armed with her "Why?" It was a "Why?" that was crafted following a year of medication, therapy, and time off from medical school to address her depression.

Gupta wrote a beautiful summary in her JAMA essay:

> "I admit openly that I am just as vulnerable to the elements of life as are my future patients, hoping that others will do the same. I do so in the hopes that the culture of the medical profession will evolve to value imperfection as the harbinger of humanity, and that this value will be exemplified by the way that we judge our students and residents. If I have learned anything after spending most of my short life in pursuit of academic distinction, it is that the appeal of the dividends—good grades, high praise, awards—is as ephemeral as the warm glow felt on their receipt. Not so with the call to protect human life; that's something truly worth living for."

Gupta's "Why?" incorporated a focus on process over results, as well as a focus on kindness and self-belief. Gupta's perspective is remarkable, just like Kevin Love's. The only way their essays could be better is if they ended with standing ovations.

It's Different for Everyone

We have gone through the whole mental health spectrum at one time or another. For David, it was anxiety. He just didn't know it at the time.

In 2010, he was a law student cowering in the back of the Criminal Law lecture. It was the first day of law school. Up to that point, he had been in thousands of lectures with no issue during his academic career. But that day, everything changed.

Law school uses the Socratic method, which often involves one student being "on call" for the duration of a class. What does that mean in practice? If your name is called, you better know your stuff.

And when it came to law, David didn't know crap. He was coming from a science background. Law was foreign. His heart started racing.

As students filed in, a wave felt like it was building deep in his chest. Just when it seemed it couldn't get higher without cresting, it'd gain extra steam. The professor sorted her notes, and the wave rose higher. He was underwater. He took his heart rate—140 just sitting there.

Even then, he knew it was ridiculous. This didn't matter! Shut up, brain! That didn't help, though. The professor began to speak . . .

"Johnson, the facts of the case, please."

David's name isn't Johnson, right? No, it's not. That's one question he can answer. The wave crested, and he breathed. He was safe.

Suddenly, another wave rose on the horizon. What the heck? There was nothing to worry about! Brain, turn yourself off!

The anxiety attack persisted, even as the "danger" vanished. For the next two weeks, his heart rate seemed to never go below 80. He could barely run. It would be really hard to live like that for a long time.

That was September 2010. What changed two weeks later? He met Megan. A switch flipped, and the anxiety attack subsided. Periodically, that feeling comes back, usually for just a day or two. Knowing what we know now, he is lucky. He is lucky to only have minor mental health issues (thus far in life) and lucky to have a partner who understands. But even with all that luck, occasionally the wave rises ever higher, and it's a couple days in the pounding surf trying to stay above the water.

For Megan, it's a little bit of both. When she was in middle school, she was assigned a presentation on the Gettysburg Address. She forgot her lines. That moment was one score and negative four years ago, and it has haunted her ever since.

Now, the thought of giving a presentation will send her heart rate rising. What if she forgets her words? Have you ever thought about how complex language is? And the only thing more difficult than remembering lines is improvisation. Agh! Sometimes, anxiety around a presentation will seep into the rest of her life, a couple weeks of social anxiety that is functional but not fun.

It's kinda funny from an outside perspective. She is a perfectly fine public speaker once she gets going, overcoming that initial surge of adrenaline and inability to put sentences together. But the combination of performance and social anxiety can turn her into a different person anyway.

What's a bit less funny are her brushes with depressive episodes. Every once in a while, she'll have a day when it takes all of her energy just to move. She objectively knows everything is awesome, but it just feels awesomely heavy and hopeless. Usually it leaves as quickly as it came, but there have been a couple times when it lingered. Once, it was overtraining that left her in the dumps for a month. When there's no trigger, it might be even scarier. *What is wrong with me?*

Both of us have learned over time that there is nothing wrong with us. We are enough. Also, fun fact: An hour of crying is a great ab workout. It's just not the most fun ab workout (possibly the only thing harder than planks).

Often, no amount of thinking on mental health can prevent these issues from arising.

Bradley Stulberg, an expert on these issues and coauthor of the book *Peak Performance* with Steve Magness, opened up about his own experience with anxiety in 2018. He literally wrote the book on the psychology of performance, and that couldn't prevent him from experiencing mental health issues. He wrote a beautiful essay in *Outside* detailing his experience:

"I thought about running—an activity I've done nearly every morning for the past ten years—but felt terrified that if I did, something awful would happen. I resolved to go for a walk. I went to put my shoes on, my hands trembling. Once I finally got them on, I realized I'd forgotten socks. Finally, I made it outside. But no more than a quarter-mile into my walk, the top of my head began to tingle. I felt detached from my body, as if I was in a virtual-reality video game. Soon I was completely paralyzed by the sense that I was losing my mind. I decided that better than a walk was to find the nearest psychiatric crisis center, which, thankfully, was only a mile away."

Stulberg has done amazing work to help remove the stigma around mental health, and he got help. He is still dealing with anxiety, but by writing about mental health openly, responses poured in about people going through the same thing. Our favorite, from an athlete we coach: "Thank you, Bradley. Your story changed my life. I now know I'm not alone."

Runners, like all people, face this sort of process of reckoning with mental health issues all the time. Sometimes it's part of their psychological makeup, other times it comes from running itself. Of course, comparing depression to a running injury or poor performance or other running-related setback is like comparing a tsunami to a splash in the kiddie pool. Depression strips you down to the core, while something like a running injury just strips your tibia, or your femur, or your left butt cheek.

But both *can* offer interesting similarities in perspective. Sometimes the vantage point gained from depression can provide a rocky pathway to developing a beautiful "Why?" Depression can be a super-power. Like Gupta finding her "Why?" or a runner reaching an epiphany about long-term process over results, the tough times can lead to a little bit of transcendence.

Other times, though, the vantage point is actually rock bottom. And that's okay too. Everyone's experience with mental health is different.

To see just how different mental health issues can be for different people, music provides an example. The song "Hurt," written by Trent Reznor of Nine Inch Nails, is about grappling with depression and addiction. The exact meaning of the song is debated, but that's the point—it can be different to everyone.

Watch a live performance by Nine Inch Nails on YouTube now. In the song, you can feel the pain and loneliness coming through Reznor's writing. Hearing him sing it, you hear emptiness and forward motion as the song builds to a crescendo as he talks about starting all over.

The song took on a different meaning when covered by Johnny Cash in 2003 as his health was declining. He was 71 years old, seven months away from his passing, and grappling with the transience of life and the inevitable decay of death. With a change in tone, he transformed the same lyrics to reflect the sadness of his decline. It became about death.

If you haven't seen Cash's music video produced by Mark Romanek, puppy ear this book right now and check it out. As you watch the music video, notice the "closed to the public" signs on the Cash Museum, the smashed record labels, the dusty trophies. The implication is that these experiences are ephemeral and that his era is over. Or as Cash sings, "What have I become?"

Trent Reznor, Johnny Cash, and Mark Romanek each interpreted the same lyrics a bit differently. Everyone suffers differently. Everyone lives a different narrative in their own heads.

Or as Bono put it, "Trent Reznor was born to write that song, but Johnny Cash was born to sing it, and Mark Romanek was born to film it."

If different people listen to "Hurt" and come up with different meanings, think about what that means for how individuals experience depression as a whole. Or think about how they experience anything. It's all remarkably different, because we are all remarkably different. After all, we each have complex neurobiology that becomes intertwined with unique life experiences, 86 billion neurons that are wired in a unique combination of nature and nurture.

When you think about it, this complexity is beautiful. Heck, it's what allows Rahael Gupta and Trent Reznor and everyone else to produce incredible art and do great things. But it also means that we can't judge others for what they are going through using the lens of our own experience.

We shouldn't judge ourselves, either. It's part of being a human.

So there is nothing wrong with mental health issues, for runners and everyone else. It's normal, it's a part of being a human being. It's part of being a runner or a medical student or a songwriter.

Alone, mental health issues can feel all-consuming. The message from Kevin Love and Rahael Gupta is that you don't have to go at it alone.

Together, runners, doctors, athletes, and everyone else can remove stigma and help each other through this crazy thing called life. Even if it literally makes you crazy sometimes, there are a lot of people there alongside you, including us.

But that doesn't always make it easier to live and run through mental health struggles. That's where giving yourself grace and developing a support system comes in.

Mental Health Support Systems

"Get some exercise and you'll feel better."

"Smile and act happier to feel happier."

"Your life is great, think of all the people less fortunate than you."

"Suck it up, and grow thicker skin."

The first three of those statements are true utterances that athletes with mental health struggles have told us they hear all the time. The last one wasn't said out loud (that we know of), but it's implied in the first three.

Mental health issues all fall on a spectrum, and sometimes it's impossible to use logic and reason to escape the struggle. Depression and anxiety can make your skull feel like a prison, with no hope of *Shawshank Redemption*ing your way out. Often, the answer can't be found between your two ears, and in those cases, it's essential to develop tools that help you escape that prison. Or, better yet, tools to help you turn that prison into a beautiful mountain cabin with hundreds of miles of trails out your back door.

That is where talking to trusted partners, professional therapy, and prescribed medication come in. The exact treatment option depends on where a runner is on the mental health spectrum. A case of the Mondays might be treatable with a smile and a run. A case of the permanent-never-ending-terrible-Mondays might require some extra help from the HR department.

The first step to treating mental health issues is identifying them. And the first step to identifying them is not stigmatizing them in the first place.

In SWAP, from the very first e-mail onward, we try to break down the stigma of anxiety and depression by using the phrase "brain sparkles." That phrase is silly as heck. But it's all about context. For athletes that have grown up being taught to repress their mental health struggles, it sometimes provides a gateway to being able to talk about it openly. "Feeling quite sparkly today" is a common training log entry, starting a dialogue about what it means for training and life. Some might judge mental health issues (like the medical school residency expert Rahael Gupta discussed). But no one judges sparkles. Sparkles are awesome, usually associated with unicorns and rainbows. Plus, a life without sparkles seems a bit dull, right?

Of course, that's just a gateway. Silliness is powerful because it helps break down barriers, but silliness probably won't cure an ailment unless you're playing the game Operation. Removing stigma opens the door, but it's still essential to walk through it.

The walk is not always a straight line though. It's sometimes like a catwalk sketched by M.C. Escher, twisting and turning in psychedelic fashion. For SWAP athletes, we try to encourage our sparkly runners to search for resources that can help. We've seen athletes have success talking to family members, friends, fellow runners, and professionals such as psychologists and psychiatrists who are experts in mental health. Sometimes just talking out loud to an engaged puppy can do the trick (if that fails, puppy snuggles help too). As Addie dog would say, I LOVE YOU UNCONDITIONALLY.

Therapy is indispensable for countless runners, including many of the top pros in the sport. For some, therapy is as important as coffee, a necessary element of the day. While both coffee and therapy offer performance and life benefits for these athletes, you rarely see a social media post talking about how they need therapy to get out the door each day. Meanwhile you constantly see memes on social media like "Life happens. Coffee helps." There are almost never silly, uplifting jokes that destigmatize therapy.

Way more people than you might think have been helped by therapy. Therapists help people escape the claustrophobic world between their two ears, zooming out a bit. Life happens. Therapy really, really helps.

So let's start talking about therapy for runners like we do coffee—it's serious and necessary, but we can still be silly about it. Rodney Dangerfield is a good place to start: "I told my psychiatrist that everyone hates me. He said I was being ridiculous—everyone hasn't met me yet."

Therapy isn't always enough for each runner dealing with brain sparkles. For some, medication is absolutely essential. A recent study indicated that 13 percent of Americans are on antidepressants. While it's okay to have your own opinions on antidepressants, it is not okay to criticize others for taking them. Through coaching, we have learned that so many amazing runners take a little pill each day so that they can be themselves. This is not a weakness.

David's mom had bouts of severe depression when he was a kid. It ran in her family, and it sometimes stopped her from running (or doing much else). Little David could tell when his mom woke up in a mental prison, rather than a mountain cabin, even though she was great at hiding it and being a perfect mom no matter what. A lot of his personality was dictated by wanting to help her be happy, even when it was darn-near impossible for her in the moment. You can probably trace the idea for this book back to those formative years (along with his insecurity that this book will be useless for you).

His mom was an amazing parent and teacher, and almost no one knew of her struggle. She kept it inside, struggling mostly silently so that her kids and students and husband didn't have to deal with it too. But it must have felt like solitary confinement at times. It must have been exhausting, like mile 24 of a marathon, but with no finish line in sight.

Then, she started taking a pill. For her, everything changed. Now in her late 60s, she is the happiest runner in the world, brilliant and smart and brave and strong. Anyone who meets her talks about how she lights up every room she enters. Medication let her be herself. And it let her be herself without an enormous internal battle every day to keep up appearances.

Others may have entirely different experiences with medication—it's highly individual. The point is just that lifting stigma means letting others explore therapy and medication without passing judgment on them. Or, if you are the one in treatment, don't pass judgment on yourself. It all gets back to the happy runner mantra: you love you some you, and you love everyone else too.

In his *Outside* essay chronicling his journey through anxiety, Bradley Stulberg laid out the stakes for athletes, noting that mental health struggles come from genes and environment in a difficult-to-isolate, often nonlinear way. In addition, "the same personality traits and brain chemistry that underlie our greatest gifts—for example, the ability to think obsessively and problem-solve relentlessly—can also give rise to our most awful curses."

For him, it changed his perception of anxiety altogether. "It's an overwhelming and devastating feeling that is very different from what I used to think anxiety was (feeling exceedingly nervous before a public speaking gig or butterflies on the start line of a marathon, for example). It can feel like I'm two different people."

A combination of therapy and medication helped him make progress. And as one of the foremost experts on performance, it gave him perspective to provide tips that might help others on their own journeys. His seven tips: think impermanence, let go of control, lean into it, know you're not alone, exercise, practice self-compassion, and be patient.

But as he says, "sometimes self-help isn't enough." For athletes and everyone else, "Talking to others who have had similar experiences can help. Therapy can help. Medication can help."

Our goal here is not to cover every element of depression and anxiety, but simply to let you know that you are not alone and that whatever your perspective is, it's okay. That perspective makes you who you are. It makes you sparkle.

Life is often a lot like trail running—sometimes you are climbing up a difficult, sparkly climb that feels infinite, and other times you are cruising down a delightful trail without a care in the world.

By openly talking about how we feel with family, fellow runners, and medical professionals, we can make the rocky trail feel a lot smoother, not just for ourselves, but for the entire running community.

Running and Mental Health

When asked why we listen to music sometimes when running, we quip: "Otherwise, our thoughts oscillate between super stressful and super boring." That joke underscores an important point—running is a mind game.

But it's a mind game that can be joyous, uplifting, and almost unconditionally fun once you get the hang of it. Running can even serve as a type of action-based therapy to lessen the effects of depression and anxiety. It's not a cure-all, but it's definitely a cure-some. There are several hypotheses for how exercise works to impact mood.

There's the endorphin hypothesis that explains the runner's high. As the state of Colorado could tell you, getting high has its benefits.

The monoamine hypothesis posits that exercise releases neurotransmitters such as serotonin and dopamine. In that way, it acts a lot like pizza or chocolate or sunshine or puppies.

The distraction hypothesis is that exercise is an interruption from distressing thoughts. Imagine a puppy that is struggling with learning how to walk on a leash getting down on herself and thinking she is not a good girl when suddenly SQUIRREL CHASE ESCAPE THE LEASH RUN FREE I AM A GOOD GIRL AFTER ALL.

And the self-efficacy hypothesis states that exercise becomes a task that can be confidently completed for a desired outcome. It gets back to the atmosphere of growth, discussed in previous chapters.

We've also seen great results from our trail running hypothesis that being in nature (preferably while covered in mud and eating tasty things) has the power to make you feel small and ridiculous. For our athletes making big life decisions, we ask them to think about it when outside, preferably in a forest or on top of a mountain. Nature has answers. Namely, that there are no answers, and that's okay.

There are, however, a few caveats to these hypotheses. Fudgewaffles! We were *that close* to a universal solution to many of the world's problems.

Running is often helpful when feeling blue or even when experiencing cases of mild depression or brain sparkles. But it should never be a stand-alone treatment for moderate to severe depression. In these cases, getting out of bed to run even 20 minutes a day can feel like summiting Everest while wearing open-toed sandals.

Also, to our knowledge, almost all scientific studies analyzing exercise and mood incorporate controlled exercise programs. Human subjects follow walking and running programs that work up to a few miles a day. Mice run predetermined quantities of time on adorable mouse treadmills.

We haven't studied what happens when we start piling on the mileage. Do endorphins ever get hungover? If we trained a mouse on a hamster wheel (hopefully with a Netflix subscription) to run 100 miles, would they experience the same effect?

Or, you could take the self-efficacy hypothesis a bit further. What happens when a runner completes a race and accomplishes their goal? Will the process bring them enough joy? Or do they have to run longer and faster in another race to get the same satisfaction?

There's a fantastic article called "The Spiritual Life of the Long-Distance Runner" by Adam Alter published in the *New Yorker*, which discusses the dispositions of ultra-runners. Alter references a psychologist named Marvin Zuckerman, who noticed that some people favor extreme emotional highs and lows in comparison to those who favor emotional stability. Zuckerman labels these people as "sensation seeking." He found that extreme sports enthusiasts "have a higher optimal level of stimulation."

Alter writes, "[Ultrarunners] are willing to endure the protracted discomfort of an ultramarathon in exchange for the scattered moments of extreme joy that arrive during and after the race. . . . Maybe ultrarunners are like extraverts with respect to sensation. They long for, and are energized by, extremes of elation, exhaustion, suffering, and joy."

Extremes of exhaustion and suffering? That sounds remarkably similar to elements of depression.

> Rob Krar, a two-time winner of the Western States 100 who openly suffers from depression, talks about the suffering he experiences in running and depression in a short film by Joel Wolpert called *Depressions*. Krar talks about going into "this dark place" during runs and races that relates back to his depression.
>
> He credits running with helping him manage his depression and depression with helping him face the pain that he experiences in the last quarter of ultra races
>
> Krar talks about his depressive episodes in this video: "I used to fight it. The biggest change for me was to accept it, recognize that I am going into the hole and just embrace it. Allow myself to think that, 'Yes this really sucks. I wish that this didn't happen to me.' And that has been a huge coping strategy for me. I have been able to shorten the episodes to as short as a day sometimes."
>
> The way that he embraces those episodes parallels how he manages pain while racing. Krar says that he reframes the struggle as something to be embraced, a privilege to be appreciated. That gave him power for running performance, and it also gave him the power to manage his depression.

Anxiety and depression can't be trained away, but training might help manage them. So embrace running as one element of a mental health strategy. It works. If we could bottle running up and sell it (probably through a partnership with Roche Pharmaceuticals), we'd be billionaires with private jets to improve our happiness. But running should probably not be the only strategy you use for your mental health, especially if you are trudging through struggles.

Be mindful about how you feel. Give yourself the grace to be imperfect. And be willing to ask for help anytime you feel like you aren't enough.

Because you are enough. No matter what.

Eating Disorders and Body Image

Mental health issues like anxiety and depression are just some of the obstacles facing happy runners. It's like the steeplechase! One of the highest barriers to jump (the steeplechase water pit) is having a healthy respect for your body no matter what it looks like, or no matter what you think it looks like. Does your body run, or has it run in the past, or will it run in the future, even just a single step? Then you have a runner's body type. You are perfect the way you are.

Of course, that is practically a Mr. Rogers quote. In practice, it's more complicated than that. So let's break it down.

Among runners, there is a common (and sometimes subconscious) perception of what an "ideal" body type looks like: a small frame with low body fat. Essentially, it's the human equivalent of a greyhound in racing flats.

This is one of the most widespread and dangerous misconceptions in running. Because genetics vary from person to person, the "ideal" body type might be downright unhealthy for some people. And trying to achieve this body type could lead to dangerous consequences for long-term health.

It's like a golden retriever trying to get the body type of a greyhound. It might work for a few weeks, but eventually there will be long-term consequences for energy levels, bones, and even happiness.

You almost never see a sad golden retriever. You almost never see a golden retriever skimp at the dinner table. Just saying.

PREACH, Addie dog says, PREACH.

Still, body image issues are shockingly common among runners. In 2015, a study performed at the Comrades Ultramarathon, found that 44 percent of female participants had disordered eating behaviors, including abnormal thoughts about food and its relation to body image.

Disordered eating and body image issues are also common in men. Studies suggest that males account for 5–10 percent of eating disorder cases, which is a universally agreed-upon underestimate given the lack of recognition and support for males with disordered eating behaviors; 45 percent of those males are involved in a sport where weight is tied up in performance.

The stats are staggering. Even runners who don't have clinically diagnosed disordered eating behaviors—runners that might not show up in these statistical analyses—can unknowingly have negative energy availability from unintentional and inadequate caloric intake. We see it constantly among athletes. Break down the barriers and form intimate relationships with runners, and most have their stories to share about body image and disordered eating.

Whatever the label, many runners struggle between what their brain (consciously or subconsciously) wants and what their body needs. Or as the R. Kelly song "Bump N' Grind" goes, "My mind is telling me no, but my body, my body is telling me yes." You need to sing it dramatically to a bowl of pasta for full effect.

But no matter where you land on the spectrum of body image and eating behaviors, you are not alone. It's like mental health. There are large numbers of professional and recreational runners who are experiencing the same thing. Our goal as a running community should be to lift the stigma and foster a community ethos of unconditional support.

Megan experienced firsthand what it meant to unknowingly slip into disordered eating in college. She went to Duke as a field hockey player. Field hockey rewards endurance, but it mostly favors speed and strength. Adequate nutrition is essential for staying fast and strong, and so Megan viewed the extra serving (or six) on Taco Tuesday as beneficial to her ability to throw some 'bows on the field hockey turf.

As a field hockey player, Megan never really thought deeply about nutrition. She ate healthily, practicing the Oscar Wilde diet—"Everything in moderation, including moderation." Midnight pizza was her friend. And so was leftover pizza. And pizza with beer. And pizza with ranch dressing. And you get the point. She was a golden retriever in mind and body (and field hockey shorts).

That all changed her junior year of college when she had the crazy idea that it would be fun to try and walk on to the track team after her senior season of field hockey. The track and cross-country team would work out on a gravel loop around the field hockey turf and Megan would always watch them in awe. She thought of them as greyhounds in mind and body (and very short shorts).

Megan started to run more seriously that junior year of college. Long-distance running and field hockey don't exactly complement each other, so she entered various local races as either "Megan Beavis" or "Megan Butthead" to avoid any issues with the field hockey team.

Around the time that Megan walked onto the track team her senior year, she started to think a lot about running. She was clueless back then. But she did know physics. So she began to think of long-distance running as a physics equation, with speed equating to a power-to-weight ratio. In retrospect, she probably should have considered that physics was her worst grade in college.

There was no particular moment it all came to a head, but eventually pizza and ranch dressing blinked out of dietary existence. It was like how a star burns through its fuel and either blows up in a supernova if it's big enough, or fades away in a white dwarf. Megan didn't make a big, momentous decision to change her body. She just kinda faded away.

Later on, all meals were essentially a variation of salad with different protein sources—breakfast salad, snack salad, lunch salad, dinner salad, and dessert salad. Taco Tuesday slowly morphed into Ensalada Martes. ¡Ay Caramba!

It wasn't about body image, and it had nothing to do with the track team culture at Duke. Megan didn't even think of her nutrition choices as problematic. She simply thought it would make her faster.

And she did get faster.

Megan hopped on the track and ran some decently respectable times, at least for a field hockey player transitioning from 50 meters in wind sprints to 5,000 meters on the track. She began to drop her meals to three a day, simply keeping the breakfast salad, lunch salad, and dinner salad.

And she continued to get faster.

But then strange things started happening. Her third and fourth metatarsals broke during the NCAA Regional 10K Championships. She attributed it to a training error. While injured, she took her burgeoning power-to-weight ratio to the bike for long hours of cross-training. Eventually, it all fell apart. It felt like her whole body shattered into a million pieces.

And she had to stop.

It wasn't a choice. She literally couldn't move. Going to class was hard. Hiking was hard. Watching *The Voice* on the couch with a bowl of popcorn was hard. At the time, it was thought to be an overtraining syndrome with components of depression. And perhaps it was. But in retrospect, it all stemmed from a persistent catabolic state. The body was breaking down from negative energy availability. Her body was consuming itself.

She took two weeks totally off and her symptoms improved, but she could never perform at the same level the rest of her collegiate track career. In one of her last few track races, the Stanford Invitational, she had an epiphany. Her beloved power-to-weight ratio was a fallacy.

Professional runners were dominating on the track. They were strong and durable. It seemed that it took a certain level of strength and resilience to survive for long as a healthy and happy runner.

The night of the Stanford Invitational, Megan ordered a pepperoni pizza (with ranch dressing) and never looked back. The equation had failed her—running was far from a power-to-weight ratio. It took a healthy energy availability to have a successful running career. For Megan, it also took a healthy energy availability to be able to run (and live) with joy.

And so she celebrated Taco Tuesday again. And again. And again.

It took a lot of Taco Tuesdays to recover—12 to be exact. Megan wound up taking the entire summer off from training after graduating from college. She knew she wanted to run with joy again and in order to do that she had to drag her body out of the hole she was in, one taco at a time.

That fall, she got into trail running with a newfound love of the sport and all it can do for her mental and physical health. She wondered what she could have done in her short college career if she was able to run with full health. At first, she had regret. And then she realized that sharing her story could help others.

Megan was lucky. Her brief journey into what was clearly disordered eating in retrospect was centered on that darn physics equation and a misconception, rather than body image or self-esteem. That's why she was able to rapidly change direction once she realized her mistakes.

This luck is not always common. Megan entered competitive long-distance running at age 21 with the support of David, who loved her for who she was and who was breaking her tendencies for perfectionism one expletive phrase at a time ("why the [fudge] does it matter?"). On top of that, Megan was only in the collegiate running world for a year and a half before moving on to medical school and adventuring in the mountains.

Megan's story probably would have been different had she decided to go to cross-country preseason as a high school freshman rather than grabbing a field hockey stick. These issues often hit hard in the adolescent years as the body and brain develop and outside demands like college scholarships and peer pressure emerge.

The running community is making great strides in opening up conversations about disordered eating and eating disorders. We recommend that all young athletes read Lauren Fleshman's piece on MileSplit.com called "Dear Younger Me."

Fleshman writes, "You can be fast *and* a developed woman. In fact, you can only reach your ultimate potential if you let your body go through its changes. If you get to the dips and valleys and fight your body, starve your body, attempt to outsmart it, you will suffer. You will lose your period. You will get faster at first. And then you will get injured. And injured. And injured."

Lauren Fleshman, initiatives like the Lane 9 Project, and others are leading a charge to fight back against the body image misconception, and they are changing everything, for women and men alike.

In SWAP, we openly talk about disordered eating and body image, right alongside everything else. From talking with experts (including some therapists on the team), we have four simple keys to reinforce healthy behaviors.

1. **The first key is eliminating tools of self-judgment.** Our rule for athletes is that unless they are losing weight at the discretion of a medical professional, they should disregard the scale. Numbers are difficult when wrapped up in performance and body image. So consider getting rid of numbers altogether.

If you have a bathroom scale, this is your moment to pick it up and toss it in the trash. You could also give it to Goodwill and give a middle finger to weight by snagging a tax-deductible donation.

2. **The second key is understanding triggering events.** Even seemingly innocuous comments or comments intended as praise can cause body image concerns. "You look stronger and healthier" or "you don't look like those other unhealthy runners" should be avoided alongside "you look so skinny" or "you could really use a heaping slice of chocolate cake."

On the flipside, runners who are coping with these sorts of comments should try to give each comment the weight it deserves. That weight? *None.* The comments should be tossed in the trash, alongside your scale. In addition, talking about it with others who understand is an essential step in the process.

3. **The third key is reinforcing that all food is good food.** Research shows that compulsive dieting, as well as labeling certain

foods as off limits, can lead to disordered eating behaviors (or be a stand-in for eating disorders). We emphasize the importance of well-balanced, nutrient-dense, and freaking delicious food choices for runners.

In her "Dear Younger Me" letter, Lauren Fleshman urged young athletes looking at colleges to think about this topic. "But before you choose a school, you will go on visits. You will have meals with the teams and notice they do things differently. There is the school that has 'salad with dressing on the side,' the school where everyone orders 'no gluten and no dairy,' the school where girls bring their own food from home to the restaurant. . . . Go to the school where people order a variety of things: the burger, the chicken sandwich, the salad. Go to the school where you can order French fries and do it without shame."

Food is fuel, sure. But it's also friends and family and fun AF (as fudge). Rather than restricting, try to set up a framework and support system that help you embrace all the good stuff about food.

4. **The final key is understanding you are not alone.** Talk openly with running partners, family, and medical professionals. Usually, it's the first statement or admission that's the hardest. When you give people a chance, they often have a vast reservoir of empathy.

If you don't feel comfortable with any of those options, the National Eating Disorder Association has a free helpline. The Lane 9 Project has a website with helpful resources. You can e-mail us anytime, too.

And, on top of all that, Instagram has thousands of accounts that feature golden retrievers. Frolicking puppies don't make everything better. But they might help get your tail wagging.

You Are Enough

There are tons of other things that could be written on happiness, mental health, eating disorders, or any other topic we have touched on. Hopefully we stumbled into some truths that apply to you, and if we accidentally stepped in some dog poop along the way, we apologize.

Before moving on, let's conclude our story. Last week, David slept a couple hours one night, his heart racing for no good reason. Megan cried for an hour when dealing with an injury. Addie dog WAS LEFT ALONE IN THE HOUSE FOR TWO HOURS WITH THE BLINDS DRAWN—IT WAS HORRIBLE. We don't have the answers, we haven't reached nirvana.

But we are happy. Happy doesn't mean living in a fairy tale; it means accepting ourselves when we can, knowing that even those times when we don't love ourselves will pass. Megan finished medical school, we threw all our worldly possessions in a Subaru (INCLUDING ADDIE), and moved to Boulder, Colorado. We finished this book with a kiss while looking up at the mountains. We traveled a long way, and we finally made it home.

This is where the book takes a sharp turn. Most of the rest is on running training, mixing in some of the happy runner principles along the way. But sometimes the principles fall away from center stage in favor of things like aerobic threshold and running economy and other training minutiae.

So before flipping this page, remember one final message.

You are enough. You are perfect. You love you some you, and you love everyone else too.

Philosophy and science mostly agree on the idea that there is no inherent, proven, objective definition of "enough" or "perfect." They are undefined impossibilities. So maybe, over time, with practice, you can begin to make your own definition that applies to you, a universal truth in your own head.

What is perfect? What is enough?

It's wherever you are right now. And now. And now.

WE LOVE YOU.

PART II

THE HAPPY RUNNER TRAINING PRINCIPLES

This section is not a unified theory of training. We aren't the Einsteins of training methodology, even if we often share Albert's hairdo. Instead, this section is a primer for people looking to understand the building blocks of training theory, with some humor thrown in to keep your eyes from glazing over.

"Rats!" a reader may think. "Why are there no training plans to use?"

The reason we don't summarize our approach to training in complete detail is that it'd be both mind-numbing and not totally helpful, like studying the tax code of Colorado. Yeah, it would work if you are Coloradan, but most people are not Coloradan, otherwise Subaru would be the biggest company in the world. For most runners, what's more important than the day-to-day specifics are the general principles over time that allow them to find their potential.

The main training ideas to start with: Think about what you are doing, be flexible, and go easy on yourself. When it comes to training methodology, it's easy to get so bogged down in the minutiae that it all becomes like trying to teach yourself differential calculus. Before all that, it's good to remember that some basic training math is most of what you need to know.

So let's rewind to the beginning. Why does a happy runner need to know about training methodology at all? Shouldn't a runner who is truly at peace with the process-oriented mindset just do frolicking-in-a-field-of-lilies intervals with giggling-like-a-schoolchild recoveries? No, it's important to go deeper than that for most runners.

Because running is not all giggle-frolics, a happy runner cannot be a blissfully ignorant runner. You have to think long and hard about what you are doing and why you are doing it for your running house not to blow over at the first sign of wind.

It's a lot like spirituality. David's dad went to a draconian Catholic school in the 1950s, so he was no longer a practicing Catholic by the 1960s (just in time for psychedelics). For him, the strict dogma of the church at the time (and the corporal punishment at his school) overshadowed the loving philosophy of the church. So when he started to understand the complexity of the world as a teenager, through the prism of Vietnam and political upheaval, his rigid, fearing faith could not handle the new information. Faith without philosophical grounding risks oversimplifying a complex universe.

So it goes with running. Running is not all puppies and unicorns, just like life. As a result, Addie dog will be a much more minor character in this section of the book. I STILL LOVE YOU FOREVER, she says to us and all the readers. AND I'LL BE HERE FOR SNUGGLES WHEN YOU FINISH READING ABOUT ZOOMIES.

The complexity of a running life can manifest itself in decreased motivation, injury, aging, poor performances, nipple chafing, or just about anything else. If your approach to running isn't built on a solid philosophical foundation, it may crumble when you face adversity. Instead, you want to think like someone with lifelong faith, who elevates open-minded principles over strict dogma, who takes in all of the available information and comes to a place of belief and love, rather than disillusionment. All with no funny 1960s mushrooms needed!

Thinking about your running can often be a slippery slope, though. If you read popular Internet forums, you'll see that specific training approaches can become belief systems for some people. Belief is good, but it needs to be open-minded, especially in a field like training where multiple approaches work and knowledge evolves. It's a good general life rule that if you think lots of other people are stupid, you may need to check your presuppositions about your own intelligence.

Because no one approach works for every runner (or even the same runner at different phases of development), a happy runner cannot be an inflexibly certain runner, either. You have to accept the fickle uncertainty of a running life and be patient with a worldview that adapts as you do (and as training knowledge evolves).

It's a lot like politics. If you vote for a political party in every election but don't examine the issues to escape the tribe mentality, you could find yourself on the wrong side of history, supporting injustice, without noticing the change.

For example, after the Civil War, the Republican Party of Lincoln supported civil rights. As the years went by, Reconstruction failed, and the unjust Jim Crow South took hold. When the 1964 Civil Rights Act was passed by Democrat Lyndon Johnson, a bloc of people previously known as Southern Democrats shifted voting allegiances overnight. Chances are that a Southern Republican in 1866 supported a more just society. A new Southern Republican in 1966 may have changed parties to support disenfranchisement and discrimination. And the parties continued to evolve since then—that's why any argument that calls a modern political party "The Party of [insert historical figure]" is disingenuous. A binary worldview does not hold up in a nonbinary world.

In running, your exact approach won't be the same year-to-year as you grow and change. In the face of an ever-changing you, it's essential to have a worldview that flexibly changes too. When our athletes go through crises, we try to calm them with a dose of perspective. "The only people that think they have all the answers are narcissists."

Or, "If someone acts like they have all the answers, you probably shouldn't trust them with your credit card number." Being willing to change your approach to running and life over time is the only way to hold onto what brings you contentment in an ever-changing world.

Admittedly, that's some heavy stuff to start a conversation about running training. If we brought up your sex life, it could have been the trifecta of taboo topics.

But there's a reason this section starts with faith and politics, two of the topics you should never bring up at a dinner party. So why did we throw two proverbial turds in the dinner party punch bowl? They are both parts of identity, and examining your identity is a necessity to being a happy person long term.

It all gets back to one of our big themes: Whenever you can, zoom out. That means viewing yourself and your decisions with a universal perspective, through a lens of kindness and enthusiasm. As said by Socrates in Plato's *Apology*: "An unexamined life is not worth living." The premise of this book is that an unexamined running life often becomes an unhappy running life, too.

Self-examination of your running life is about more than over-arching philosophy. The first part of this book set up one possible happy runner's philosophical approach, which acts as the foundation and frame of a house. You can picture it—a house skeleton, well-constructed and sturdy, but not yet habitable. Now, you need to add the roof and the walls.

What actually holds the philosophical foundation and framework of a happy runner together? The walls and floors are made up of general training principles designed to foster a lifelong, adventurous approach to running.

These training principles aren't a strict set of rules. They won't lay out a training plan. They might not even be right for everyone, especially pro athletes who have advanced beyond Training 101 and 201 and 301 and are now applying for PhDs in Butt-Kicking.

So what are these principles? They are a general set of guidelines to consider as you learn about what makes you tick as a runner. Use what you want, discard what you don't want. There is no one-size-fits-all approach to training because running backgrounds and goals range in size from field mouse to elephant.

The principles are based on science, medicine, and philosophy, with a dash of spirituality thrown in for good measure (there will be no more politics, we promise). They are flexible and sustainable. They are fun (most of the time).

And, oh yeah, these principles may make you way faster too.

—5—

Principle 1:
Easy Means Easy, Not the Absence of Pain

Take a chill pill and wash it down with some loose juice. That is the central premise of running training—easy, chill running now begets fast, fun running later. It helps to think of intensity and aerobic development in the context of how you are treating your body. Do you train in a way that supports self-acceptance and love? Or is it more like self-destruction?

Let's think about what that all means when it comes to training. The opposite of love is indifference. Loving running and being indifferent to running cannot be farther apart, like galaxies that went in divergent directions at the big bang.

No, indifference isn't the problem for most runners. Instead, it's something a lot closer to love . . . hate. Hate is like a galaxy that went the same way, but is spinning in the opposite direction. Hate is often just love with anger management issues.

Love is passionate, but patient and kind. Hate is passionate, but forceful and mean. And when many runners put on a heart rate monitor for the first time, they find out that what they thought was loving was actually hatefully destructive all along.

The story plays out so often that it's like the coaching equivalent of the movie *Groundhog Day*. A runner loves what they are doing, and they want to go faster, so they run a bit harder. Without realizing it, what they thought was easy effort becomes something that is not so easy at all.

The heart rate monitor brings in some objectivity to the love/hate game. The runner puts it on, only to find out what they called "easy" was actually physiologically difficult. With each step, stress mounted and running became a destructive relationship. Their body was flooded with the stress hormone cortisol, the lack of polarization of effort led to stagnation, and eventually it was all going to culminate in overtraining, injury, or burnout. They were hating on their running selves without even realizing it.

But before we get to the soap opera details of the love story gone bad, it's important to understand why easy is so important in the first place.

More Running Means Better Running . . . to a Point

Nearly every runner who probes the limits of their genetic potential has a story to tell about the "Trial of Miles."

The Trial of Miles is the superhero origin story of countless runners. In John L. Parker Jr.'s cult classic novel *Once a Runner*, the protagonist Quenton Cassidy is expelled from college, moves to the woods, and simply begins running lots. As described by his spiritual mentor in the book: "The only true way [to maximize your running potential] is to marshal the ferocity of your ambition over the course of many days, weeks, months, and (if you could finally come to accept it) years."

As Cassidy learns, the secret of running training is simple: it's the "process of removing, molecule by molecule, the very tough rubber that comprised the bottoms of his training shoes."

Spoiler alert! That book ends with Cassidy winning an Olympic medal. But the main theme is that what comes from the Trial of Miles is beyond the point. The Trial of Miles is the point.

When you think about it, every complex skill in life works similarly. You never read about a well-balanced piano prodigy with a flourishing social life. You don't want a surgeon who inconsistently wields a scalpel. Running is the same. Practice might not make perfect, but it makes better. And lots of better over time will eventually get you as close to perfect as you can possibly get.

What separates running from the piano and surgery is the potential for physical breakdown. Heck, that is also what separates running from other endurance sports like swimming and biking. In running, each step involves a big impact. All of those impacts add up to a lot of pounding on the body over time. In cycling and swimming, meanwhile, the body doesn't bear the weight of impact and you can do a lot more before the point of no return. The most a runner will train (outside of outliers) is 10 to 15 hours a week consistently. Some cyclists and swimmers train upward of 30. Surgeons might be up over 100. There's a reason medical training involves something called "residency"— historically, they expected young doctors to live at the hospital.

Even at a relatively measly 10 hours a week (when compared to other sports), running is risky unless you do it strategically. You have 206 bones, and lifelong runners can learn a disturbing number of them from stress fracture injury scares. If a runner Google searches their symptoms enough, they could probably pass a med school anatomy test after a few years. Or, at the very least, they could ruin anatomy nursery rhymes. "The hip bone is connected to the . . . *femoral neck, which I learned from doing too many track workouts in 2008."*

The key to running development is balancing risk of injury and burnout with your own personal Trial of Miles. How does it all work? It's all about a progressive series of adaptations that happen as you run more over time. Disclaimer: These are complex physiological processes that could each take up 10,000 words and be the subject of an entire episode of *The Magic School Bus.* So we will gloss over some of the details for the sake of not making you get really sleepy and involuntarily snoozle like Addie dog with your snout in the spine of the book.

First, there's aerobic development, primarily via the cardiovascular system. As you run more, your body improves oxygen processing capacity and your ability to handle fatigue. At the easy end of the spectrum, you develop more capillaries and mitochondria that

Glossary of Key Physiology Terms

Your body is a very cool machine that can turn Frosted Flakes into the energy to run farther than almost any animal on earth. To understand how the human machine works, a few terms are important to understand.

Running economy: the energy demand for a given velocity of submaximal running. Picture a star runner bounding over the trail effortlessly, like a super-antelope. Now picture a beginner runner, slogging like a rhino, using twice the energy to do half the work. How do you go from rhino to antelope? It's all about improving your running economy.

+O$_2$max: the maximum amount of oxygen a person can use, expressed in milliliters of oxygen per kilogram of bodyweight per minute. In basic terms, the more oxygen you can take in, the faster you can run. +O$_2$max generally corresponds to an effort an athlete can sustain for seven to 11 minutes (with variance due to physiology and how +O$_2$max is being measured). While most people have +O$_2$maxes around 30–55 ml/kg, trail runner Kílian Jornet has an astounding 89.5 ml/kg +O$_2$max. Matt Carpenter, who currently holds the record for Pikes Peak Ascent, was at 92 ml/kg in his peak fitness. A typical Iditarod sled dog tops the charts at 200 ml/kg. Meanwhile, Addie dog tops the charts for +O$_{poo}$max.

Lactate threshold (LT): the tipping point when your body produces more lactate than it can use and waste products accumulate without being cleared. Contrary to conventional wisdom, lactate is a fuel source, not a boogeyman that forces you to slow down. However, it is associated with waste products that force you to slow down, so for most runners it's a distinction without a difference. In lieu of lab testing, LT usually corresponds to an effort you could hold for about an hour, though it varies based on physiology, training background, and the LT definition you prefer. One important note to distribute throughout this section is to not get bogged down in "energy systems" like lactate threshold. In practice, the body doesn't care about how we define or measure things in a lab, but they can provide a helpful framework to get started with this topic.

Aerobic threshold: the intensity range at which the body switches from primarily relying on fat oxidation for fuel to primarily relying on carbohydrates. Below aerobic threshold, the body has enough oxygen to function without producing significant amounts of lactate and other associated byproducts that build up with harder exercise. Above aerobic threshold, breathing rate increases and lactate levels begin to build up, plus there may be a bit more muscle damage. It's generally an effort you could hold for 2–3 hours, depending on background.

Blood volume: the sum of erythrocyte volume (red blood cells) and plasma volume (mostly water plus some dissolved proteins, glucose, clotting factors, electrolytes, hormones, carbon dioxide, and oxygen). Red blood cells transport oxygen, while more plasma lets your heart pump more volume per beat per minute (greater cardiac output). Red blood cell increase usually occur over weeks and months, while plasma volume responds more rapidly (days or even hours). Blood volume responds substantially with consistent training, and it drops rapidly with a stop-and-start approach. For most athletes, the big takeaway of the literature on blood volume is just to train consistently, not shying away from heat or mountains, while eating enough iron-rich foods (or supplementing) to get the maximum bang for your training buck.

Glycogen: a branched polymer of glucose stored in the liver and muscles that acts as a fuel source for exercise. While the glycogen-to-fuel process is complex enough to fuel many PhD dissertations, the basic takeaway is that excess carbohydrates are stored as glycogen, turning pasta into performance. Think of fat and carbohydrate burning on a spectrum, with high-intensity efforts involving mostly carbohydrates and low-intensity efforts involving mostly fat. Both energy sources are important for running, with glycogen stores lasting just a couple hours at high intensities and fat stores lasting all day at lower intensities.

Think of training like a big salad, with time below aerobic threshold being the greens, time closer to lactate threshold being the dressing, and time above lactate threshold and $+O_2$max being the bacon. A salad with just greens isn't going to get a five-star Yelp review; likewise, a cup of dressing and bacon might taste okay, but it's not a well-balanced meal. The goal is to structure training to run faster at those same effort levels, thereby improving your running economy.

supply and process fuel for working muscles. Capillary growth is called angiogenesis, and recent studies indicate that angiogenesis is impaired by too much intensity. While the hare focused on impressing its training partners, the tortoise must have been studying exercise physiology.

At moderate intensities, your body gets better at using fat for fuel at faster paces, which means you can go farther and more efficiently before bonking. All these adaptations support harder workouts that improve lactate threshold (essentially how well you buffer against fatigue-causing chemical byproducts of intense exercise) and $+O_2$max (raising your aerobic capacity). It's like a 100-story skyscraper—the first 80 stories are low-level aerobic development, and that allows the top floors to reach higher.

Bones, joints, and tendons get stronger as you run more too. The best example of what happens when you start running may be from the TV show *Parks and Recreation*, where the lovable Andy Dwyer tries running for the first time. After one lap around the track, he stops and begins to take off all of his clothes. "This is horrible! Ugh, I'm going to die! I'm so tired, everything hurts!" And when he finally gets all of his clothes off, he lays down on the track in his underwear. "Running is impossible!"

What Andy would have learned with consistent running is that it starts out impossible because the body first needs to adapt to the mechanical load. Repetitive bouts of low-level stress provide a stimulus that strengthens the musculoskeletal system to handle more impact. Running plus adequate recovery promotes development of osteoblasts, which become bone cells called osteocytes, which become stronger bones. After stress and recovery, the body repairs damaged muscle fibers to become new muscle strands called myofibrils that are stronger than before. A similar process can occur in tendons and ligaments. Meanwhile, enzymatic activity and angiogenesis spur aerobic development. Essentially, the body makes itself anew to respond to repeated bouts of low-level stress. That's why frequency and consistency are so important for runners, and why working up to five or six shorter runs a week is usually better than three longer runs.

At the same time, when you run more, your muscle fibers can actually change their properties altogether to become progressively better equipped for endurance exercise. We all have a genetic predisposition to certain types of muscle fibers, generally broken down into fast-twitch (FT) and slow-twitch (ST). ST fibers are full of mitochondria and capillaries, using oxygen and built to withstand fatigue for longer distances. FT fibers generate more force, but it comes with a catch—they get tired quickly. Type IIx FT fibers use carbohydrate fuel and are anaerobic, meaning they can only go for a short time. A good example is a swimmer competing in the 50-meter sprint at the Olympics. They are recruiting type IIx FT fibers, so some can go the entire distance without taking a breath at all. Meanwhile, type IIa FT fibers are intermediate, using aerobic energy sources in a generally more sustainable way.

A Primer on Muscle Fibers

Muscle fiber composition and recruitment plays a large role in determining the design and execution of running training. If you want your improvement to stay regular, you should understand how muscle fibers interact with your training plan.

There are three types of muscle fibers. Slow-twitch fibers (Type I) use oxygen, relying on aerobic energy processes to do work. They contract less forcefully but are filled with capillaries and mitochondria that make them more resistant to fatigue.

Fast-twitch fibers are broken down into two subgroups—Type IIa and Type IIx. Type IIa are wannabe FT fibers, always trying to butt into conversations at FT cocktail parties. They are intermediate, with some properties of ST and FT, using aerobic energy processes and with high capillary and mitochondrial density, but capable of producing more power than ST fibers. Type IIx are the real deal—all power and using anaerobic energy processes.

Distance running is mostly a slow-twitch sport, even for the fastest pro running a 10K. Those type IIx FT fibers fatigue too rapidly to use a bunch outside of sprints. Meanwhile, to paraphrase Sir Mix-a-Lot, ST and Type IIa fibers can go long, they can go strong, and they're down to get the friction on. He was probably knighted for his work in exercise physiology.

Thus, most of your training should be focused on optimizing ST and Type IIa fiber recruitment. But it goes beyond that, because there is evidence that muscle fibers can actually change their type (or act as if they change) over time with consistent aerobic training. A 2018 study measured ST muscle fiber expression in two twins, one of which did decades of endurance training, and the other of which was sedentary. The Cheetah twin had 55% more ST muscle fiber expression; the Cheetos twin had more bodyfat, worse genetic markers of performance, and worse aerobic abilities. Consistent training can lead to physiological (and genetic) breakthroughs.

Consistent aerobic training makes a runner more ST (and type IIa FT) than their genetic predisposition. That sounds weird, right? Don't you want fast-twitch to go fast? David's experience shows why hard-running FT fibers are not optimal for endurance running.

After he graduated high school, David was a protein shake–based organism. He was under six feet tall and weighed 200 pounds of thick muscle, as if a pot roast was granted its wish of becoming a real boy. His training consisted of explosive movements like sprinting and weightlifting.

As a result, he was a good sprinter and mediocre football player, landing himself a spot on the Columbia football team. Now, stop right there if you think that's impressive. At the time, Columbia football was one of the worst sports teams in the country, like an opposite-world Harlem Globetrotters, getting dunked on repetitively by opponents in increasingly humorous fashion. Still, David couldn't cut it for the Washington Generals of college football. So he was left with lots of FT muscle fibers and nothing to do with them unless someone needed help moving their couch.

His dad had always been an endurance athlete, and David had run as a kid, so he chose his next adventure. He was going to be an endurance runner. Don Quixote would have been proud of his hubris. What would happen when a sprinter chased the windmill of endurance running?

The results were predictably Quixotic. Six months after quitting football and not running a step in the interim, he laced up his lifting shoes and ran out the door; 300 meters later, he stopped, winded and sore.

That sounds like an exaggeration, but it's true. David literally got less than a quarter of a mile on his first endurance run as an adult. Most embarrassingly, it left him sore for days. We are talking "can't walk in a straight line" sore. We are talking "calf muscles lose all ability to function" sore. To paraphrase Andy Dwyer, running was impossible.

Little by little, David's body adapted. Over the next few years, he'd lose 60 pounds of muscle and fat. The pot roast gradually became a veggie burger. The changes were all small and gradual, happening at the cellular level. He probably got a bit more ST-oriented as muscle fibers adapted over time. His joints and tendons adapted to the impact forces. He no longer felt like he was breathing through a crazy straw when jogging as his aerobic system became less feeble.

But perhaps the biggest change wasn't in the muscles, but in his understanding of running. He read every book there was to read and constantly listened to running mentors to learn what he missed by not having teams in high school or college. And he came upon the same epiphany as Quenton Cassidy. It's all about the Trial of Miles; Miles of Trials.

Training Books to Read

There are tons of great books that can help you on your training journey. For example, *The Art of War* may teach you how to attack at night with fire, when the enemy is fatigued and hungry. That seems important! Just possibly not for training. Here are some books that are narrowly tailored to help you create your training plan (night-fire attacks not included).

Daniels' Running Formula: One of the most important figures in the development of running training, Dr. Jack Daniels provides an accessible, flexible approach to getting faster at any distance. Yes, he has the same name as the whiskey, and yes, reading his writing is also a great way to start a party off right.

Science of Running: Steve Magness breaks down running training to its component parts, reconciling physiology and coaching in a way that extracts the best of both worlds. Coach Magness has an open-minded approach to performance that could serve as a model for all athletes and coaches looking to develop over time.

Running to the Top: The father of running training, Arthur Lydiard, breaks down his approach to periodized training that revolutionized the field. Most modern training approaches evolved from Lydiard's philosophy.

The Lore of Running: Dr. Tim Noakes gives an overview of how the body responds to training, and provides a "Why?" for everything athletes do.

Run Faster From the 5K to the Marathon: Top coach Brad Hudson lays out a philosophy that can work for any level runner.

To take your training knowledge to the next level, google "Renato Canova training" to dive into the deep end of understanding modern elite marathon training, consisting of long tempos near marathon pace and epic specific blocks that will light your freaking eyes on fire. Or, if you want to look at a completely different approach, check out "Mihaly Igloi training," which would talk about a top-down, interval-based approach popular in older training systems, but still influencing some elements of training philosophy today.

Training and medicine share a lot in common. Both involve physiology. Both involve performance. Both involve getting comfortable with bodily fluids. And perhaps most importantly, both involve evolving knowledge systems based on a combination of empirical and laboratory data.

With medicine, we know bloodletting isn't the best approach, just as we know that a training system based on tons of intervals three times a week with rest on the other days isn't right for runners. At the margins, though, there are lots of different treatments that work for some people, and there are lots more that are being tried out all the time. Staying open-minded (à la author Magness) on top of a base understanding of physiology (à la authors Lydiard and Daniels) is the best way to evolve with the field.

Easy Running Means More Running

So we only have 10 to 15 hours a week, tops, if we are lucky? And way less time when we start out? Shouldn't we just hammer until our asses are in the grasses?

In a perfect world, there could be some justification for going moderate or hard often. Swimmers, for example, will do intervals most days. Surgeons have incredibly intense training. So do cyclists and chefs and basketball players and pianists.

But running involves those pesky impact forces. Go too hard too often, and your body will rebel against the work, usually before your brain does. "Running hard is spiritually cleansing," your brain may scream with dopamine.

"Shut your trap, you overenthusiastic dingus," your tibia may respond as a stress fracture forms.

"It doesn't feel painful," your brain may say in a future training cycle. "Any slower and I'd basically be walking!"

"Then walk, you lopsided clown," your adrenal system may whisper as you sink into overtraining.

The goal of running training is to avoid having your brain write checks that your body can't cash. Because when you overdraft as a runner, you get hurt. And when you get hurt, you lose some of what you worked so hard to gain.

Running easy limits injury risk. There is no greater challenge to a happy runner than being injured. You'll be driving down the street when you see someone jogging along, smiling obliviously, only to find yourself wishing the worst upon their extremities. "No one deserves nice things" you'll think, like Gollum wanting the one true ring all to himself. It gets really hard to see the brightness in the sport when your own running is bathed in the darkness of a health-related setback.

Injuries Are Inevitable

A side effect of being a runner is that you will get injured, and you may have burnout too. The severity of the injuries or burnout episodes will vary. But the only runners that don't have setbacks are the ones that aren't pushing themselves, or they're very experienced and already got over the initial injuries common for runners. As the Twitter account Thoughts of Dog said about a doggo with a torn knee ligament: "it is better to zoom. and tear something. than to never zoom at all."

The first key is trying to limit the damage. We have a set of questions for an athlete debating running when they are tired, injured, or sick. Answer yes to any of them, and you don't run.

If you're tired:

1. Does the thought of running make you unhappy?
2. Has fatigue lasted for more than one day?
3. Does the fatigue not improve after one mile?
4. Have you not been eating enough?

If you're injured or sick:

1. Are you uncomfortable walking?
2. Has pain/illness lasted greater than one day?
3. Does pain/illness get worse while running?

If you're tired and injured or sick, definitely don't run.

Even if you do everything right, you'll still have setbacks. The second key is knowing that your current physical health doesn't define you as a runner or person, just like the mental health discussion in chapter 4. You are enough no matter what.

The final key is prioritizing treatment to get better, along with cross-training to keep moving forward. Work with experts to determine what's the best course of action. If you get the green light to cross train, get to it! You can grow as an athlete even when sidelined from running.

Cross-training can help because in addition to making you good at that specific activity (biking, swimming, tug-of-war with your dog), it supports physiological adaptations that play a role in strong, healthy running. Let's break it down.

Value in Cross-Training

Aerobically, cross-training could improve oxygen-processing power, enhance capillary growth, and help build blood volume, all adding up to maintaining or improving $+O_2$max and lactate threshold, among other variables. To put it another way, the aerobic stimulus is similar (and can be better), even if the activity is different.

Cross-training diverges from running for biomechanical and neuromuscular adaptations. To simplify it, the movement patterns are different, so cross-training alone will probably not make you faster. However, there could be benefits for leg muscle strength depending on the activity.

We are big cross-training fans for injured and uninjured runners alike. Our preference is high-cadence cycling on the stationary bike, which we theorize has better neuromuscular transfer to running. Cat Bradley and Clare Gallagher did blocks of high-cadence cycling through injury scares before winning big races in 2017, among tons of others. A typical three-day progression might be:

Day 1: 30–60 minutes easy to moderate

Day 2: 10 minutes easy, 10 to 30 × 1 minute hard/1 minute easy, 10 minutes easy

Day 3: 10 minutes easy, 1/2/3/4/3/2/1 minutes hard with 1 minute easy between, 10 minutes easy

Easy is 90+ revolutions per minute, moderate around 100, and hard 105 or above, adjusting resistance to keep effort appropriate. The exact approach or activity is up to you—there is no magic to this one. Find what you enjoy, load some good music onto your headphones, and go.

It sounds strange, but injuries can be an opportunity for aerobic development. Just make sure you have fantastic bike shorts.

Independent of injury risk, easy running is indispensable for long-term speed development. That seems counterintuitive. But if running training were an episode of *MTV Cribs*, when they got to the room with easy running, you'd say "This is where the magic happens" as you winked at the camera. Easy running enhances capillary development and aerobic enzyme activity—introduce an anaerobic stimulus to the mix, and it all gets mucked up. It also increases your running economy, reducing the amount of energy it takes to go a given pace.

But it isn't always that simple, especially as runners start out. It's kind of like how kids rebel against their parents, only to become their parents later on. As David started running as an adult, he was in a rebellious phase. "I gotta go hard to get fast," he thought, the equivalent of a 16-year-old getting a barbed wire tattoo and stealing Hennessey from the liquor cabinet.

About a year into his running journey, he went on a run with a friend and an older acquaintance who was faster. We'll call the acquaintance Virgil, after Dante's guide through hell and purgatory in the *Inferno*. That sounds melodramatic (because it really, really is). But in both stories, Virgil understood all about playing with fire.

As they jogged around at what David thought was a slow pace, he ran a few steps ahead, probably flashing his barbed wire tattoo in the process. Behind him, the wise Virgil whispered: "He'll learn eventually."

Virgil thought David didn't hear, but he did, and fury rose inside him. Later on, after the run, David talked to his friend when Virgil left. "No, he will learn. He may be faster than me now, but I'll be faster than him soon."

That story is embarrassing. The ending is perhaps most embarrassing of all. David didn't realize he was playing with fire, and he got a severe IT band issue shortly thereafter and wasn't much of a runner for the next couple months. It wasn't until he adopted Virgil's advice after doing the years of research that he got faster. If only David had listened the first time, he could have avoided those years of running purgatory.

Or perhaps it was all a part of the process. Like in *The Matrix*, when the Oracle tells Neo he is not the one. "Sorry, kid. You got the gift, but it looks like you're waiting for something . . . Your next life, maybe. Who knows? That's the way these things go." It turns out that the Oracle was merely telling Neo what he needed to hear at that time to realize his ultimate destiny. Maybe Virgil was just telling David what he needed to hear in the way he needed to hear it to fully internalize the advice later.

Or maybe David was just being a rebellious idiot.

Either way, lots of runners go through a similar phase, chasing short-term gains from harder running over long-term happiness from easier running. In the process, they get neither.

Why? Easy running correlates directly with health. Health correlates directly with how much you can run in a mentally and physically sustainable way. And how much you run sustainably correlates directly with how fast you get.

The goal is not to go harder, it's to go faster. Easy running is where you learn that hard and fast don't have to be synonyms.

Easy Is an Effort, Not a Pace

Now for the most difficult part, like getting to the end of a video game only to face off against the hardest boss. After accepting the importance of easy running, how do you actually know what easy is?

The answer is not a "yo momma" joke. It's in an understanding of the physiological processes at play when doing endurance exercise.

Aerobic threshold is the intensity range at which the body switches from primarily relying on fat oxidation for fuel to primarily relying on carbohydrates. For training purposes, it's not helpful to think of aerobic threshold as a specific point. Instead, think of it as a range of intensities that vary slightly over time, depending on age, psychological stress, weather, and many other variables. Bottom line: it's when you transition from easy to moderate exertion, to a slightly harder effort with deeper breathing and a less-sustainable pace.

Training too often above aerobic threshold is like venturing into the abandoned chainsaw warehouse in a horror movie. Yeah, something bad may not happen, but there are freaking chainsaws, man. Stop messing around!

The chainsaws in this instance are musculoskeletal damage and the stress hormone cortisol. Too much chronic cortisol exposure from too-hard training can cause a cascade of negative effects, culminating in the mind and body blow-up that is overtraining. On top of that, every time you play fast and loose with higher levels of musculoskeletal damage is like playing Russian roulette with your health. You may get away with it most of the time, but that doesn't mean you should play with it often.

This is where the heart rate monitor test comes into play. Once, a top pro athlete joined SWAP after a few months of rough races, along with some emotional difficulty too. So we had her put on a heart rate monitor for an easy run. And the results were astounding.

On a normal easy run, she was well above aerobic threshold. On each hill, her heart rate went even crazier. Miscalibration of easy was making everything hard. It sent her to the brink of physical and emotional downfall.

Fortunately, with the heart rate monitor, she was able to learn what easy actually meant for her. Like a dog running into an electric fence, every time it buzzed, she knew to slow down. Now, she no longer needs the monitor at all, becoming one of the top trail runners in the world in the process. And it was all because she found out that easy doesn't mean the absence of pain, but the absence of overexertion.

A problem arises for some runners, though. When you get joy out of pushing yourself, what is to stop "mission creep" in your daily run? "Mission creep" was originally a military term for when objectives start limited, like a peacekeeping mission, and evolve gradually to be expansive, like regime change. For a runner, getting stronger over time can make faster paces feel a bit easier. As you develop more, you might find you can run even faster each day. Eventually, you are running every day as if it's your last without that being the goal in the first place.

How can you calibrate your easy? The simplest way is the talk test—you should be able to hold a conversation on most of your runs. Remember, "easy" does not mean the fastest pace you can go while finishing the run intact, but something truly relaxed, with no urge to stop.

You can step it up a notch with a heart rate monitor. We have our athletes start by calculating their lactate threshold heart rate (LTHR) using a method pioneered by Coach Joe Friel. Do a 30-minute time trial. Your average heart rate in the last 20 minutes of the test is your LTHR. Multiply that number by around 0.85 to find a good cap for easy runs, adding a few beats if you are inexperienced, and subtracting a few if you have a lot of miles on your legs. An even better way to calibrate heart rate zones is with lab testing (which involves blood tests during exercise, as opposed to the more entertaining lab test of seeing how long a lab retriever can snuggle).

The goal is not to run at aerobic threshold all the time, but to have a general understanding of what is actually easy for your physiology. There is no magic to a specific heart rate number or effort band. Next, you simply hold yourself accountable to your physiological definition of easy.

David had that thought in his mind one morning when he went out on a trail run with Matt Daniels. Now, Matt is no beginner. He is a sub-4-minute miler with work ethic and talent spilling out of his ear holes. So it made sense that he took the lead on the single-track trail, cavorting over rocks like he was more antelope than human. Around halfway on a 10-mile easy run, he gapped David. About 10 seconds opened up between them on the uphill. Matt is a freaking beast, so it made sense, right?

After the run, David loaded his GPS to Strava. And on that segment of trail where he got his butt dropped like a bad habit, he had run one of the fastest times ever. Matt is a better runner than David (and more handsome and smells better and is smarter and . . . okay parenthetical, you can stop now, you are just rubbing it in). But even with that fitness offset, no one should be setting records on easy days.

David immediately texted Matt after seeing the GPS. "Wanna run again tomorrow?" He added, "[Dog emoji] [Pizza emoji] [Flexing arm emoji]." Matt agreed, and they ran together. Only now, something was different. David took the lead. They ran the same route more than 10 minutes slower. And they had a conversation about why easy is important.

"Going faster on easy days always backfires in the long run," David described. He and Matt got real with each other, talking about a past running history where burnout was a constant companion, where great race results were followed by subpar ones and DNFs, especially at longer races that required higher training volumes. They talked about the physiology, and Matt's history, and it all came together. His ability to run so fast on easy days was actually a hindrance to long-term growth. With that, Matt got way, way slower . . . most of the time. His normal run became a dawdle in the park, barely breaking a sweat. He even got passed by other runners once or twice, a first for him.

And he found himself loving it. His body had what it needed to repair itself, and he got excited to go out the door every morning. His workouts got faster, his long runs stronger. Most importantly, by taking easy days and turning them down a bunch of notches, he found joy in the consistent daily grind of training. Easy running unlocked a new love of running along with performance breakthroughs.

That's not to say Matt didn't go really hard sometimes. He just avoided going moderately hard most of the time. Cool epilogue: Matt has become a kick-ass coach since.

No matter what training approach you use, around 80 percent or more of your running should be easy. That will help you unlock your long-term potential, pursuing your own Trial of Miles, all while staying healthy and developing over time.

Training philosophy gets a lot more complicated than that at the margins. But at its core, it's really simple. Author Michael Pollan coined one of the most famous sayings in nutrition in his book, *The Omnivore's Dilemma*: "Eat food, not too much, mostly plants." That is incontrovertibly true according to most experts. For running, the equivalent phrase might be: "Run lots, not too much, mostly easy."

A happy runner finds training nirvana only after they find their easy. Do that, and everything else starts to fall into place.

Consistent Beats Epic Because Epic Is Not Consistent

Structuring your own approach to easy running depends on your background and goals. Four general rules can help you put it all together. Just remember—different things work for everyone, so think of all this as a general template, with rules that are meant to be strategically broken.

1. **First, work up to running five or six days per week to support aerobic and biomechanical adaptations.** Even 10 minutes counts if you are time-strapped or starting out. Once you are advanced, you can even add "doubles"—second runs that add an extra aerobic stimulus, plus could facilitate more hormone production. We recommend one complete rest day each week year-round to prevent injuries and burnout. That being said, some runners thrive off of running every day like it ain't no thang.

> If you look at 100 training logs of pro road runners, probably 70 or more would include "doubles"—two runs in one day two to five times per week, usually totaling 30 to 60 minutes at a time. Most recently, 2:03 marathoner Eliud Kipchoge's training log for the Berlin Marathon became public, showing mind-blowing workouts and long runs. But buried in there was a seemingly simple addition—he would run 35 to 50 minutes slowly (for him) most afternoons after longer morning runs.
>
> Why do so many pro road runners do doubles? The answer is a bit unsatisfying . . . no one is 100 percent sure. The increased overall aerobic volume could enhance aerobic development

while minimizing injury risk and recovery cost from longer single runs; they could aid in glycogen replenishment; they could simply be more convenient for some runners. So if you have time to burn, you can consider adding short second runs, especially on days you are doing a harder workout (in order to optimize hormone production). But if running twice in a day sounds like too much, forget we ever mentioned it. For most runners, the second run may be best replaced with a first beer anyway.

2. **Second, on most easy runs, start slow, with the option to end faster if you feel perfect.** Running easy doesn't mean you can't find flow and enjoy the good days. That will be more fun, and it will also provide some extra gas for your aerobic engine. As you develop, do some of your easy runs over hills to mix up movement patterns and build power. The old saying is that "hills are speedwork in disguise." They provide a good bridge to faster workouts. However, with faster finish runs and hills, never force harder efforts when you don't feel like it, trying not to start the process of letting mission creep seep into your training.

3. **Third, aim to run as many easy miles as you can within the context of your life.** It may help to think of it in 20-mile increments. The first big breakthroughs happen at 20 miles per week, the next at 40, the next at 60, and most people will get super close to their potential at 80 (especially on just six days per week). Above 60, and you're really starting to juggle with fire swords, so make sure you are experienced or have a good juggling coach. And if you are under 20 miles per week, you win the jackpot! At that point, every mile you can add healthily will lead to major progression. So it's great to do 5 miles per week, but get to 10 and you may see your speed skyrocket. Later on, runners start chasing marginal gains. Those runners are suckers in comparison, as the people that are just considering ramping up can experience growth charts like a Silicon Valley IPO.

Keep in mind that there is no magic to weekly mileage, but it's a helpful framework to think about when determining total training load. Training load leads to aerobic development, and aerobic development leads to faster, stronger running. More is not always better. But more is usually better.

The tricky part is staying healthy, happy, and motivated while running more. The common wisdom is to avoid increasing weekly mileage by more than 10 percent at a time. While that number is not set in stone, it's a good guideline to avoid pushing yourself (and your grocery bill) too far. Pay special attention to your injury history and total stress load. If you have stress fractures or other overuse injuries in your past, be more careful about increasing mileage. And always remember—the body knows stress, not mileage. So if stress is high, don't expect your body to be able to mimic the training of other athletes that might get to wear sweatpants and watch *The Bold and the Beautiful* all day.

Start where you are (don't jump immediately to 50 miles a week) and spread out your mileage, being sure to take time off at the first sign of injury or burnout. You can even use run/walk methods, like those pioneered by Coach Jeff Galloway, especially if you are getting started or getting back into it. Every third or fourth week, decrease mileage slightly (a "down week") to make sure you are fully recovered and absorbing the training. And most importantly, make sure it's fun. As soon as running becomes a chore, your training plan might as well be an epitaph. "Here lies a once-happy runner"–inducing plans are basically the only objectively wrong approaches to training.

Here is a general template for spreading out your mileage that works most of the year for many athletes.

Monday: Rest: Just chill!

Tuesday: Aerobic: 15 percent of miles

Wednesday: Aerobic or Workout: 20 percent of miles

Thursday: Aerobic: 15 percent of miles

Friday: Aerobic or rest: 0–10 percent of miles

Saturday: Long Run or Long Run Workout: 25–35 percent of miles

Sunday: Aerobic: 15 percent of miles

Later on, you can add some spice:

· Strides up to a few times per week, usually Tuesday and Sunday in this template (chapter 6)

· Workouts one or two times per week (chapter 7)

· Longer, harder long runs when training for long races (chapter 8)

Adaptations of this template have been used for most SWAP athletes, including top pros and people in their first year of running. Just make sure whatever plan you use supports puppy-like joy, or eventually you'll find yourself feeling cat-like apathy.

4. **Fourth, do one long run a week that is anywhere from 20 percent (for very high mileage runner) to 40 percent of your weekly volume (lower mileage runners).** Long runs provide a super-charged aerobic stimulus, spurring glycogen depletion (which

has been shown to enhance adaptations to exercise in some studies) and adding moderate stress to the musculoskeletal system. A bit of extra, controlled stress can help you bounce back stronger.

If you just run easy, you will get faster. It seems weird, but it's the universally true paradox of running training. Slow begets fast. But to jump-start the process and reach your true potential, you don't want to just run slow all the time. Now, it's time to add another, sexier element to the mix.

—6—

Learn How to Run Fast Before You Practice Running Hard

Picture a little kid running at recess. What do you see? Chances are it's a child effortlessly frolicking across the grass, looking like they aren't even trying. And, of course, they're smiling.

Zoom forward 30 years, and picture that same kid running after a bus. What do you see? Maybe that same kid is now pounding the pavement as if they're tenderizing a pork chop, taking all the effort in the world to sprint a few blocks. Of course, they're grimacing.

What changed in the time between the two vignettes? Well, maybe that grimacing adult watches TV news instead of cartoons. But more likely, somewhere along the way, the adult lost the natural joy of running.

When you begin looking at adult runners on a routine basis, you start to see a similar pattern. There is a lot of slogging, few smiles, and what seems like a lot of effort with each step. The kids look like they have joyous springs in their legs; the adults look like depressed, overused Slinkies.

It doesn't have to be like that. The key to put some juice in your caboose is just to actually do some recess running in your training.

Running Fast Is a Skill, Not Just a Talent

You've heard that practice makes perfect. For running, a sport that relies heavily on biomechanics, that phrase needs to be clarified. Instead, think of it as the inverse: bad practice makes imperfect.

That goes for any complex skill, right? Take jazz. In the movie *Whiplash*, the young drum prodigy joins his art school's ensemble. He plays with immaculate skill. Or so it seems to the casual listener. But his instructor has a special ear and stops the prodigy with each small mistake. The corrections seem minor, but to the instructor, they are everything. He doesn't want the prodigy to internalize bad habits. As he says in a climactic scene: "There are no two words in the English language more harmful than 'good job.'"

The instructor causes the prodigy to burn out instead of pushing him to perfection. Somewhere between being a drill instructor and a yes-man, there would have been a healthy medium, where the instructor could say "Awesome job!" and still help the prodigy develop good habits.

The problem with removing that external feedback is that gradually we will seek out the path of least resistance. The prodigy started like the kid at recess, flying over the playground naturally and effortlessly. But if his mistakes were not corrected, he would have become the plodding adult, playing lazily and without inspiration.

You see it with any skill-based activity. Surgeons spend a decade of training in the hospital under the watchful eye of superiors, chefs apprentice for years, comedians do open mics every night, musicians constantly seek out feedback. Meanwhile, in running, there is rarely that external guidance outside of high school and college programs. So little by little, a bad habit can become an ingrained movement pattern. Effortlessly fast can become hard work. The joyous kid can become the adult in quicksand.

It's all about the magic phrase of developing as a runner long term: running economy. Running economy is "the energy demand for a given velocity of submaximal running." To put it simply, it's how hard you have to work to go fast.

Running economy can continue to improve for decades, long after other factors of running development have stagnated. For example, $+O_2$max (a measure of upper-end aerobic capacity, essentially how much oxygen you can process) will jump up 15 to 30 percent when you start running, then level off. Paula Radcliffe, the world record holder in the marathon, had a $+O_2$max of 70 ml/min/kg in 1991 when she was a world-class teenager. A researcher tested her each year thereafter, and that number didn't budge. But in the process, she got immensely faster. So what changed?

Her oxygen consumption at 6 minutes per mile pace went from 205 ml/kg/km to 175 ml/kg/km. Radcliffe's running economy improved about 15 percent, so she did too.

But now comes the tricky part. We know that running economy matters; so how do we improve it?

Practice. As Allen Iverson famously said, "We're talking 'bout practice."

The studies are all over the place, but the general thinking has coalesced around a few ideas. Running economy is influenced by biomechanics, neuromuscular circuitry, and aerobic development. All too often, runners focus on that last element, aerobic development, pounding out tons of hard miles, without thinking about the first two. As a result, they reinforce bad habits, and they find themselves running in quicksand, eventually.

This principle is especially important for runners who didn't start as kids, being funneled through running programs and learning how to run the right way as they went. How can you become a jazz expert when you never learned to play the recorder?

It's easier than you might think. First, think about biomechanics. Running speed is essentially a simple equation: the number of steps you take multiplied by the average power per step. One of the easiest ways to tell an advanced runner apart from a novice runner is their cadence—how many steps they take per minute. Novices usually plod a bit, closer to 150 or 160 strides per minute. That slowing over time likely happens partially because they don't think about it, and it's easier for many runners to slow down their turnover on days they feel less than spry. As a result, over time, every

The Happy Runner

Running Form Tutorial

Running form and dancing share a lot in common. Some people prefer the salsa, others hip-hop, and others Gangham style. But they're all working with the same general principles, just applying the principles in the best way for their backgrounds.

Studies usually show that changing form doesn't improve running economy overnight. That offset is likely because the body adapts to whatever form you use, so any deviation makes you less efficient temporarily. So improving form is something you have to commit to, likely for many months. There are no universal rules, though, so don't get caught up in the specifics, or what a pro runner does, but in finding what dance works for your body.

- **Quick and soft strides:** Measure your cadence by counting the number of single-foot falls you take on one side in 30 seconds, multiplying that number by four (or let your smart watch do the work for you). Most runners should try to be around 170 or above on their everyday runs. The specific number is not that important, just the principle that more strides decrease impact forces per stride, which could reduce injuries for some runners (though the studies are all over the place).

- **Run tall through the hips:** Good posture opens up your breathing and prevents your hips from sinking an excess amount with each stride. Plus, you'll look like a beautiful, majestic ostrich for any mid-race photos. Some runners have success with a slight forward lean, particularly on uphills.

- **Relax and let it flow:** Removing tension will let your body channel more energy into forward motion. Start at your feet and focus on one body part at a time, as if you're in a meditation practice on the move.

day becomes a less-than-spry day. Faster runners are usually at 170 to 180 strides per minute, with a lot of individual variance around those numbers.

For power, after a certain amount of progression from easy running, you will plateau, and no amount of slow running will give your muscles and tendons the "spring" to increase average power-per-stride to new levels. You need an extra-strength stimulus from faster running to get extra strength.

Next, think about neuromuscular development. Running is a skill-based activity, far more than a sport like cycling where the machine does most of the work. In running, you are the machine. If your transmission is faulty, it won't matter how strong the engine is.

Cadence and power output both have large neuromuscular components. For turnover, the brain and body get better at moving quicker. At first, increased cadence may make you feel like a placenta-covered baby gazelle. But over time, as you adapt to the new stress, it becomes natural. For power, ground-contact time and force generation can increase just from improving neural circuitry that sends signals related to the complex skill of running. It's like a dance—miss a step by a fraction of a second, and eventually you'll be completely off rhythm.

The final major component of running economy is aerobic development. This is the straightforward part that is often overemphasized. If you run lots and run hard, you'll improve until you don't, usually stopped by burnout or inefficiency. So the key needs to be transitioning from running hard to running fast, learning to make that speed take less effort. Only then will improvement be sustainable over time.

Here's the happy runner magic: most runners can improve their running economy rapidly. Running can get easier while it gets faster, no matter what background you bring into the sport.

Because you are faster than you think.

Improving Speed Makes
Every Pace Feel Easier

Speed is really complicated. But it's also not complicated at all.

First, think about some of the complications. Your neurons send signals to your legs to exert force into the ground, powered by blood pumped from your heart and oxygen processed by your lungs. You evolved for millions of years to be able to perform this complex task of bipedal locomotion. Before that, stars had to explode to create heavier elements like iron, which is essential for oxygen transport in blood. As Avril Lavigne said, "Why do you have to go and make things so complicated?" (If you want to feel about the same age as those long-dead stars, here's a fun fact: that song came out in 2002.)

Fortunately for us, it doesn't need to be that complicated. Most of what goes into running fast doesn't require conscious thought. You don't have to tell your heart to beat or your lungs to expand. Instead, you just have to run fast, and your body does the rest. But here's the idea of this chapter—you have to take that first step. You have to remember in your training to tell your body to run fast.

In December 2016, at 35 years old, Andrew Skurka was a 2:44 marathoner (run on a downhill course in Colorado). That is a blazing fast time in the big scheme of things: 6 minutes and 15 seconds per mile for 26 miles. In his first e-mail to David, he laid out his goal: breaking 2:40.

That is a big leap, especially for someone with his background. Andrew was no spring chicken. Heck, with his history, he was more like an autumn peacock, thinking it was almost time to retire his plumage entirely. He had over 100,000 training miles on his legs, and his endurance exploits as a backpacker earned him the 2008 National Geographic Adventurer of the Year award. How could he improve enough to break 2:40 before Father Time caught up with him?

David felt like channeling "The Answer" himself, Allen Iverson, when responding to Andrew's 2:40 goal. "We're talking 'bout [running economy] practice."

Instead, he had a different type of answer. "Long story short: I think you can run 2:32 in Boston."

So Andrew got to work on improving his running economy. His training for Boston started with a few presuppositions. One, he was already aerobically developed close to his capacity. Like Paula Radcliffe, his $+O_2$max wasn't going to skyrocket, and it's unlikely that more miles would make a big difference. Two, all of those years of training may have ingrained bad habits. Like the adult chasing the bus, he was trapped in a bit of quicksand from years of focusing on running hard, not fast. Three, he had the happy runner approach of focusing on the process, not results. The time mattered to him, but only because it structured the running life he loved.

Andrew ditched the hard running in favor of fast running. Whereas his previous workouts would look like hard efforts that are familiar to any student of pro athlete training, like 10-mile tempos and 6×1 mile intervals, he now started doing lots of short strides and intervals between 20 and 60 seconds. He was learning to run again, going back to recess.

At first, instead of 10×1 kilometer workouts, he was doing 10×30 seconds fast. The goal was to add extra strength all along the biomechanical chain, to rewire his neuromuscular approach to running, and get some added aerobic development from short, fast intervals. Within three weeks, things started to change.

"That felt easy," he said after a 16-mile easy long run at a faster pace than he used to run. "I don't know what's happening to my body, but I'll take it."

His heart rate data backed it up. On December 10, he ran 16 miles at 6:40 minutes per mile pace at 162 average heart rate. On March 3, he ran 16 miles at 5:54 per mile pace at 161 heart rate. The autumn peacock was strutting, plumage blossoming under the new approach.

At Boston, he ran that 2:32, a 12-minute PR at 36 years old. But that wasn't the end of the story. Six weeks later, he won the Bighorn 100 Trail Run in a four-way tie for first, showing that running economy matters even at slower mountain speeds.

But he had more left in the tank. After a summer on trails guiding backpacking trips and finishing the Ultra-Trail du Mont-Blanc, a single-stage 103-mile ultramarathon, he wanted to swing for the fences one last time. In October 2017, Andrew laid out his goal:

"I really want to go sub-2:30 before I'm old and slow."

It was 85 days until the Houston Marathon, and the summer on trails had reduced his running economy back to where he started the year before. And Father Time was chasing fast.

So Andrew got to work. With the base of running economy training from the year before, his body adapted rapidly to the new stress. He got to the Houston start line ready to target 2:30.

In a prerace e-mail, David assessed his chances. "I think you have the fitness for a 2:28, but let's be safe and go for a 2:30."

Andrew agreed in writing, but clearly had other plans. He was going to go for it.

At 6 a.m., David turned on the marathon live tracker, waiting for the first split. Around 17 minutes, Andrew crossed the 5K timing mat. At 1 hour, 14 minutes exactly, he crossed halfway.

"Stop running so fast!" David screamed at his computer. "You are risking everything!"

Andrew ignored the disclaimer on David's advice, fixating on 2:28. Unlike 13 months prior, when he had a PR of 2:44, his legs were now able to cash the checks his aerobic system wrote. He had learned to run fast at 36 years old.

His final time? 2:28:24. Sixteen minutes faster than he had been just over a year earlier.

The lesson of Andrew's story is that raising the speed ceiling provides more room to play in the aerobic house. Many studies and stories support rapid improvement in paces and races from speed endurance training.

That's not to say Andrew focused on short, fast stuff at the expense of traditional marathon workouts—he did plenty of mile repeats and long tempos. He just did them faster by incorporating some recess running along the way.

So, what exactly are strides? Strides are short, fast bursts of running that are a unifying factor in most elite training plans across the last 50 years. While they are important for pros, they may be even more important for regular Janes and Joes who might not practice speed as often.

There are lots of ways to run strides, but here is what we have found works best for our athletes. Place them some time in the second half of a run, which helps to break up the day and add some spice to your run guacamole. Accelerate gradually, taking around five seconds to get up to the fastest pace you can hold without straining. For most athletes, that will equate to anywhere from ½ mile race pace (for beginners) to 1-mile or even 3K race pace (advanced). The exact pace doesn't matter as long as the athlete can stay relaxed and smooth, like a puppy that had some espresso in their kibble.

Each stride lasts 15 to 30 seconds depending on the goal, on flats or uphills. Shorter time is good for maintenance or during heavy training; longer works when an athlete is focusing on running economy development rather than lots of hard workouts. Hills are good to minimize impact forces and build strength; flats are good to work on speed. Between strides, go back to your normal easy pace for one to two minutes. If you can't go back to easy pace, you may be going too hard on the strides. Anywhere from 4 to 12 strides one to three times per week does the trick.

And that's all it takes. You might think you have lead legs. But for those leaden quads, strides can seem like alchemy. Practice the speed skill, and keep reinforcing the skill year-round, and you might find that your lead legs can turn to golden gams.

Learning the speed skill can make every effort level faster because it increases power output per stride (letting you go incrementally farther with each step), cardiac stroke output (how much your heart pumps with each beat), neuromuscular and biomechanical efficiency and countless other variables.

The problem with a training approach that skips the speed step is that it presupposes you have already grabbed these low-hanging fruit. For pro runners coming from college track backgrounds, maybe they have. But most runners are leaving those juicy mangoes sitting there for the taking. And even those pro runners are doing a lot of running economy–oriented work their entire careers, it just seems less impressive than the 10-mile tempos and 6 × 1 mile track runs.

A universal truth of running training is that the little things are actually the big things. Run easy a lot, learn to run fast sometimes, and you'll get 95 percent of the way to your potential. That next 5 percent is just icing on the cake.

Hard Running Chases Marginal Gains; Fast Running Chases Breakthroughs

You never hear someone say that the stew has just one drop of rat poison. Similarly, bad habits from failure to develop running economy are like a contagion spreading through all of your running.

It gets back to the kid at recess. All they know how to do is run fast. It's natural and playful. The adult, meanwhile, may lose the play aspect and focus solely on the miles and the longer workouts. Perhaps their running is just 1 percent less economical than needed as they get farther from faster running. The adult can hide that loss in economy by doing hard workouts like 10-mile tempos and 6×1 mile intervals, which raise lactate threshold and $+O_2$max. They might even improve their race performances while their economy drops. However, eventually, lactate threshold and $+O_2$max will start to plateau, like 35-year-old Andrew Skurka saw. Then, you're just left with crappy running economy. You spend your running time thinking you are slower than you are. Bad genetics, maybe. Better luck on the parent lottery next time.

But what if the focus is on improving that running economy the entire time? Being 1 percent more economical makes those 10-mile tempos and 6×1 mile intervals faster. Faster workouts improve economy a bit more, so maybe you're now at 2 percent (along with a higher lactate threshold and $+O_2$max). Do some more economy-oriented work and now you're at 3 percent. Some workouts raise it to 4 percent. The fitness snowball starts to roll downhill, and that's how a 35-year-old 2:44 marathoner can become a 2:28 marathoner while working less hard than before.

It all gets back to the simplest principle of running training: all stress must have a purpose. And as Coach Jack Daniels says, training should strive for the least amount of stress possible to achieve a given adaptation. Training stress causes physical breakdown. In moderation, that's a good thing. The body comes back stronger. But breakdown without a purpose just becomes self-destruction.

It's not just physical breakdown, but mental breakdown too. An emphasis on long and hard workouts is extremely grueling. Meanwhile, easy running and recess running bring fun to the forefront. A training approach that elevates fun is more sustainable for body and brain, and that's what a happy runner is all about.

Hard workouts, like those tempos and mile intervals, are a big stress. They have rewards, sure, but their risks are immense. Stress fractures, overtraining, and burnout almost always correlate with an increased amount of time above aerobic threshold.

By optimizing the time you spend below aerobic threshold, you can strategically use that time above aerobic threshold to perform at your maximum potential.

Some runners can learn to run fast in as little as 10 minutes a week. That sounds like an infomercial, but it's true. Andrew Skurka would do 10×20 seconds or 8×30 seconds a few times per week when he was starting out with the new approach. Add easy running, then add workouts, and viola! A new runner can be born pretty quickly.

By learning to run fast, you can chase breakthroughs. By solely practicing running hard, you may sink into quicksand.

A Sample Skurka Week

When Andrew Skurka started focusing on running economy, he spent six weeks avoiding longer, harder workouts in favor of easy running mixed with short, fast strides and intervals. Many runners in a similar rut could see big breakthroughs with that approach too. However, everyone has different physiologies, so it's never the same for every athlete. At first, a typical week for Andrew looked like this:

Monday: rest and recovery

Tuesday: 12 miles easy with 8×20 seconds fast/2 minutes easy in the second half

Wednesday: 10–12 miles easy

Thursday: 12 miles easy with 10×30 seconds fast/1 minute easy in the second half

Friday: 8 miles extra easy

Saturday: 16 miles easy/moderate (option to speed up in the second half)

Sunday: 12–14 miles easy with 6×30 seconds fast/2 minutes easy

After he absorbed the new stimulus, he added more traditional workouts back into the program. When he did, he noticed that his body could hold faster paces for longer without a significant amount of hard work in the preceding months.

Get Fast and Stay Fast Year-Round

Albert Einstein's study habits are probably not instructive for a person without an intellect the size of a galaxy. Similarly, the training of Olympic champions is not necessarily the best way for most runners to train. A universal truth of self-improvement is that you should not interpolate from outliers.

This outlier phenomenon is especially evident for running training. A prime example is how professional runners approach off-season. Every winter, mountain runner Kílian Jornet hangs up his shoes. He is so good that when the shoes come off his feet, doves sing and angels play harps. Before the doves get hoarse or angels get carpal tunnel, he puts on ski-mountaineering boots and won't touch a trail again until spring.

When he returns to the trails, he is as unstoppable as ever. Sometimes, people will say, "It must be the ski-mo," just like people used to say of Michael Jordan, "it must be the shoes." Then, normal runners will imitate Kílian's off-season plan, only to find themselves playing catch-up to their previous running fitness all season long. Their running economy suffers, and because economy is everything, their speed suffers too even as they develop aerobically. Aerobic development without top-end speed development will usually make a runner slower overall.

So when in doubt, always remember the training skeptic's questions: Are the pros successful because of what they do, or in spite of what they do? And if it's because of what they do, can that approach work for everyone?

It gets back to genetics and background. Kílian works his butt off, and has since he was a kid, but is also a freak of nature, an outlier among outliers. In road running, Olympic medalist Bernard Lagat famously took six weeks without any running at all each year. Of course, he was practically breaking 4-minute miles in diapers. Someone with that talent and work ethic could probably do competitive Scrabble six months a year and be a world champion the rest of the time. Bernard works his butt off, but he also came out of the womb with a fantastically fast butt to work.

The average person is genetically average. That sounds obvious, but interpolating training methods from genetic outliers ignores that reality. In the process, it's easy to lose some of the incremental gains that come from consistent development of running economy over time. Don't skip a step—you have to methodically go from average to above average to great to exceptional. Then maybe start applying the training methods of outliers to make the leap from exceptional to world champion.

It's a scene that plays out all the time. Runners take months off during winter, only to regress, pulled back by genetic inertia. Kílian and Bernard have genetics that need to go fast, whereas most of us have genetics that would prefer to Netflix and chill. For most runners, a consistent focus on speed development over time is the best way to unlock genetic potential that even your double helixes aren't sure you have.

That doesn't mean you should train your butt off all year. You may even need a complete off-season of weeks or months, physically and mentally. It just means to make sure you don't regress needlessly.

In SWAP parlance, it means you should periodize big-T Training, not little-t training. Periodization is a concept brought to the forefront by the father of modern running training, Arthur Lydiard. All consistently successful training systems rest in part on the philosophy he helped develop. When you periodize training, you build one block on top of another, generally starting with easy running, working up to faster running, layering hard intervals on top of aerobic base.

We call that big-T Training, essentially focused "Training blocks." It's *Training* as a proper noun, complex and often hotly debated on Internet message boards.

In contrast, little-t training is the process of consistently running. It has complex underpinnings, but it's not complex in execution. Run lots, not too much, mostly easy. Take breaks when needed, but don't take breaks needlessly.

To develop running economy over time, most runners should be doing consistent training almost all year. It's the background drum beat on top of which the sweet guitar solo gets played.

Consistent training is all about developing the aerobic system with easy miles and low-level stress. On top of that, short, fast strides get the running economy positive-feedback loop looping. So, let's break it down with some sweet, CliffsNotes–style action:

- Do lots of easy running, and your aerobic system and running economy develop over time. Those adaptations are sticky—they don't go down much with age, and they allow you to run more and run faster.
- Build your speed with short, fast strides and intervals (while avoiding going too hard too often), and your running economy

rises like a full moon tide. In the process, it takes the aerobic ship with it, allowing more aerobic development.

- Run more over time, and your aerobic system improves even more. As your economy improves, you get faster without even trying. Do that for a few years, and you can chase breakthroughs rather than marginal gains. That is what we mean by consistent training.

- Background mileage fluctuates with more complex training blocks. But to keep your running economy train chugging, you should never get too far away from the speed you worked so hard to develop. That can be as simple as a couple sets each week of 4×20 to 30 seconds fast during runs most of the year. Just don't derail your running economy train without a good reason.

Corrine Malcolm is a prime example. When she joined SWAP, she was a top biathlete, skiing and shooting her way onto the U.S. Olympic development team. Badass! However, as she put it in her initial e-mail, "I am not fast."

Or was she? We set out to answer that question. Over the next couple years, Corrine ran almost all year-round (with lots of rest built into training), mostly easy, sometimes fast. She emphasized strides and easy miles to improve running economy. Even when she spent the winters skiing, she'd usually run consistently and do strides a couple times a week. Eventually, her old moderate pace became her new easy pace. The miles got easier. The strides got faster. So the miles got even easier, which again made the strides even faster.

She planted a tree in 2013. Corrine was going to get fast and stay fast year-round. That tree grew as if it was sprinting toward the jungle canopy, spurred on by her talent and work ethic. And in 2016, she won the U.S. 50-Mile Trail Championships.

Get fast and stay fast year-round, and you may discover a secret. All this time, you thought you had average genetics, playing around at the margins of your fitness, looking for a second or two of speed. But in reality, you had the potential to be an outlier, running joyfully and effortlessly beyond what you ever imagined. Those low-hanging fruit are really yummy.

Develop the Speed Skill

Smooth is fast. That's the mantra to use when learning to run fast in a sustainable way.

To make smooth fast, you have to make a complex skill take less effort. It's just like piano, dancing, or surgery. To get proficient at those skills, you have to tickle the ivory, cut a rug, or saw the stranger. And you have to do it so often that it becomes second nature, rather than an awkwardly forced behavior. Three guidelines can guide your journey to speed. As always, the big disclaimer applies—these are generalized rules, and what works for you could be way different.

1. **First, start on hills.** Uphills reduce impact forces and optimize power output, reducing injury risk while providing a safe bridge to faster work. After your total weekly easy running volume feels sustainable, add short hill strides where you go the fastest pace you can without straining. That is the key—no strain. If you are pumping your arms in a sprint, it's too hard. If you're begging to stop at the end, too hard. If you upchuck your Cinnamon Toast Crunch, way too hard. But great cereal choice.

At first, most SWAP athletes do 4×15 seconds fast with full recovery (usually 1 to 3 minutes of easy running) a couple times per week at the end of runs. Work up to 8×30 seconds fast with full recovery over time. Advanced athletes can just do short hills for a few days before progressing. Athletes just starting out or over age 40 should focus more on hills, which reinforce proper biomechanics with less injury risk.

2. **Second, move to flats gradually after the easy miles and hills feel completely sustainable.** When doing flat ground strides, you will be moving substantially faster, and it opens you up to injury risk if you aren't careful. So treat your body like a precious family heirloom, an urn that should in no circumstances be handled recklessly.

On each flat stride, ease into the effort, with the first five or so seconds just building up speed, then settle in to the fastest pace you can go comfortably. Think about effortless form, avoiding swinging your arms like a sprinter. You're a kid playing tag at recess, not an adult running from the cops.

At first, most SWAP athletes do 4×20 seconds fast with full recovery (around 2 minutes usually) in the second half of runs. Eventually, that will progress to 8–12×30 seconds fast with full recovery, still focusing on smooth speed, not strained speed. Counterintuitively, faster is not better because go too fast, and you will be going anaerobic and recruiting too many fast-twitch muscle fibers. Generally, runners over age 40 will spend less time doing flat strides and more time on hills to emphasize improving power output safely.

3. **Third, as a bridge to more complex training, shorten the recovery times between strides.** Wait until the neuromuscular and biomechanical adaptations are mostly absorbed, where strides feel effortlessly smooth like you are a beautiful puma-person. The shorter recoveries let the puma's aerobic engine start to purr, working running economy.

Start with just 1 minute recovery after 30 second strides (on hills or flats), shortening it down to 30 seconds over time. Most SWAP athletes will build up to 10–15×30 second strides with 30 seconds easy recovery, done just once or twice a training cycle. On one island is your smooth speed; on the other is your velocity at $+O_2$max. These short-rest strides provide a bridge for you to access your speed to go faster for longer.

Sample Economy Build

Okay, so you've got the easy running down. You feel comfortable running a good bit. You're becoming a running boss.

Completing the promotion involves learning to run faster. On top of your normal easy running, a five-week economy build that works for many athletes is outlined below. Each workout is in the context of a normal easy run.

Week 1: 6×20 second hills fast with 2 minutes easy recovery (economy workout 1) and 8×20 second hills fast with 2 minutes easy recovery (economy workout 2)

Week 2: 6×30 second hills fast with 1 minute easy recovery and 8×30 second hills fast with 1 minute easy recovery

Week 3: 6×20 seconds fast flat with 2 minutes easy recovery and 8×20 seconds fast flat with 2 minutes easy recovery

Week 4: 8×30 seconds fast flat with 2 minutes easy recovery and 10×30 seconds fast flat with 1 minute easy recovery

Week 5: 10×30 seconds fast flat with 1 minute easy recovery and 15×30 seconds fast flat with 30 seconds easy recovery

The build can be shorter for athletes who have developed their speed skill or longer for athletes doing it for the first time. Afterward, fast should feel easy, and an athlete can jump into longer workouts.

As always, there are a million ways to go about developing the speed skill, and the specifics are all about personal preference and background. Instead, focus on the principles.

No matter who you are, you can get fast. A little bit of practice is all it takes to have major breakthroughs.

—7—

Principle 3:
Build Strength From Speed

If your car has a top speed of 80 miles per hour, holding 70 on the highway is probably going to cause it to quake and shake before it sputters to a stop, seemingly exhausted by the effort.

The same principles apply to running. Higher top-end speed endurance (prolonged time near maximal speed) will usually make lower speeds more sustainable. Yet all too often, runners focus on putting all their weight into the gas pedal rather than working on the engine. When they sputter to a stop, they might say, "I should have pushed on the gas pedal harder" rather than "I need each push of the gas pedal to be more efficient."

To put it another way, you ain't no Ford Pinto. You aren't going to explode on the interstate. You're a Tesla—sexy, sleek, and strong. That sounds simplistic, but internalizing the principle that your potential is higher than it seems at first is key to finding your potential at all.

We call the relationship between smooth speed and sustainable speed the "20 Percent Rule" for endurance running. It's not exact whatsoever (it could easily be called the "15 Percent Rule" or the "25 Percent Rule" or the "Magna Carta Part II: More Magna, More Carta"), but the principles behind the 20 Percent Rule have formed the basis of lots of breakthroughs.

Here's how it works for us: after an athlete joins SWAP, we'll often have them do a series of workouts to evaluate their current fitness level.

- **Sustainable top-end speed endurance test:** In the middle of a run, they will do 8×20 or 30 seconds fast with equal easy running recovery after each. The short recovery times are to make sure they aren't sprinting like they are doing the 40-yard dash at the NFL Combine, but rather using their top-end long-distance running form—smooth and quick. This gets back to the purring puma in the previous chapter, plus it doubles as a great intro-to-running-economy workout.
- **Lactate threshold test:** 30-minute time trial at a hard but not all-out effort. This test is useful because most runners will gravitate toward their race effort for a 1-hour event, a key marker of endurance performance. It also lets us calibrate their easy run pace, as described in chapter 5.

Across the athletes we have tested, the average speed on the lactate threshold time trial is around 20 percent slower than the average peak speed on the short little strides (plus or minus based on genetics, gender, and background). Generally, more slow-twitch-dominant athletes will be a lower percentage, and fast-twitch athletes will be higher. As the athletes develop, that baseline percentage rarely changes much outside of minor fluctuations within training cycles. How can 30-second speed correlate with 30-minute effort?

It's all about running economy. On those short strides, most runners will gravitate toward an effort they could hold for 5 to 8 minutes. On the longer tempo, most runners will gravitate toward their 40-minute to 1-hour effort. On top of that, studies show that the 1-hour effort will often correlate pretty closely to performance at every distance longer than that, from half marathon to 50 miles.

So, to summarize: short distance (but still aerobic) running economy seems to correlate with long-distance running economy for an athlete over time.

Now, what to do with that information? It's intuitive, right? Faster top-end (but still smooth) speed makes slightly slower (but still fast) speed feel easier.

Well, let's look at what happens when you focus on those energy systems. If a runner starts by doing lots of moderately hard intervals focused on long-distance effort, those paces will improve as they get more comfortable. Eventually, though, the improvement stagnates when neuromuscular and biomechanical adaptations lag behind aerobic adaptations. To put it another way: the brain and legs can no longer cash the checks written by the aerobic system.

If the athlete focused on long-distance efforts retested, you'd see the offset. The 30-minute time trial may now just be 10 percent slower than the short strides. That is great if a long-distance race is upcoming, but it can be disheartening if the ratio persists. At some point, there is a cap where an athlete cannot get significantly faster at steady efforts without raising their top-end speed, like the car struggling to hold 70 mph on the highway.

Meanwhile, improving top-end speed endurance usually does distribute to faster steady efforts with training. If those 30-second strides get faster and you add some steady efforts later in the training cycle, the 30-minute time trial usually gets a bit faster too, especially for beginner or intermediate athletes. Support that with lots of aerobic development across training cycles, and overall potential skyrockets with it.

The takeaway: Your strength will usually be a certain percentage of your smooth speed, give or take based on your genetics, background, and training approach. Hard, grueling interval training may raise that percentage, but it comes with risks of injury and burnout, plus there is an underlying cap on how high it can go before you stagnate. So how do you solve the equation?

Always start with speed.

In September 2016, Kimberley Teshima faced the unfortunate reality of being a lifelong runner. She failed.

At the Cascade Crest 100 Mile Endurance Run, Kimberley didn't finish. She had planned for this moment for so long—her first 100 miler!—and her plans were dashed. Not only that, it happened in the public eye. Kimberley is a major figure in trail running media, with over 100,000 subscribers on the YouTube channel she shares with her husband, "The Ginger Runner" Ethan Newberry.

She felt like she let herself down. She felt like she let her fans down. We've all been there, upset and lost. As she wrote:

"I know DNF's happen. I know they happen to most (if not all) of us, and I know I should be celebrating the small victories in life. But ugh, I'm having a tough time. Any advice on how to move on? It feels silly to be so upset still, the logical side of me keeps saying that. But the waves of despair seem to keep coming. Thoughts? Eat a pizza, drink a beer, suck it up and carry on?"

It's the happy runner dilemma. Do everything right, only to have everything go wrong. How do you respond?

David wrote back: "Nothing in life is worth 'sucking it up' unless it's a milkshake."

After going back and forth, they came to a conclusion that became the subject of their e-mail chain: "LET'S GET FAST!"

Instead of focusing on long-distance stress, Kimberley focused on learning the speed skill. Only after ingraining new, speedy movement patterns did she go back to her old strength-oriented approach. What happened?

In six weeks, she set big personal bests at every distance from 5K to half marathon.

Learning to run faster let her access her true strength, rather than wallow in the reduced strength she thought she had. For professional runners, it's incredibly complicated, because they've often developed their speed. But for Kimberley, she found out what many runners discover by using speed to access their true strength. Her spirit animal was not a sloth. She had a super-puma lurking inside her all along.

Strength and Speed Training

To go fast, many runners first have to learn to go fast. There is another sentence written by Captain Obvious, who apparently just got a coaching certification. But it's true, and it's a step many skip.

For those runners, no amount of running at a 10-minute pace will make an 8-minute pace easier until their body can run an 8-minute pace without impersonating one of those inflatable wavy-arm men outside of a car dealership. How can you go from flailing around wildly like you are trying to sell used Hondas to smooth, effortless speed? Build strength from speed.

Two weeks with similar training volume might show the contrasting approaches at work.

Strength-focused week

Monday: rest

Tuesday: 2 miles easy warm-up, 2×10 minutes moderate/hard with 5 minutes easy recovery, 2 miles easy cool-down

Wednesday: 5 miles easy

Thursday: 10K moderate

Friday: rest

Saturday: 5 miles easy

Sunday: 18 miles moderate

That's a lot of moderate and hard volume. With that amount of moderate, the body will usually fall back on old habits, going a bit slower to complete the runs and avoid breaking down.

Speed-focused week

Monday: rest

Tuesday: 6 miles easy with 6×30 seconds fast/2 minutes easy

Wednesday: 3 miles easy warm-up, 3/2/1 minutes fast with 2 minutes easy after each interval, 3 miles easy cool-down

Thursday: 6 miles easy

Friday: rest

Saturday: 16 miles easy/moderate over hilly terrain

Sunday: 6 miles easy plus 6×30 second hills with 2 minutes easy recovery after each

Kimberly made a change like this, and polarizing her training speeds let her achieve breakthroughs. Coolest of all—over the course of a few months, not only did her fast paces get faster, but her easy paces got faster too.

The goal is to start at a low volume of intensity, then build up as the body adapts. So eventually, an athlete advances to being able to handle high volumes of intensity, but it sometimes takes many months, especially for athletes who are fully developing their speed for the first time.

Velocity Matters

To understand how it all fits together, let's dig into that harbinger of endurance performance, $+O_2$max. $+O_2$max is the maximum amount of oxygen a person can use, expressed in milliliters of oxygen per kilogram of bodyweight per minute. In basic terms, the more oxygen you can take in, the faster you can run.

The problem with $+O_2$max is it doesn't predict how fast you will go, just how much oxygen you will use. What's much more interesting is running economy—how fast you can go using the oxygen you have.

The offset is related to velocity. $+O_2$max is a largely genetic variable that doesn't improve much with training after an initial jump. Meanwhile, velocity at $+O_2$max ($v+O_2$) can improve long after the raw oxygen-processing number has stagnated.

The same goes for lactate threshold (LT) and aerobic threshold (AeT). vLT and vAeT can improve even as the baseline LT and AeT numbers stay the same.

That explains why stride pace correlates with LT time trial pace in the athletes discussed above. Faster strides do not improve the raw LT number. Instead, they improve biomechanical and neuromuscular variables that can make that raw LT number equate to a faster pace with focused training.

Let's look at an example of how this all works at the pro level.

In 2016, Patrick Caron ran 14 hours, 51 minutes for 100 miles. It's astounding when you think about it—faster than 9 minutes per mile for 100 miles. That same year, he ran the Boston Marathon in 2:46:59. In training, he worked from the top-down, doing lots of miles and sustained intervals.

But in December 2016, he tried something different. Patrick went from using brute force to build strength to using his speed to access his strength. He still ran a lot of easy miles, but fewer than before. And those hard intervals were replaced by shorter and faster efforts. Instead of doing 120 miles per week, he was now doing 90. Instead of doing 6×1 mile workouts with 1 minute recovery, he was now doing 12×1 minute workouts with 1 minute recovery. The entire goal was to raise his top-end speed endurance, hoping to spur a breakthrough.

And break through he did. Off a training emphasis on making fast paces smoother, he ran 2:40 at the 2017 Boston Marathon. But that was just the beginning. He ran personal bests at every distance from the 1 mile and up, culminating in a shocking 13-hour, 51-minute 100 miler at the same race from the year before. Patrick went from a kid trying to find his way in the sport to a professional runner sponsored by Salomon.

It's easy to think of training as a mixed martial arts fight to bring your body into compliance with your mission. You attack it, you get it into a triple suplex throat-lock, you wait for it to tap out, then you move onto the next fight. You can probably tell we don't know much about MMA, and that's for a reason. If you view training as a fight, eventually your body will fight back through injuries, stagnation, or burnout.

Instead, think of training as a dance. You move to the music, feeling the rhythm with your body, applying general rules but being flexible to create something that is uniquely your own. Sometimes, that might mean ballroom twirls. Other times, it might mean dance-club twerking. Viewing training as a dance will let your body grow with you as the music changes over time.

Back in 2016, Patrick loved running, but there was some fighting going on without him realizing it. His mileage- and workout-heavy program often looked like this:

Monday: 10 miles easy

Tuesday: 14 miles easy/moderate (a.m.) and 6 miles easy (p.m.)

Wednesday: 3 miles easy, 2×5K moderate with 5 minutes easy recovery, 3 miles easy (a.m.) and 6 miles easy (p.m.)

Thursday: 16 miles easy

Friday: 10 miles easy

Saturday: 24 miles easy/moderate with second half steady

Sunday: 16 miles easy

When we first saw his training, we were in awe. The mental toughness and physical talent to complete that plan is astounding! But it had already left him stagnating a bit due to the volume of running and the lack of polarization to practice the speed skill. A new week looked more like this:

Monday: 8 miles easy

Tuesday: 12 miles easy with 8×20 seconds fast/40 seconds easy

Wednesday: 3 miles easy warm-up, 15 minutes moderate/hard (1-hour effort) with 5 minutes easy recovery, 8×1 minute fast (5K effort)/1 minute easy/moderate (50K effort), 3 miles easy/moderate (a.m.) and 5 miles easy plus 4×30 second hills (p.m.)

Thursday: 10 miles easy (a.m.) and 5 miles easy (p.m.)

Friday: 8 miles easy with 4×30 seconds fast/2 minutes easy

Saturday: 16 miles easy/moderate (20 minutes at 1-hour effort in the middle)

Sunday: 12 miles easy plus 6×30 second hills with 90 seconds easy recovery (a.m.) and 5 miles easy (p.m.)

His training volume dropped by about 20–30 percent, he emphasized developing his running economy at faster paces, and his performances took off. After developing the speed skill, when he would do workouts from before (like $2 \times 5K$), they were 30–45 seconds faster per mile. That improved running economy distributed to all of his races, from 1 mile to 100 miles, and now he is one of the rising stars in ultrarunning.

It all gets back to the 20 Percent Rule. Patrick's heavy emphasis on longer intervals and tons of miles made him stronger than he was fast, which capped his ultimate potential. Kimberley was on the same trajectory. By working on getting faster, they built breakthrough strength from newfound speed.

Build Strength From the Bottom Up

Consistent training is the most important part of development as a runner. Run lots, mostly easy, not too much, all while working on smooth speed with strides and hills. That is the cake.

The icing is more complex training blocks focused on longer intervals and lots of effort. These training blocks are really important for long-term development too, and for most professional runners they are the most important of all. But it should not come first. Cake without icing is still delicious sweetbread; icing without cake is the sweetest path to diabetes.

Let's look at two different cakes that use similar ingredients.

Super-talent Scott Trummer joined SWAP in 2016 as a promising athlete looking to reach the next level. He had finished 4th at the 2016 U.S. 50K Trail Championships, but he didn't know how to make the leap. Scott had oodles of speedy noodles in his legs, and a few years of running experience.

His new training approach focused on building up easy aerobic mileage, working up to 80 to 90 miles per week from 60 to 70. He did some short, fast strides, but not too many, since he had so much natural speed. Instead, he focused on building strength from his speed, doing lots of intervals between 2 and 5 minutes with lots of recovery. The goal was not to go hard and struggle, but to go smooth at longer distances.

Meg Mackenzie was an entirely different athlete when she joined SWAP in 2016. She had promising results in her native South Africa, but she kept getting injured and had stagnated over a couple-year period.

Her new training approach only had her running five days per week, with less total mileage than before to minimize injury risk. She purely did hill efforts, starting with short hill strides and working to longer, tougher workouts. Meg's go-to workout was the appropriately named Hill Beast, which involved a 20-minute easy warm-up, followed by 10/8/6/4/2 minute hills with run down recovery after each, before a 20-minute cool down. Instead of raising top-end velocity like Scott, she was focused on raising top-end power, then using that power to build race-ready strength.

Scott's progression culminated in winning the 2017 American River 50-Mile Endurance Run, one of the most storied ultramarathons in the United States. Meg's journey led her to international success, culminating in a win at the Otter Trail Classic, a big race in South Africa and a major event on the international race calendar.

Their secret sauces were totally different. Scott focused on smooth speed, building into improving velocity at long-distance effort levels (vLT and vAeT). Meg focused on effortless power, building into better climbing at those effort levels. The training tasted different, but the results were equally delicious.

In other words, there are tons of different ways you can do workouts to reach your goals. It's like eating at the Whole Foods salad and hot food bar—you can make hundreds of different meals that are all equally delicious with just a few overlapping ingredients.

Given the unlimited options, what matters is not the specific approach, but the general principle that **fast needs to feel smooth, or eventually hard will become slow**. To put it in technical terms, if v+O2 slows down substantially due to neglecting speed, vLT and vAeT will probably slow down, even if the actual numbers for $+O_2max$, LT, and AeT stay the exact same. That's why pro runners will almost always do some short, fast speed work, even when they are training for marathons. For normal runners, it's even more important, since unlike pros, that speed development has not been honed for most of us over many years.

How does it work in practice? You can almost never spend too much time on consistent training, doing easy running and fast strides. Once that prerequisite is satisfied, it should still occupy at least 80 percent of the running you do each week. With the other 20 percent, you can do hard intervals and more sustained tempos that focus on strength. Because those harder efforts come on a base of aerobic development and speed development, fast will feel smoother and easier, which means it's more sustainable, which means your overall potential goes up.

With most of your running at an easy effort, you will stay healthier. By focusing on improved running economy, you will use less effort at faster paces. And healthy, effortless running is happy running.

This Is How We Do It

There is no right way to train. Even the band Train probably agrees with that. There are a bunch of different ways to reach your potential as a runner (or as a pop-rock supergroup), all of which can lead to breakthroughs.

The exact approach that works best is tough to determine, since it's always an experiment of one, which means you can't have a control group. In the face of all this uncertainty, the key is simply finding a method that supports long-term consistency and growth. None of what we do is unique or particularly interesting, so feel free to skip this section like a commercial on your DVR.

The SWAP approach generally mixes styles of some of the top coaches in running history: Arthur Lydiard, Jack Daniels, Renato Canova, and Mark Wetmore. On top of that, we add some wrinkles that are specific to athletes who are specializing in trail races and ultramarathons.

Breaking down the SWAP approach would be its own book, so we won't go into much detail here to avoid boring you to tears. Before getting to the phases we use, there are a few overarching principles:

1. Maximize total aerobic volume that an athlete can do over time while staying healthy, happy, and motivated. That includes cross-training activities like biking, skiing, and aggressive dog cuddling. Periodically, athletes will do down weeks where total volume and intensity are reduced (as often as every other week for injury-prone or busy athletes, to every sixth week for resilient professional runners).

2. Practice a year-round emphasis on speed endurance outside of race-specific training blocks. That means strides or short intervals 1 to 4 times per week after the aerobic base is strong.

3. Long runs are quality efforts. Most long runs are the second workout of the week (on top of a midweek speedy session), involving workouts that are tailored to an athlete's goals.

4. Rest from running consistently. Almost every athlete has a complete rest day (or two) every week, though some pros will rest less often if they have stayed healthy for an extended period of time.

5. Emphasize sustainability and qualitative metrics, rather than performance metrics. How something feels matters more than splits.

In practice, the phases we use blur together, particularly for athletes who have been developing with us for multiple years. An overview of the five phases is shown below:

1. **Aerobic Phase:** maximizing aerobic volume before introducing short, fast hill strides, followed by flat-ground strides, with easy/moderate running over hills introduced on a couple runs later in the phase. The weekly long run usually involves short fartlek efforts as a bridge to the next phase. Trail runners will begin training to run downhills fast in the context of a couple runs a week (including the long run). Duration is usually 4 to 10 weeks, though an athlete can't really spend too long developing at this stage.

   Spirit animal = border collie puppy getting trained not to pee in the house

2. **Economy Phase 1:** emphasizing strides and short intervals with shorter rest to improve v+O2 running economy (approximately), primarily through neuromuscular and biomechanical adaptations. Volume drops by 20–40 percent at first, then gets back to peak levels. The weekly long run usually mixes light-tempo efforts and fartleks, and there are some sustained efforts over variable terrain. Duration is 2 to 8 weeks, depending on the athlete's background and goals.

   Spirit animal = golden retriever puppy learning how to fetch

3. **Economy Phase 2:** emphasizing vLT (and similar effort levels) through tempos and hills, improving the pace an athlete can run without tipping the lactate curve, while keeping v+O2 speed through periodic speed endurance work. Total aerobic volume usually increases 10 to 20 percent above previous peak levels from earlier in the training cycle. The weekly long run usually involves grueling tempos of 20 to 60 minutes total work with short recovery. Trail runners will start doing extra-long runs with downhill emphasis. Duration is 2 to 6 weeks. In practice, athletes will oscillate between these first three phases most of the year.

   Spirit animal: husky sled dog preparing for the Iditarod

4. **Specific Phase:** developing for goal event by emphasizing metabolic efficiency at race effort. For trails and ultras, that means improving power output at AeT by mixing long runs over race-specific terrain with sustained tempos to turn them into a fat-burning monster. For marathons, that means speeding up vAeT, improving the pace they can run while using fat as a primary fuel source. For much shorter races, it means focusing on workouts where total volume equals or exceeds race duration at similar intensities with as much recovery as needed to run efficiently. Duration is 3 to 8 weeks.

   Spirit animal: golden retriever puppy celebrating dinnertime

5. **Pizza Phase:** eating lots of pizza to recover and rebuild. Depending on the athlete and their goals, they can substitute burgers, tacos, or cake. Duration is a couple days to a couple weeks.

   Spirit animal: ADDIE DOG

Each phase could be the subject of 50 pages of text (especially Pizza Phase). But we are fully aware this section is more effective than a sleeping pill, so we'll stop now in case you are planning on operating heavy machinery.

More Climbing May Make a Slower Climber

If you focus a lot of your training on going up and down steep hills, you may eventually discover the climbing paradox: more climbing may make for worse climbing.

It's a variation of the same discussion above, but with velocity replaced by power. On flat ground (like road racing), what matters is not your $+O_2$max, LT, or AeT—it's your velocity at those effort levels and in between. In other words, it's your running economy.

On very hilly terrain (like trail racing), those raw variables don't matter either. Instead, what matters is your power output (and resilience) at those effort levels. In other words, it's your climbing (and descending) economy.

In SWAP, we use the measurement "vam." The term is based on an Italian acronym short for velocità ascensionale media, used in cycling to equalize climbing strength across different ascents. In cycling, the unit is meters climbed per hour. For running, the unit is not important, but the principle is. Optimizing power output will improve vam at different effort levels.

So grab your slide rules and let's go further down the acronym rabbit hole. Before, we talked about $v+O_2$, vLT, and vAeT to describe running economy. Now, we are focused on vam$+O_2$, vamLT, and vamAeT to describe economy over variable terrain. We apologize for the convoluted terminology; we promise it'll make sense soon.

You can think of running economy as focused on the horizontal vector—how fast can you go forward?

Climbing economy focuses on both the horizontal and vertical vectors—how fast can you go forward *and up*?

So back to the original question: Why can too much climbing make for a worse climber over time? It's all about those pesky vectors.

Consider a rather steep 12 percent grade, the type of hill that would make you nearly go sideways on a bike. Even though it's steep, the vertical vector is only a relatively small percentage of the horizontal vector. For that vertical vector, power matters most. For that horizontal vector, velocity is still really important, even at slower paces.

In other words, speed still is one of the most important factors in how quickly you climb except at the steepest grades where you can no longer run (studies indicate that happens around 15–20 percent gradient).

If you climb incessantly, you eventually stop working on velocity. Since that is a big component in vam at all but the steepest grades, your vam may drop over time even as you climb more. Layered on top of that is the previous point about the 20 Percent Rule, that top-end power output needs to be optimized or vamLT (or other climbing economy variables) can drop over time even as LT stays the same. Conversely, if you focus on climbing efficiently, rather than climbing hard, vamLT can improve while LT stays stagnant.

Wow, that involved so many acronyms that your eyes probably got glazed over like breakfast at Dunkin' Donuts. So let's see how it works in practice.

Hillary Allen joined SWAP in 2016 as a top international skyracer, a sport involving steep mountain climbs. Her previous training strategy had emphasized lots of climbing all year round. She was focused almost entirely on strength. That makes sense, right? Why do mountain climbers need to be fast?

Eventually, though, that strength plateaued. She was amazing, but not getting stronger on climbs or faster in races. So she changed course and started focusing on building breakthrough strength from newfound speed.

Hillary started by raising her top-end on top of her already-developed aerobic system, with short strides and hills (Aerobic Phase). Then, she worked her running economy, honing $v+O_2$ and vLT through shorter, flatter intervals on roads around Boulder, Colorado (Economy Phases 1 and 2). With her horizontal vector better than ever, once her first big race was six weeks out, she switched to a $vam+O_2$ and vamLT emphasis (Specific Phase). Immediately, she noticed something shocking. She had become one of the best climbers in the world while barely climbing at all in training.

After adding some power to the mix, she went on to have one of the best seasons in the history of U.S. skyracing. She was third at the Transvulcania ultramarathon, won Madeira Island Ultra-Trail, and was ranked no. 1 in the world in the skyracing discipline in August 2017.

In one of her final big races of the season, she suffered a tragic accident, falling 50 meters and fortunately living to tell the tale. After a long recovery period, she's returned to the mountains she loves, bringing her beautiful spirit and talent back to the trails.

Sugar, We're Going Down

Reference to a song by early aughts pop-punk group Fall Out Boy in our book = tween versions of ourselves would be in heaven.

Going downhill is a chance to capture free speed. On downhills, most athletes will find their heart rates way lower, especially in trail races where the descents are steep. So unlike going fast on flats or putting out power on ups, it's not a big aerobic stress. Instead, it's more of a biomechanical and neuromuscular stress.

Biomechanically, downhills involve eccentric muscle contractions, where muscles (primarily the quadriceps) lengthen under load. That causes microtears in muscle fibers. Have you ever had Jello legs after some downhills? That is probably your quads going to mush from eccentric muscle contractions. You'll know we found the culprit if 24 to 72 hours after the downhill stimulus, your legs lose most of their capacity to bear your weight and you become a jellyfish-person (the jellyhuman phenomenon is called delayed-onset muscle soreness, or DOMS). On top of DOMS, downhills involve significantly higher impact forces, which requires every part of your body, from your feet to your back, to be more resilient.

Neuromuscularly, downhills require a blend of focus, agility, and speed rarely exhibited out of a puppy playpen. Comfort with pushing on downhills is a learned skill that requires practice.

You can develop your downhill skill on long runs. Run downhills with a purpose on all weekend runs—not to push, but to flow. That concentrates the stimulus on a two-day block, allowing adaptation without overstress. Later on, do moderate tempo runs over hilly terrain. Combine those two stimuli, and you can become a downhill expert without doing specific downhill intervals or substantially raising injury risk.

Getting Strong From the Ground Up

It's okay to ignore the specifics of that last discussion. Instead, think about the big takeaway from this chapter: strong running must be efficient, or eventually your strongest efforts will get slower. And running hard, but going slow, is one of the most frustrating obstacles facing a happy runner.

The following four guidelines can help turn your Pinto into a Tesla.

1. **First, always focus at least 80 percent of your time on the aerobic development-to-running-economy positive feedback loop,**

which is formed with lots of easy running and short, fast strides. Going harder all the time may provide some short-term rewards, like investing in a get-rich-quick scheme. Just like a pyramid scheme, it'll eventually become too top-heavy, and the whole thing will come crashing down.

Spend as much time as you can increasing total easy running volume and getting comfortable at faster paces for short distances prior to stepping up to strength-based workouts. The goal is not to put the cart before the horse, but to give the horse's engine some nitrous.

2. **Second, on top of the easy running, begin the transition to strength development by running slightly more moderate on one or two runs a week, ideally over hilly terrain.** These unstructured runs provide an introduction to strength without risking physical breakdown. They are best done as easy–moderate progression runs, with the first half relaxed and the second half purposeful but not hard.

After building up easy running volume, do most of your long runs with this easy–moderate approach, with trail runners focusing particularly on running downhills with purpose. It builds up resilience and provides a base of low-level strength that makes for higher-quality intervals later. Think of easy running as assembling the ingredients for the stew—it's required if you want to eat. Then the short, fast strides and hills are searing the meat, taking the stew's taste potential to another level. More sustained running is putting it all in the crock pot and letting it simmer.

3. **Third, add intervals and tempo runs that emphasize efficient running over hard running.** The biggest mistake athletes make in workouts is pushing to their limits. The body adapts to gentle prods, not torturous pokes. If you go too hard, form breaks down and you undermine the economy you worked to build.

Focus on more recovery and controlled efforts for workouts. For example, 6 × 3 minutes fast with 1 minute easy may cause a beginner athlete to start running with poor form and slow down immensely. 6 × 3 minutes fast with 3 minutes easy may let that same athlete run faster, with less effort, reinforcing smooth and fast running. Later on, when there is a focus on a race, things will get more specific. For example, Hillary's 8 × 3 minute moderately hard hills with full recovery became 30-minute moderately hard hill climb tempos in the final month before Transvulcania.

4. **Fourth, do not overemphasize specificity.** Running is running, whether it's on roads or trails, long or short. Running and climbing economy involve many of the same input variables. Focusing too

much on specificity for an event can sacrifice long-term development and possibly make the race less fast as well.

Spend most of every training block focusing on running or climbing economy, rather than race-specific training. Then, in the 3 to 8 weeks before the race, the specific training becomes more valuable because the harder workouts take less effort.

The key is to work smart, not hard. That sounds like an awful TED Talk, but it's true. Lots of smart running can make fast feel easier, then later on can make hard running far faster. The next step is like a caterpillar going into a cocoon, full of smooth speed and economical strength. How does it emerge as a race-ready butterfly?

—8—

Principle 4:

Specificity Matters, But Less Than You May Think

Specificity is the training concept of preparing specifically for the demands of a race or event. Hilly race? Run lots of hills. Ultra race? Run until the cows come home. Rainy race? Practice chafing now so you're not surprised by it later.

For a happy runner, specificity raises a few concerns. First, it puts all of your training eggs in a race basket, which can stall long-term progress since it may overemphasize results over process. Second, for long races (or races with lots of climbing), specific training is slower training, and slower training can stall progress too. Third, even for shorter races, peak performance requires cultivating a broad set of skills before narrowing focus close to race day. In other words, too much specificity can be like a get-rich-quick scheme, with immediate results offset by longer-term physical and psychological letdowns.

This may seem like a small point, but it's a story that plays out over and over. Runners focus a lot on races, train specifically for the races at the expense of developing a broad skill-set, and sooner or later they stagnate or burn out. In the process, they lose some of the joy of focusing on the process of being a lifelong runner.

To see how it works, let's take you back to school. Running training and education in any field share a lot in common. A general education almost always precedes specialization because specializing too soon limits ultimate potential. First-graders don't go straight to coding school, because to develop a good app they first need to know the basics of math, science, and even social studies. If they did become coding savants at the expense of all else, they might have skills but they will probably not be able to apply them outside of a narrow range of circumstances, and their talent will have trouble growing over time.

Running training is the same way. Overspecialize now, and it's possible to lose the broad skills necessary for growth later. Law school is based wholly on this principle.

In the first year of law school, students spend a lot of their time looking at books from the 1700s, where every disagreement is a crossover episode of *Downton Abbey* and *Jerry Springer*, involving cases about things like over-boiled goose. After reading ye olde dispute, the real learning begins.

The trembling students all sit in a big lecture hall, when an authoritative professor comes in with swaggering confidence and surveys the audience. The first five minutes of each class are tense with nerves. Up front, the professor is about to unleash the scariest element of law education: the Socratic method (as talked about briefly in chapter 4).

"Johnson," the professor says. "The case about the over-boiled goose."

Somewhere in the crowd, poor Johnson's heart sinks to her feet. For the rest of the class, she is "on-call," requiring a front-to-back understanding of the case and the legal principles. The professor asks questions ranging from facts to law to esoteric philosophy, all designed around the Socratic ideal of argumentative collaboration.

"At what temperature is boiled goose best served? What is the standard of care for goose cooking in 18th-century England?"

Meanwhile, if Johnson can avoid peeing herself, she stumbles through some answers about boiled goose. Even if she does pee herself, she stumbles through answers, just with a wet seat.

That seems really strange, right? What does boiled goose have to do with being a contracts lawyer, or divorce lawyer, or environmental lawyer?

Everything, it turns out. Many say the goal of law school is to learn how to "think like a lawyer," not to actually learn the law. The Socratic method applied to obscure cases allows Johnson and her classmates to understand how it all fits together, how the law evolves over time, and how to articulate their thoughts. It's not just a boiled goose, she'll learn. That goose could just as well be a surgery gone wrong or an iTunes user agreement where clicking "Agree" gives Apple the right to harvest your organs.

Legal education and legal practice are immensely different, but the base of knowledge can be applied to any field afterward. There is no such thing as a good environmental lawyer, just a good lawyer that applied their knowledge to environmental issues.

Medical school is similar, with four years of general education before specialization. Heck, culinary school works the same way. Good French or Italian or Japanese chefs are just good chefs that applied their expertise to a specific discipline. But all of the best could cross over to other cuisines with just a bit of training. If the lawyer or the doctor or the chef specialized entirely, they'd only be able to learn the narrow range of subjects they are taught directly. They'd have trouble learning and growing to their full potential over time.

So it goes with running. If law school is about thinking like a lawyer, medical school about thinking like a doctor, and culinary school about thinking like a chef, training is about thinking (and running) like a runner.

Used in moderation, specialization can lead to breakthrough fitness and performances. But neglect being a good runner in favor of being a good specialist for too long, and eventually you will just be left with a plate of over-boiled goose.

Back in 2016, Cat Bradley thought of herself as a specialist—she was an ultrarunner. She trained slow so she could race far, conquering mountains almost every day. Training was all geared toward her goal of covering the mountain terrain she loved efficiently.

What did that mean in practice? Lots of climbing and descending, with epic long runs and races. After all, running a 5K fast doesn't matter when there are 33 5Ks in a 100 miler. Run a fast 5K and you still have 97 miles to go.

That makes intuitive sense. A luminescent track star is going to be a dull red dwarf in the Hardrock Hundred Endurance Run. So Cat's training was like a lawyer who went straight to environmental law and skipped the intro classes. She was really good at ultras, but nothing mind-blowing.

In August 2016, she shifted her focus. She went back to the basics and developed her speed skill while simultaneously running fewer mountain miles. And the next year showed what can happen when specialization plays a narrower role in training.

With less than two months of specialized training prior to the Western States 100, she shocked the ultra world by winning. With just a few weeks of specialization before attacking the Grand Canyon, she set the fastest known time (FKT) from rim to rim to rim, covering 42 miles and 15,000 feet of climbing in a record-breaking time. In between, she essentially developed her 10K speed with a weekly run of 14 to 20 miles in the mountains and the rest of the week focused on making faster paces feel easier. A lot of overall development coupled with a little specialization made breakthroughs possible.

Reaching Your Running Potential Is Not Event-Specific

An old truism in running training is that everything shorter than 800 meters is a sprint, and everything above 800 meters is a fast jog. What that is getting at is that all endurance running relies on similar physical variables. It's why the 20 Percent Rule connecting smooth speed to sustained endurance applies to most runners. It's why the best marathoners are usually the best 10K runners plus a bit of training. And it's why overspecialization could sabotage ultimate potential.

The explanation revolves around running economy. Over the course of many years, running economy can continually improve. Developing it to your max potential requires an emphasis on consistent training, with lots of miles and speed development, mixed with cycles of more complex training blocks, focused on improving economy at different effort levels.

Overspecialization involves emphasizing race-specific training blocks instead, constantly reinforcing adaptations related to a specific event (like velocity at $+O_2$max for a 5K or mountain adventures for a 100 miler). A specialized approach will provide lots of gains at first until the body's potential gets tapped out entirely and a broader focus is needed to improve more.

It's like the saying "give a man a fish, feed him for a day. Teach a man to fish, and you feed him for a lifetime." Improving overall running economy by building general skills over time is like learning to fish—it may be a bit slower at first, but it'll provide sustenance for your running life for much longer.

You see this constantly in trail running. Fast road runners come to the sport and immediately have success with a minimal amount of specialized training. Their overall running economy is sky-high, they add some hills and rocks, and they are world-beaters.

Then, something strange happens. Their results might level out. After a few years of mountain adventures, they might just be another trail runner, good but not great. At first, time spent on trails and away from speed is like feasting on fish that have already been caught. If they aren't careful and focused on constantly improving running economy, the fish usually runs out, eventually.

When David was starting out and learning about running training, he was all about specificity. It seems logical, right? Train for an event to improve for an event. First, it'd be a trail 10K. He'd do mile repeats at 10K effort on trails, limiting his overall mileage so he could crush workouts. Then, after the 10K passed, it'd be a marathon. Now, lots of miles to get the endurance to run 26.2 miles. Specificity led him to short-attention-span training, which led him to stagnation.

What he should have been doing instead was building his overall mileage and top-end smooth speed without worrying so much about training specifically for races. It took a few years for him to figure it out—all that time in his early 20s was wasted in a specificity

Groundhog Day, thinking he was moving forward but he was actually spinning his wheels.

Eventually, he realized his mistake. He started running more, doing strides, and focusing on long-term development of running economy over short-term race performance. In a year, just by jumping off the specificity train, he went from an okay runner to a national-class racer (though still getting his butt kicked plenty).

Think in Years, Not Months

The specialization dilemma all gets back to time horizon, one of the most important elements of happy running. Happy runners think long-term, emphasizing process. Others are like David in his early 20s, jumping from race lily pad to race lily pad, hoping they don't fall in the water.

The dilemma is most clear for ultramarathons. The best way to maximize short-term performance for an ultramarathon is to run lots of miles around aerobic threshold on terrain that is similar to the race. For the Hardrock 100, a race with 34,000 feet of climbing, that means going up and down big peaks until moving efficiently through the mountains is second nature. For the Lake Sonoma 50, a race with 10,000 feet of climbing, that means getting proficient at running downhill fast and uphill strongly on tired legs. Do that for a year or two, and you'll reach your potential.

Or will you? That is the question that counts. When you stop building your base and working on all-around running economy, you cap your ultimate potential without realizing it.

It's helpful to think of your long-term development as building a wall. Imagine that you start with 100 bricks, just lying there on the ground in a pile.

Specialized training builds the wall. Meanwhile, training focused on long-term development of running economy through a balanced approach to training adds more bricks to the pile.

Focus on specialized training, and in a relatively short time, you'll have a solid, 100-brick wall. You might have some good results and satisfying races.

But instead, if you focus on consistent training and long-term development, you'll add a bunch of bricks to the pile. You still need to build the wall, though.

Given this hypothetical exercise, what's the best method to build the biggest wall? You mix a long-term focus on developing running economy at all distances and specialized training to improve event-specific performance in cycles over the course of a year.

At first, your wall might not be as big as it could be if you spent all your time with specialized training. But over time, you'll have so many bricks to work with that you could just be using half of them and have a bigger wall than you ever imagined possible.

To put it another way, with smart training emphasizing long-term development, your new okay day can become your old top performance. Later on, if you add a bit of specialization to that longer time horizon emphasis, your new top performance can be unimaginably strong.

From Base Fitness, You Can Be Ready for Almost Any Event

Building that wall when you have the bricks assembled doesn't take all that long. That is the primary thing to remember about specialization: You don't need to specialize for long to get close to your current potential.

While there is a lot of variation across methodologies, the general way most training systems work is to go from less specific to more specific closer to race day. So on the background of consistent training, if you're training for a marathon on up to 100 miles, you start by focusing on $+O_2$ fast efforts, working to LT tempos, before progressing to AeT longer runs on race-specific terrain.

For a 5K, off the same consistent training base, you start with LT tempos before working down to $+O_2$ for race day. In between, you can mix approaches, working from the top down or bottom up depending on your background and physiology (generally, more slow-twitch athletes will work from the top down, and fast-twitch athletes from the bottom up).

At most, off a solid base of consistent training, these more focused training blocks are 12 to 16 weeks. Of that time, usually 6 weeks will be the absolute most for specific training focused on the exact stresses of race day. Any more time than that, and it's wasting valuable bricks that could be accumulated in the meantime.

The big takeaway is that the benefits of specificity only come from the long-term aerobic development and improving running economy. The problem arises because specificity does work—it will lead to big jumps in performance when done right. If an athlete thinks that the improvement comes from what they just did most recently, rather than what they've done for years, they might make conclusions that sabotage their long-term performance.

Instead, remember that fitness is not based on your most recent training any more than being a good chef is based on the meals you just cooked. Continue to build skills, using a happy runner's long-term thinking, then save specificity for when it counts.

K eely Henninger is the type of athlete whom coaches dream about. She didn't run for her college team, getting to the sport a bit later than most. What she lacked in experience, she made up for in toughness, intelligence, and talent.

The first time we saw her run, our jaws dropped. It was poetry in motion, like seeing Bach at the piano or Addie dog at the dinner table. After picking our mandibles off the floor, we told her something a bit crazy: "You can be one of the best ever."

At first, she was hesitant to embrace that vision, and for good reason. She was really strong and fast, but there were people finishing far ahead of her in big races. How could she make up that gap?

We sat down together and laid out the long-term vision—develop running economy over the course of three years. But there was a catch. Focusing on running economy would mean focusing less on race specificity for her major ultra races.

Keely was all-in. As a biomechanics expert at Nike, she understood the method behind the madness. For the next couple years, she never spent more than a month focusing on race-specific adaptations. Instead, she aimed to get faster year-round, with races serving as transition periods between training blocks rather than as the sole focus.

That may have tamped down her short-term potential. In 2016, she was good, but not a world-beater. In 2017, she made Team USA for the World Trail Championships, but she suffered from cramps on race day. Later that year, though, she showed a glimpse of her ultimate potential. She was fourth at CCC, a major international 100K race in France, and just a few minutes behind the leaders. The whole time, she was getting faster and faster, running PRs at every distance from the mile to the half marathon in training.

In 2018, a few years after shifting gears, she broke through. Against one of the strongest fields in the United States, she won the Chuckanut 50k in the second fastest time ever. Then she repeated the feat at the Lake Sonoma 50.

Eventually, Keely will stop getting so much faster (one would assume). Then, she'll do a bit more specificity to get the final few percentage points out of her legs. But for now, by emphasizing long-term growth over race-specific gains, her normal day has gone from really good to world class. The few percentage points she could gain from specificity is offset by the few dozen percentage points she has gained from long-term development of running economy.

The truly scary thought: What might her normal day be like in 2020? We are already getting our popcorn ready to watch the show unfold.

Integrate Long-Term Development With Short-Term Performance

Thinking long-term doesn't mean sacrificing in the short-term. It means continually building your overall, long-term potential so that at any point, your short-term performance is better than it would be otherwise. Strategically implementing principles of specificity can let you have your wall and build it too. Again, there are a million ways to think about it. Here is one approach that might be helpful for you.

First, choose the adventures each year that matter to you most. If you have too many important events, it'll be tempting to jump from lily pad to lily pad, changing approach and thinking short term instead of piling up training bricks over time. There's a reason that professional marathoners usually only have two key races each year—it's because spending too much time specifically training for a fast marathon eventually slows them down or breaks them down. Race prioritization doesn't mean you can't race a lot, it just means that only a small number of races will divert your attention away from long-term improvement.

Most athletes we know usually think about their one to four key adventures at the start of each year. In between, it's okay to race a lot, just not with a full training block. In other words, they keep "A" races focused, with an emphasis on specificity in training. "B" through "Z" races are just hard training days. Races 50 miles and up are always considered "A" races to avoid overtraining (unless they are viewed as a key training day for a 100 miler).

Taper Breakdown

Tapers are complicated as all get out. A lot of athletes have a misconception about what a taper is, thinking that it's all about recovery. But that's not usually the goal, especially for non-pro runners who aren't doing 120-mile weeks. Instead, tapers are about sharpening and getting a final stimulus to make race effort feel easy.

The problem arises because taper theory is largely derived from pro athletes doing massive training. Consider one athlete doing 100 miles and two big workouts each week and another doing 30 miles per week and one smaller workout. If that 100-mile athlete does a 2-week taper, cutting 25 percent in week 1 and 50 percent in week 2, they are still doing 75 and 50 miles, solid stimuli that let them maintain sharpness for race day. Meanwhile, the 30 miles per week runner will be barely running in the second week relative to their usual training load. There's a good chance they show up with quads that feel like a bucket of soggy noodles.

So it may be helpful to reframe the taper as a sharpening period. What you do to feel sharp varies a lot based on background and race goals, but we have found the following principles work best.

- *Principle 1:* Cut volume by 20 percent in week 1 and 40 percent in week 2 if you run more than 50 miles per week; 10 percent in week 1 and 25 percent in week 2 if less than 50 miles per week (if races are longer than 50K, cut volume by 10–25 percent more in week 2).

- *Principle 2:* Cut down intensity similarly, but make sure there is still a healthy dose of intense workouts. Plus it's okay to do a big workout 10 days out.

- *Principle 3:* The week before the race, still do a long run.

- *Principle 4:* Don't rest the day before the race, which could cause leaden legs on race day.

Putting it all together, for a 60-mile per week runner training for a marathon, it might look like this:

Monday: rest

Tuesday: 8 miles easy with 4×30 seconds fast/30 seconds easy in the second half

Wednesday: 3 miles easy, 5 miles moderate/hard (at half marathon race effort), 3 miles easy

Thursday: 6 miles easy

Friday: 5 miles easy with 4×20 seconds fast/40 seconds easy

Saturday: 14 miles easy (4 miles in the middle at marathon effort)

Sunday: 6–8 miles easy

Monday: rest

Tuesday: 5 miles easy

Wednesday: 2 miles easy, 3 miles at marathon effort, 2 miles easy with 4×30 seconds fast/30 seconds easy

Thursday: 5 miles easy

Friday: rest

Saturday: 4 miles easy with 4×20 seconds fast/40 seconds easy

Sunday: Marathon!

There is still volume, but nothing tiring. There is still intensity, but nothing crazy. The goal of sharpening weeks is not to hibernate like a bear on Lunesta, but to get to the start line wide awake and excited, like a grizzly on caffeine pills.

Every bear is different, though, so find what works for you.

Second, when you don't have an "A" race in the next few months, think about improving your 10K fitness. The 10K is the bellwether of performance at almost all distances—a better 10K means more half marathon potential or 100-mile potential. It rewards lots of easy running, well-developed top-end speed, and running economy at all effort levels, so it supports sustained development over time. And you can do 10K-style training for ages before burning out. After a month or two with no key event on the horizon, you can cycle back to an easy training block focused on building mileage and speed development, oscillating between those two approaches almost indefinitely without too much worry about stagnation. There is no magic to the 10K specifically (you could think shorter or longer or no distance at all), rather the concept that speed takes practice and development.

After optimizing consistent training of easy miles and strides, SWAP athletes usually default to 10K-style training before training specifically for an event. Before the 2017 North Face 50 Miler, for example, Clare Gallagher built up to 10K training. She started with short intervals between 1 and 3 minutes with lots of recovery, optimizing $v+O_2$ (sample workout: 10×2 minutes around 5K effort/3 minutes easy). After adapting to that, Clare did slightly longer intervals with less recovery (sample: 8×3 minutes at 10K effort/1 minute easy) and slower tempo runs (sample: 20 minutes at half-marathon race effort). Finally, she put it all together with some 10K-paced tempo runs of 10 to 30 minutes. That 10K training plus just a few weeks of specificity led to a second-place finish at one of the biggest 50-mile trail races in the world.

Third, don't overemphasize extra-long runs for extra-long races or crazy-vert training for crazy-vert racing. The longer you go or more you climb, the slower you have to go. Eventually, that will catch up to you and slow you down across the board.

All year, it's good to do a long run that is 20 to 40 percent of your training volume each week. But when you start going 20 miles and up, make sure that your running economy is already in good shape, or you'll just get better at slogging. For this reason, the Hanson's Distance Project has mentored Olympic marathoners without any long runs over 20 miles. The same goes for the races themselves—too many long races will eventually undermine your speed unless they are separated by enough time to avoid overtraining and rebuild running economy.

Athletes we work with almost never train specifically for a long race for more than 6 to 10 weeks. It's not that a longer specific focus wouldn't be helpful short term, it's that going too far, too often might undercut long-term development. Instead, they focus on accumulating as much aerobic and speed development as possible, improving running economy as much as possible, and running really far as little as possible.

At the end of the day, it's all about the happy runner principle: Dream big and believe in your long-term potential. Then plan and train for that exhilarating future.

No matter what you do in training, though, one thing matters most of all—health. And health should be the focus of every decision you make for running training.

—9—

Principle 5:
Healthy Running Is Active and Earned

The body doesn't know miles. It knows stress. Adjust your training based on stress and don't mimic the training of someone living a different life.

Those words are simple to say, but they are hard to understand, let alone put into practice. What do we mean when we say "stress" in the context of running? There are two main components: musculoskeletal and systemic.

Musculoskeletal stress is the breakdown of muscles, tendons, and even bones that occurs when you run. A little breakdown plus time to recover can do a lot of good—the body builds itself back stronger. But push a bit too hard, and a bit too long, and things fall apart in the form of overuse injuries.

Running also causes the adrenal glands to release a stress hormone called cortisol, causing what we call systemic stress. Cortisol increases at the onset of exercise in order to help regulate glucose concentration in the blood.

A little bit of cortisol is necessary. But too much leads to a progression of maladies. Think of your cortisol reserves like a reservoir: It may be full during hard training, but if the dam floods it can cause major destruction.

Stress overload starts with decreased performance. You'll often notice the symptoms in everyday life before you notice them in your running. For example: abnormal fatigue walking up stairs, disrupted sleep cycles, or legs that involuntarily clench while sleeping. Keep pushing, and the body can essentially shut down as a defense mechanism, culminating in overtraining syndrome.

That said, in order for the body to adapt, it needs to be stressed. So when we are talking about how to structure your training, we are essentially talking about how to distribute stress in a sustainable way.

Put it all together and it's like a big pepperoni pizza. If you're like us, your first thought might be: "A life of pizza? Yes! Heaven is on Earth!"

Each week, you have just that one pizza. "No! Just one pizza a week? But I want *all* the pizza!"

Every activity you do takes a slice out. A 10-mile run? A big slice with lots of toppings. A board meeting? Maybe even a bit bigger slice than that. Sleep-deprived baby feeding? Two slices. "There's plenty of pizza! I can do it all!"

Eventually, the pizza starts running out. "A humanitarian crisis!"

The pizza represents the amount of stress you can absorb without breaking down. If the pizza is finished before the week is done, everything goes to crap, with injuries, burnout, and overtraining. To borrow from the movie *Ghostbusters*, it's "human sacrifice, cats and dogs living together, mass hysteria!"

Here's the catch. You aren't 100 percent sure how big the pizza is each week. It could be an extra-large, with plenty to go around. Or you could be at risk of trying to make a small pizza fit a big life.

The Perils of Balancing Stress

We both saw the world's saddest pizza party play out firsthand—you might remember parts of these stories from Part I. In 2013, David was working in Washington, D.C., commuting an hour each way. It was his first year out of law school, and he thought he could take it.

"This is called being an adult," he'd think. "Everyone does it."

At the same time, he had big running dreams. Every day, twice a day, he'd run. One hundred miles per week? Sure, why not? That's what adults with big dreams do.

All the while, the background stress was mounting. He didn't realize it at the time, though. That's the thing—you almost never realize it until it's too late.

For David, it was officially too late one morning in November. His hip ached as if a family of squirrels was nesting for the winter in his upper thigh. The pizza ran out. It was a fully torn hip labrum, likely out for a few seasons at least.

In 2016, Megan was working endless hospital shifts. The only time she would see the sun was when medication posters in patient rooms showed people with hemorrhoids playing at the beach. (The fine print for pharmaceutical advertisements should have to explain why everyone is frolicking in the surf with serious medical conditions.)

"This is called being a doctor," she'd think. "Everyone does it."

All the while, she ran her butt off (which sounds satisfying for one of those beach-goers with hemorrhoids). Twelve miles around a 1/3-mile loop at 3 a.m.? You'd better believe it.

For Megan, it was officially too late at a race in August. Her body felt like she was giving a piggyback ride to a silverback gorilla. The heaviness enveloped her whole being.

The pattern constantly repeats itself. One top athlete joined SWAP two months after a breakup. The sense of loss was so all-consuming that her body rebelled, along with her heart. She thought she was just out of shape. Turns out that the stress of a broken heart can make running up a hill feel impossible.

It's not just bad stress, but good stress too. The euphoria of a new child throws a smorgasbord of ingredients into the stress crockpot. So does a fun job, a night out at a club dancing vertically, and a night in bed dancing horizontally. Stress is a part of life; if you don't view it as a part of training, you could end up sabotaging both.

Now for the tricky part. Different people absorb stress differently. Even the same person will absorb the same stress differently depending on the biophysical context for it. And sometimes, you can feel like you do everything right and still end up screwed anyway. This is the world's most complicated pizza party!

How We Handle Stress

Everything matters. First, think about genetics. Countless articles on CEOs talk about how little sleep they need to thrive, as if self-deprivation is strength of character. In office, Barack Obama slept six or fewer hours a night. Donald Trump is often cited as needing just three or four hours of sleep a night, though perhaps a day spent watching Fox News accomplishes the same thing. Elon Musk sleeps just two hours a night while listening to an audio tape of *The Art of War* to sub-consciously develop business strategy. That last one isn't true, but it feels like it could be.

Those sleepless CEOs likely have some genetic predisposition to being able to operate on little sleep. A few genes have even been isolated that may explain the "sleepless elite"—people who can function optimally with less than the recommended eight hours a night.

Genetics apply to everything, from bone density to how stress itself is absorbed. DEXA scans are used to measure bone density, with Z-scores explaining variance around the mean. Positive scores mean better than average bone density; negative scores are worse. We have seen Z-scores that are off the charts in both positive and negative directions, with little explanation aside from genetics. It's telling that when we survey injury history, previous experiences with stress fractures are the best predictors of future injury risk. There is some genetic factor at work, determining how stress is managed at the cellular level.

Second, think about background. You are shaped by your experiences physically and psychologically. A great example is how children learn language. If a toddler learns multiple languages early enough, that style of pattern recognition ingrains itself in the structure of the brain. That's one reason why some people can learn eight languages without much effort, and others can barely speak one.

Physical traits work the same way. There is some evidence that children who run a lot at a young age can develop differently than they would otherwise, even stunting growth if endurance running is not accompanied by adequate energy intake. David is a great example of the opposite situation. His big, meaty frame probably led to some big, meaty bones, like a fossilized brontosaurus came to life as an awkward human child. While he has had his fair share of injuries, those Jurassic-style bones have never faltered . . . yet (*knocks on wood like a furious woodpecker*).

Third, think about sex. If your ears perked up, sorry, it's not *that* type of sex. Sex differences lay across a spectrum, and even at different points on the spectrum bodies will respond differently than what may be expected. Generally across the population, women have lower $+O_2$maxes, lower testosterone, and higher essential body fat to maintain healthy bodily function. Usually, that means female runners are at a higher risk of overstressing their bodies. However, not every general rule applies to every person.

Blood tests for iron show how sex differences can change the dose-response curve for stress. Iron is essential for hemoglobin, which is how the blood transports oxygen. Low hemoglobin means less oxygen transport. Often, before seeing a blood test with low iron, a person will complain of extreme fatigue, as if an orangutan is doing pull-ups on their eyelids.

All runners, male and female, lose iron through foot strike hemolysis, wherein blood cells break down upon footfall. Sweating causes some iron to leach away too. Just women, though, have the menstrual cycle, and blood loss takes iron away with it. On top of that, the average man will absorb iron more readily than the average woman (with outliers in both directions). As a result, female runners are iron deficient more commonly than men.

This phenomenon has implications for everything a runner does, from supplementation to nutrition. For example, meat intake is one predictor of iron levels because "heme" iron from red meat is more readily absorbed. So female vegetarians may have to think more about what they are eating than a male vegetarian.

The general rule we tell our athletes is that sex differences mean that the average man has more margin for error than the average woman. The average man may not need to supplement with iron, to start. Their body fat percentage can drop lower before essential bodily functions begin to shut down. Testosterone means men may be able to withstand more hard runs. Women are freaking rockstars, but physiology can be unfair sometimes.

Sex, genetics, and background all are stirred together into the stress stew. Add in life circumstances, and it gets really complicated to figure out what is too much, what is too little, and what is just right.

Goldilocks herself would struggle to make a burnout-proof training plan.

When in doubt, remember a central principle of happy runner training: overtraining is 1,000 times worse than undertraining. Lots of little bricks over time add up to a really big wall, eventually. But try to stack up too many big bricks all at once and it can come crashing down in an instant.

When Stress Leads to Injury

The most obvious ailments that can make like the Kool-Aid man on your training wall are injuries. Soft tissue injuries result from tendons, ligaments, and muscles being overstressed, usually by repetitive loading. Think of your connective system like a rope—you can lose a strand or two and be fine. But push beyond that, and the whole thing starts to unravel. Tendinitis is the most common soft tissue injury, usually feeling like one of your extremities is an out-of-tune guitar trying to play country music. Instead of a pleasant twang, it's a screeching scream, often coming from the shin, knee, or hip.

Hard tissue injuries are the next level up. Stress causes cellular-level deformities in the bones. A little bit is usually unnoticeable. A bit more might feel like a bruise on top of a bone. A lot feels like someone took a sledgehammer to your skeleton. At a minimum, a stress fracture takes weeks to heal, and some (like those in the femur and pelvis) can take months.

Even more insidious than musculoskeletal injuries is overtraining syndrome. With overtraining, chronic exposure to stress essentially causes the hormonal system to turn off the lights and the central nervous system to put up a flickering "Closed" sign. At its worst, overtraining manifests itself as horrible depression. Getting out of bed is a chore—going out for a run is all but impossible.

Overtraining, like soft and hard tissue injuries, falls on a spectrum. Before a runner is doing their hardest intervals just to get up in the morning, they are feeling a bit more tired on uphills, or a bit more lethargic at their desk. The brain feels groggy, the muscles feel soggy. And if the goal of happy runner training is to embody the joy of a doggie, there is no greater obstacle.

The problem with all these risks to health is that you're usually fine, until you're not. Plus, sometimes it's all a matter of luck and chance. Training needs to balance the reward from pushing with the risk of pushing too far. The line between healthy and unhealthy is blurry, and it keeps moving. So it's absolutely, unequivocally essential to err on the side of health. Your monkey brain that strives for success may disagree.

Your shin hurts. "Run goshdarnit or you're a failure!"

Hills feel harder than usual. "Run harder or you will disappoint your loved ones!"

You only slept three hours. "Run normally or you don't deserve to call yourself a runner!"

Happy runner training turns that monkey brain off. That is the most important element in long-term success. Why? Because consistency is all that matters. What you can be tomorrow, or next month, or next year is nothing compared to what you can be in five years or 10 years. And you'll be exponentially more happy on the journey if it's not spent feeling like a smoldering dumpster fire. So how should you rewire your monkey brain?

Your shin hurts. "I'll rest today, maybe hop on the bike or go in the sauna, and wait until I don't feel it at all."

Hills feel harder than usual. "Time for a burger and a movie instead of a hill workout."

You only slept three hours. "Snoozle intervals sound way more productive than mile repeats."

When in doubt, do less, go easier, eat more, sleep in. An ounce of preventative actions now are worth a pound of doctor's bills later.

Rest Days Are the Best Days

Injuries are sometimes unavoidable. They can pop up suddenly, a chain reaction that is unstoppable once it is set in motion. You can do everything right and still have everything go terribly wrong. In those cases, stay positive, cross-train if you can, and you'll come back stronger than ever after the layoff. Shalane Flanagan won the New York City Marathon after an uncharacteristic layoff due to a stress fracture. Des Linden did the same at Boston after her own break. There are tons of stories like that, so take heart—what seems like a setback may actually fuel a leap forward.

Even though injuries can be opportunities, staying healthy is a lot more fun. While some injuries pop up quickly, others are more gradual, the result of multiple fail-safe systems that don't work when it counts. Rest days are the preventative mechanisms—the maintenance and rebuilding you don't always know you need. To see a higher-stakes setting when a small problem led to a chain reaction that ended in disaster, rewind to Pennsylvania in 1889.

The South Fork Dam on the Little Conemaugh River was constructed in the mid-1800s, with plans for a complex system of relief pipes and valves to make the dam resilient during floods. Twenty years after it was built, those pipes and valves were never put in place, even as private developers modified the dam for a group of wealthy landowners. They lowered the dam top and added a screen on the spillway to keep the lake teeming with fish. The failure to build the pipes and valves combined with the little changes to the dam design would lead to one of the worst catastrophes in American history.

But first, there were chances to prevent the disaster to come. Maintenance was ignored for years. Leaks continually sprang up, only to be patched by mud and straw. And on May 28, 1889, when a massive storm began, it was clear there was a problem.

A local landowner saw the lake nearly overflowing its banks after a few inches of rain. A group of people did everything they could to save it—trying to reinforce the banks at the locations of the old leaks, trying to unclog the spillway (which had backed up with a combination of the fish screen and a broken fish trap), even trying to plow earth to raise it higher. At 1:30 p.m. it was clear that the efforts would be futile.

They telegraphed the towns below to prevent massive loss of life. The warnings were ignored, not even passed to town officials. It was the boy who cried wolf, dam edition, with numerous similar warnings being sent over the years, but no floods to back them up.

At 2:50 p.m. the dam breached. Nearly four billion gallons of water emptied from the lake in less than an hour; 2,209 people lost their lives in what would become known as the Johnstown Flood.

Many tragedies have a similar trajectory—unforeseen circumstances interact with negligence to create disaster. Plane crashes, bridge collapses, and even many house fires have similar postmortem analyses. On an insignificant scale comparatively, many running injuries are analogous.

Think about the Johnstown Flood. For decades prior to the dam collapse, things seemed fine, but the elements of disaster were silently piling up. The lowered dam, the fish screen, the patched leaks—all weren't a problem when things were normal. Any one of those elements could have been corrected in advance to stop the eventual disaster. But when it started raining, it was already too late.

Those maintenance activities to prevent problems that don't seem to even exist yet are like rest days. Running injuries are usually a complex mix of factors that add up to a major problem when an outside force acts on them. A left ankle turn could cause a slightly altered stride, which leads to a batch of tendinitis in the right knee, which alters the stride a bit more.

Energy depletion from too little calories for a couple days could make the body ever so slightly more fragile, and some stress at work could leave no time for foam rolling for a few days. Then, on a seemingly normal run, the altered gait and vulnerable body could put a bit too much pressure on the left hip.

The bone tissue on the femoral neck might sprout a few leaks, only to be patched up with some anti-inflammatories. As the pain gets worse, warning telegraphs are sent from the hip to the brain—*stop running now*. Only, the brain has ignored the signs before, and nothing happened. So it's okay to continue, business as usual. Right?

Wrong. This time it's not a false alarm. The damage gets greater and greater, only to breach the point of no return on an interval workout three weeks later. It's a stress fracture of the femoral neck; no running for 3 to 6 months at least.

Rest days are how you can stack the odds in your favor to prevent the unlikely disasters from taking place. Consistent, planned rest can help solve problems you don't even know you have. And resting as soon as the warning signals appear can help stop small problems from becoming physical catastrophes.

It all gets back to how most injuries happen for runners. Think of baseball players. They might get injured from diving in the outfield (grade 2 separated shoulder), sprinting to first base (grade 3 torn hamstring), or putting on too-tight pants (grade 20 asphyxiated crotch). Most of their injuries are acute—single bouts of stress that cause the biomechanical chain to break down.

Now think of runners. They might get injured from running with a slightly altered gait for a few weeks (knee tendinitis), increasing mileage too rapidly (tibial stress fracture), or wearing an abrasive running outfit too often (grade 20 nipple hemorrhage). Those injuries are chronic, caused by stress over time.

Sometimes, an injury can happen all at once, and that truly sucks. Other times, an injury can just seem to happen all at once. For example, you'll be out running when your shin starts throbbing, leading to a radiologist telling you the damage has already been done in your tibia—stress fracture. But that run was probably just the straw that broke the camel's back. All the other hay before that last strand contributed just as much. In that case, preventative rest days may have healed the damage when it was unnoticeable.

Injuries are usually progressive, going from minor annoyance to major issue over weeks. For example, you'll feel a slight pressure in your shin at the end of a long run one week. Then the next week, it'll sound the alarm once, on an awkward step. The week after, it'll be tolling like a bell, impossible to ignore. That progression is the process of going from the soft tissue around the bone being inflamed to the bone itself having a stress fracture. In that case, resting at the first sign of a problem could have shortened recovery time from a few months to a few days.

As a runner, doing nothing is doing something. Rest is the most proactive way to prevent calamity before you're even aware that calamity is possible. During a rest day, damage in the musculoskeletal system can heal, inflammation can subside, and the body can restock glycogen stores to fuel the next round of training. Rest is also the time to rebuild and adapt to past training. Running training without time to adapt to stress just leads to breakdown.

Stress plus rest equals adaptation. Too much stress plus not enough rest equals self-destruction. So how do you balance the equation? You rest. It's better to be 99.99 percent too overprotective, rather than 0.01 percent underprotective.

The discipline to do nothing now will let you do something later. It'll enhance your longevity in the sport. Most importantly, planned rest days will help you feel good. And happy runners thrive off of feeling good.

Two weeks before the 2018 Chuckanut 50K, Keely Henninger felt pain in her foot. The pain rapidly spread to her shin, with swelling to match. She quickly saw a doctor and found out she had an infection.

Fortunately, she caught it early. Unfortunately, the time off would sabotage her "A" race goals at Chuckanut.

Just kidding. The five days off were a blessing in disguise, letting her mind and body recover for the upcoming race. She eased back into training carefully, then ran a breakthrough race to win Chuckanut in one of the fastest times ever.

"That's crazy," you may think. "I feel like an overgrown hippo after one day off. Don't I lose fitness in five?"

Rest days are so magical because you don't lose fitness in that time, especially if you're just taking one or two, so it's all reward with no risk. The aerobic system doesn't detrain at all; there is a minor reduction in blood volume but it bounces back rapidly, and all of the other elements of detraining usually take at least a week to kick in.

So give your body a break. Take little breaks enough to stay healthy, happy, and motivated, and you might find yourself like Keely, breaking off something really special in your next race.

Even if you have longer periods of time off, you'll be back and better than ever more quickly than you'd guess. It's always easier to get back where you were than it was to build it the first time, a phenomenon that likely has complex neuromuscular, aerobic, and possibly even epigenetic (changes in gene expression) reasons. Many pro athletes trace their breakthroughs back to what they thought were downfalls. So even time off can be a major opportunity for long-term growth.

Little Things Are the Big Things

When athletes contact us for coaching—especially elite athletes—it's rarely because things are going super swell. It's like the self-help section of Barnes & Noble. No one is paying $29.95 for *5 Ways to Overcome Your Crippling Fear of Trees* when their life is on a roll.

Usually, athletes join when dealing with long-term injuries, stress, or stagnation. Over the years, we have found that what is holding most runners back is not what they are doing, it's what they are not doing.

- They are not resting enough. Our only unconditional rules are to practice self-belief . . . and take at least one rest day every two weeks.
- They are not doing at-home physical therapy. Foam rolling takes priority over miles.
- They are not sleeping enough. No hard workouts until they can get a rolling average of adequate sleep to adapt to training.

- They are not eating enough. Every pizza is a personal pizza if you believe in yourself.

All those little things don't involve too much time investment. But for long-term consistency and happiness, they are everything.

When Meg Mackenzie joined SWAP, she was in the often-injured boat. In her native South Africa, she was an up-and-coming running star. Only her star was constantly shooting off solar flares that would devastate her running galaxy. She had stress fracture after stress fracture, doing everything right but having everything go wrong.

Her only change after joining SWAP? She started resting twice a week, every Monday and Friday. That may seem like a lot for an elite athlete. But Meg focused on a general rule of running: You'll get most of the way to your potential just by being consistent, and marginal gains after that are nothing in comparison.

Chasing marginal gains from taking risks in training is like standing on top of a mountain and seeing a hundred miles to the horizon, thinking it is the whole universe. Yeah, it's big. But look up at the night sky. There are billions more light years out there if you just broaden the horizon of your focus.

Meg started looking up, dreaming years down the line instead of looking out, thinking in terms of weeks and months. She had a breakthrough season, culminating in a win at the prestigious Otter Trail Classic.

How much should you rest? Once a week minimum, unless you have a compelling reason to run every day. Rest twice a week if you are more injury prone. And at the first sign of abnormal pain, rest until it goes away. That is the rule for happy, healthy running: Rest is the best prevention and treatment.

When Steve Tucker joined SWAP, he had the opposite problem—he rested too much. He wasn't that consistent, yet he constantly found himself felled by injuries, trying to run through them until it was too late. He was like the Black Knight from Monty Python.

His left arm gets cut off (IT band pain). "Tis but a scratch!"

His right arm gets cut off (plantar fasciitis). "Just a flesh wound!"

His leg gets cut off (IT band pain again). "I'm invincible!"

After a series of injuries, he could no longer claim invincibility. In fact, he thought that it was his destiny to be the Black Knight, getting all of his limbs chopped off every time he tried to run more than 30 miles per week.

He changed his destiny by trying something different, as if the Black Knight tried statesmanship instead. Every night, he did 10 to 20 minutes of foam rolling. He did exercises pioneered by Jane Fonda to improve his hip strength and mobility. He did some dynamic stretching. And he ran really, really easily while his body adapted.

Over the course of a few months, his old weekly cap of 30 miles became a pretty routine weekend. It was as if the Black Knight took off his helmet to reveal he was King Arthur all along. With the sustained health from at-home physical therapy, he started to realize that his potential was greater than he ever thought possible. In his first e-mail in mid-2016, his initial goals were quaint in retrospect: "Run a bit faster in the 5K" and "Run 50 miles in a week."

By April 2017, he had run 80 miles in a week. He had crushed his 5K PR nearly a dozen times in the context of training runs. And it culminated in winning the North Face DC 50 Miler, a major regional U.S. race.

What type of at-home physical therapy should you do? At a minimum, foam roll or do other daily massage techniques so routinely that it becomes like brushing your teeth. Foam rolling should be taught in schools right along with sex education. It's that important for healthy running for many runners.

On top of that, make sure your hips are strong and mobile. Coach Jay Johnson's Myrtl routine is what we recommend most. Start your runs with a solid warm-up consisting of lunges and leg swings (again, Coach Johnson's Lunge Matrix/Leg Swings (LMLS) warm-up is wonderful). After runs, do some light stretching if you're into that, some dynamic stretching if you're not. Basically, prioritize non-running stuff so injury stuff doesn't cause you to be a non-runner.

Strength Work for the Athlete Who Hates Strength Work

"Strength work sucks."

A lot of runners think that way. Or, they think that there's just not enough time in the day during their busy lives. There can be any number of reasons to neglect the little things, from good ones (gotta get to work) to less good ones (a crippling fear of foam rollers).

Because most athletes are time-limited and don't love strength work, we recommend short and sweet routines that can be done almost every day.

Prerun Warm-Up (5 minutes)

10 forward lunges

10 rear lunges

10 side lunges

10 front-to-back leg swings

10 side-to-side leg swings

1-minute very slow jog at walking pace or a bit faster

Post-Run Strength and Mobility (5 to 10 minutes)

10 clamshells, bridges, and leg raises with each leg

5 eccentric calf drops

Foam rolling of quads, calves, hamstrings, and glutes

On top of that, if an athlete has some time to spare, we'll have them do a more complete strength regimen 2 or 3 times per week.

Legs

10 forward lunges with both legs

20 rear lunges with both legs

10 side lunges with both legs

50 to 100 single-leg step ups per leg

10 to 20 single-leg squats per leg

Core

1-minute front plank (can do variations of these with movement after you gain proficiency)

1-minute side planks

30-second rear plank

Repeat

Upper Body

Push-ups to fatigue, not failure (on knees works great!)

10 to 20 dips (supporting some weight works great; you can even use a sturdy chair with handles for this)

10 to 20 above-head military presses with light weights

More complex routines are even better, like the myrtl by Coach Jay Johnson. It's kind of like cooking—people who want to be the best chefs can go to culinary school and learn what cardamom is (a type of fish?) and how to use it (carefully?). But the rest of us can use a few methods and simple ingredients to make a good meal, and to avoid burning the house down while we're at it.

Sleep Is a Performance Enhancer

Layered on top of rest and non-running injury prevention is the most important secret sauce of all: sleep. You have probably heard of performance-enhancing drugs (PEDs) that come in big, scary Armstrong-branded needles and give you back acne volcanoes that could rival Mount Vesuvius. Sleep is a PED too, but a natural one without any negative side effects. It makes you stronger and faster. Heck, it even makes you a better person. And all too often, people take pride in neglecting it.

First, let's look at how sleep acts like a PED. Sleep is essential for regulation of hormone production, including human growth hormone, the same stuff Barry Bonds used to make his head grow more sizes than the Grinch's heart. It's also key for the stress hormone cortisol, optimizing diurnal cycles to avoid overtraining. Perhaps most importantly, sleep is when repair and maintenance happens on the cellular level. Failure to sleep makes you a worse, less healthy runner. And it's so all-encompassing that messed up hormones and a tired body from too little sleep can make you a worse, less healthy human being.

Second, think about the cultural associations with sleep. Stoners sleep. Sloths sleep. High achievers don't sleep. Without googling it, how many hours do you think Steve Jobs slept a night? We are willing to bet you it's less than 6. Excuse us for a second while we Google search . . . sure enough, it's three or four hours a night while building Apple. Same with Bill Gates while building Microsoft. The same probably goes for Walter White while building his crystal meth empire in *Breaking Bad*. You may be able to build a company or drug cartel with little sleep. But you cannot build a happy runner.

Running training is the process of controlled breakdown. The key is to provide the biophysical context for the body to build itself back stronger. Sleep is when that building happens. Training hard without sleep is just self-destruction.

How much should you sleep? Most sleep experts recommend 7 to 8 hours minimum for healthy adults. We have found that 8+ averaged over the course of the week is ideal, 7+ doable, and less than 7 usually ends up being like a big injection of the drug Thissportsucks right in the butt cheek. Every body and person is different, so the exact number isn't important. What matters is remembering that running is just the process of breakdown. Without an equal focus on build-up, your body (and brain) will usually break eventually.

Adaptations Are Earned at the Dinner Table

Run long enough, and eventually you will have a dinner table epiphany. For us, it was at the 2015 World Long Distance Mountain Running Championships in Zermatt, Switzerland.

But long before that dinner table, we saw the importance of food for running performance firsthand. Starting his journey as a football player, David heard the stereotype that runners subsist on lettuce and air to stay light. So he thought he needed to subsist on lettuce and air too. As he became a runner, he'd weigh himself constantly. After nights when he skipped dinner altogether, he'd be like a kid coming down the stairs on Christmas when he walked up to the scale. Days when he'd go out with friends and eat nachos, the scale would be his atonement, like being grounded for staying out too late.

As discussed in chapter 4, when starting her running journey as a field hockey player, Megan knew she didn't look like some of the other women on the track team. At first, every day she ran in a Duke singlet felt like trying on jeans that were just a bit too tight. So her brain wanted to force her body down a few sizes. She'd eat salads almost every night at dinner.

And we both kept getting injured. We improved at the start, then stagnated, then even regressed as our bodies rebelled against having too few calories. It took a few years to realize our mistakes. Megan took a few months off entirely after graduating, lifted weights, and switched her orders from salads to spaghetti. David's meticulous workout tracking showed him that lighter bodyweight correlated to worse running performances. In 2015, we got an extra visualization.

At that dinner table in Zermatt, we sat down with our Team USA teammates for the first time. The teammates were some of the best runners in the sport, with long and happy careers. And they ate. Boy did they ever eat.

Beyoncé had hot sauce in her bag—well, one woman on the team had olive oil in her bag. She literally put olive oil in her suitcase. When her extra-large plate of pasta came out, she brought out the oil, and it began to glug. And glug. And glug. Just a few years before, David had counted calories, so his brain couldn't help but do mental math. It was like the scene in *A Beautiful Mind* with numbers and symbols flying across the screen, trying to figure out how many calories were on that plate.

All of the runners at the table were the same. One late-30s runner who is among the best in the sport said that the dinner table is a great way to tell how long a runner's career will be. The eaters last. The skimpers may be fast, but probably not for long.

The dinner table epiphany of lifelong runners all gets back to energy availability. Negative energy availability is simply running on a caloric deficit. It doesn't mean a runner is skinny or has an eating disorder, it just means that they don't have quite enough calories to fuel running when accounting for all the other things that require energy in daily life. Across countless studies, negative energy availability is shown to be one of the biggest roadblocks to performance due to increased rate of injuries and fewer adaptations to training stimuli.

Why does negative energy availability become a problem in the first place? Sometimes, runners associate being lighter with being faster, and they become unhealthy as a result. There is an iota of truth lurking here: A decrease in body fat or weight can enhance performance in some people. However, weight loss below healthy levels and negative energy availability are both ticking time bombs. Sooner or later, performance and health can suffer, leading to injuries or hormonal deficiencies.

Worst of all, the fuse seems to get shorter each time. The runner may recover and get back to full strength, but reverting back to negative energy availability causes performance to diminish even more quickly than before.

But that first experience of associating increased performance with negative energy availability can trigger habits of calorie restriction. It's a mental–physical cycle that can be very difficult to overcome, and may never completely leave.

Energy availability is the number one determinant of longevity and health in running. That doesn't mean you have to look a certain way. Every body is different. But make sure you give your body what it needs, rather than trying to fit into someone else's singlet.

How should you approach nutrition? There is no one-size-fits-all approach. But among happy runners, there is one overarching mantra: Eat enough, always. Eat too much, sometimes. Eat too little, never.

One More Thing

This chapter has almost all been about physical health. But as important as that is, it's just a small blip on the happy runner radar compared to mental health.

In chapter 4, we talked about depression and anxiety. Even short of those diagnosable conditions, most people have their own mental health struggles at one time or another. And no matter what your background, just know that it's okay. You are enough right here, right now. As we said before, you are perfect in this moment.

Running training—like life itself—is essentially one long tunnel. You can train perfectly, reach every goal you ever set through your meticulous training methodology, win the biggest races in the world, or accomplish any other unimaginable feat, and you'll be left with the same realization as countless others that have been there before you. There is no light at the end of the tunnel. There is no magical time when the outcomes of your training will bring you lifelong joy, when finish lines will make everything okay all the time.

So set up a training (and life) framework to embrace the tunnel. Get out a flashlight and find some friends. When you can, laugh along the way. When you can't, cry. And whether you succeed or fail, try to make some memories. Do that, and you may have a revelation.

The tunnel can be pretty freaking awesome.

CONCLUSION: YOU ARE AWESOME

We will end this book with a final reminder of the big theme. No matter what, just remember one thing: You're enough.

You might suck at a race, but you're enough. You might miss a run, but you're enough. You might even lose the running love for a while, and you're still enough.

Actually, scratch that. Here's a big final edit. Replace every instance of "enough" in this whole book with a different word: "awesome." YOU ARE AWESOME (said with Addie dog's joy).

So if you take nothing else away from this book, have it be this: Practice loving and accepting yourself unconditionally, knowing you are awesome . . . because you are.

Happiness is not always a choice. But over time, with practice, being kinder to yourself can be. Unconditional self-acceptance is the most important step to being fulfilled independent of the twists and turns of life. And it's also an essential step toward reaching your potential as a runner.

Being a lifelong runner involves a series of failures interspersed with momentary successes. That sounds morbid as heck, but think about it. You'll get slower as you age and get injured pretty consistently over the years. If you dream big, you'll sometimes fail to reach those dreams. You'll struggle getting out the door, you'll bail on a workout because you just don't feel like it. In the face of constant, unpredictable failure, it's easy to be a running nihilist, thinking none of it matters.

Instead, it's essential to think of running as something that adds meaning to your life, rather than showing you that your life has no meaning at all. That way, those inevitable failures are just parts of the story, adding color and interesting tidbits. You are awesome no matter how your running is going in the moment.

What happens if your self-worth is tied to your running? You are less equipped to deal with the inevitable failures, and they could derail you altogether. Not only that, the goalposts keep moving. You'll reach one milestone, just to already move onto the next, judging yourself constantly along the way.

When you accept yourself, you give yourself permission to fail. When failure loses its stigma, you can overcome all the obstacles you encounter in your running life. And perhaps most important of all— you can learn to believe.

Persistent belief relies on unconditional self-acceptance, because otherwise belief would be proven wrong, illogical, and stupid again and again. When you set up a framework to continue believing even when the evidence points in the opposite direction, you can accomplish things that might seem impossible.

When unconditional self-acceptance and self-belief mix, anything is possible. Athletes who believe in themselves are more enthusiastic, more passionate, and more confident in what they are capable of. Their workouts are better. They are more consistent. Their perceived exertion is lower. They get faster, year after year. Self-acceptance and belief are the most important parts of training.

The best example of self-belief we have ever seen firsthand is Liza Howard. She joined SWAP in 2016, a busy 45-year-old mom who was a top coach and foundation director, too. She did it all, and she thought she might be washed up as an athlete.

From her first e-mail: "I'm not sure if it's possible, but I really want to make the 2018 U.S. 100K World Championships team."

The next two years were spent on the first part of that sentence, which made the second part possible.

Through ups and downs and everything in between, Liza worked relentlessly on buying in to her own potential to do amazing things. She didn't change all that much in her training. She just changed the internal monologue about her training and self.

At 46, she won two overall national championships. First, it was the 50-mile road race. Then, in April 2018, she became the 100K champ, reaching her big goal from a couple years before. As she reset for the next phase of her running life, she summed up what she learned in her training log. "Belief in self + friend's belief = magic. Ready for some more training fun." HECK, YES!

So where does all this talk of unconditional self-acceptance and belief leave us?

It doesn't matter how lofty your goals are, nor whether you reach those goals. Just by accepting yourself and believing, you'll get closer than you would have otherwise. Belief can act as emotional alchemy that turns discouragement into confidence, and given time, that can turn the impossible into the ordinary.

So when you have a tough race, or a tough workout, or a tough work presentation, tell yourself, "Bad luck, I'll get 'em next time."

When you don't get 'em next time, tell yourself, "No worries, I'll get 'em in a few years."

Belief isn't about thinking you will win a gold medal, it's about thinking you can keep growing even when you are handed evidence to the contrary. But here's the really cool part. If you really, truly buy in to yourself, and work strategically in pursuit of your goals, those long-term dreams have a magical way of becoming reality.

Dream big and never stop believing, even if it seems crazy, and even when you fail. Accept yourself even when it's hard, and even when others might tell you something different.

Do that, and you might not reach your dreams right away, but we promise that you'll end up closer than you could ever imagine.

The final message? We haven't figured it all out. Not even close.

We don't accept ourselves all the time. We don't believe all the time. We sure as heck aren't happy all the time. But we're getting better at it all, bit by bit, trying to laugh and love as much as possible along the way. And that's the whole happy runner point.

OH, WAIT, ONE MORE THING TO TELL THEM.

What's that, Addie dog?

YOU ARE PERFECTLY AWESOME. NO MATTER WHAT.

ABOUT THE AUTHORS

David Roche started the Some Work, All Play (SWAP) team in 2013 and is a coach to some of the top trail runners in the world. SWAP team athletes have won 17 US national championships and appeared on Team USA 41 times, as well as winning races like the Western States 100 Mile Endurance Run and Hardrock 100. He is a two-time national champion, a three-time member of Team USA, and the 2014 USATF Men's Sub-Ultra Trail Runner of the Year. He is also a contributing editor for *Trail Runner Magazine*. David graduated from Columbia University with a degree in environmental science and received a master's degree and law degree from Duke University.

Megan Roche joined the SWAP coaching team in 2016. She is the 2016 USATF Women's Ultra Trail Runner of the Year and Sub-Ultra Trail Runner of the Year, a four-time national champion, the North American Mountain Running Champion, and a six-time member of Team USA. She attended Duke University, where she played on the field hockey team and raced on the cross country and track teams before graduating with a degree in neuroscience. Megan received her medical degree from Stanford University in 2018.

You read the book—now complete an exam to earn continuing education credit!

Congratulations on successfully preparing for this continuing education exam!

If you would like to earn CE credit, please visit

www.HumanKinetics.com/CE-Exam-Access

for complete instructions on how to access your exam. Take advantage of a discounted rate by entering promo code **THR2019** when prompted.

HUMAN KINETICS